POLAND

•Warsaw

DISCARD

Kharkov

U

•Lvov

CZECHOSLOVAKIA

rague

SEA OF
AZOV

Vienna

TRIA

•Budapest

HUNGARY

Odessa•

R Dnieper

BLACK SEA

RUMANIA

•Zagreb

Belgrade

Bucharest

R. Danube

YUGOSLAVIA

BULGARIA

•Sofia

Ankara•

ATIC
SEA

ALBANIA

TURKEY

•Tirana

aples

GREECE

AEGEAN
SEA

•Smyrna

Athens•

IONIAN
SEA

SICILY

RHODES

CYPRUS

Malta

CRETE

MEDITERRANEAN SEA

•Barce

GULF OF
SIRTE

•Benghazi

Tobruk

Mersa
Matruh

•Alexandria

El Alamein

•Cairo

•Beda Fomm

UNITED ARAB
REPUBLIC
(EGYPT)

Aghéila

LIBYA

R A

Generalissimo Churchill

Generalissimo Churchill

———

R. W. THOMPSON

CHARLES SCRIBNER'S SONS
New York

1 3 5 7 9 11 13 15 17 19 C/C 20 18 16 14 12 10 8 6 4 2

Printed in the United States of America
Library of Congress Catalog Card Number 73-19553
ISBN 0-684-13557-4

This book is dedicated with inexpressible gratitude to my wife, Mel, whose loyalty and fortitude have made it possible.

'At the summit true politics and strategy are one.'

WINSTON CHURCHILL

'Political and strategic preparations must go hand in hand. Failure of such harmony must lead either to military disaster or political retreat.'

SIR EYRE CROWE

'War is a choice of options.'
GENERAL WAVELL

Acknowledgments

THE EXTRACTS FROM THE BRITISH OFFICIAL HISTORIES OF THE Second World War are quoted by courtesy of Her Majesty's Stationery Office; from Churchill's *The Second World War*, by courtesy of Messrs Cassell & Co., Ltd. and the *Daily Telegraph*; from John Connell's *Auchinleck*, *Wavell, Scholar and Soldier*, and *Wavell, Supreme Commander*, by courtesy of Mrs. Ruth Connell Robertson. My grateful thanks are also due to Lady Liddell Hart for permission to quote from the late Sir Basil Liddell Hart's privately circulated memoranda, lectures, letters to the author, and published works. I wish also to thank the heirs of Major-General Eric Dorman O'Gowan, M.C. (Dorman Smith), and of Sir Desmond Morton, K.C.B., M.C., for permission to use my personal correspondence freely, and the various private papers in my possession.

I wish also to acknowledge the value of the works in the bibliography; nevertheless, as with my book, *The Yankee Marlborough*, this effort to focus on Churchill's attempt to 'command' armies in the field expresses my own personal view after many years of study and discussions with those who knew him well.

R. W. THOMPSON,
BELCHAMP WALTER,
SUFFOLK.

January, 1973.

Contents

Illustrations

PART ONE

The Long Apprenticeship

CHAPTER ONE

The Man and the Hour

IN THE HOUR OF ASSUMING THE SUPREME COMMAND OF BRITAIN, and in the hour when the British people were threatened with overwhelming disaster, Churchill recorded his feelings:

> I was conscious of a profound sense of relief. At last I had the authority to give directions over the whole scene. I felt as if I were walking with destiny, and that all my past life had been but a preparation for this hour and for this trial ... I could not be reproached either for making war or with want of preparation for it. I thought I knew a great deal about it all, and was sure I would not fail.

The simplicity and sincerity of Churchill's reaction belies the awesome magnitude of the task confronting him and the British people. It might have daunted the bravest of the brave. It did not daunt Churchill, and it might be true to say that a man feeling less than the exhilaration and the sense of destiny experienced by Churchill, would have been incapable of saving Britain. There would be many brilliant, brave and dedicated men to aid Churchill in his task, but there would not be scapegoats. It would be his victory, or his defeat. His whole life had been, as he said, a preparation for this hour, and it was already a long life, marvellously varied. He did know a great deal about it. When he assumed Supreme Command on 10th May, 1940, he was sixty-six years old.

In the first days words were his greatest weapons, almost his only weapons, making an immediate impact not only upon his countrymen, but upon the enemy. And although oratory was not

17

natural to him he saved Britain by his oratory, by his overwhelming self-confidence and by his courage. From a mind
magnificently stocked with Gibbon and Macaulay, with
Shakespeare and with the finest rhetoric of the greatest parlia-
mentarians, he set words to the music of war in rhythms to
delight the common man, and confound the enemy.

There was complete justification for Churchill's assumption
of full power by combining the offices of Prime Minister and
Minister of Defence in his own hands. In different times and for
vastly different purposes Chatham had not hesitated to do like-
wise. But whereas Chatham's purpose was to found a great mer-
cantile empire based on the military genius of Clive in India and
Wolfe in Canada, and on the unmatched daring and seamanship
of men like Hawke and Boscawen, it was Churchill's resolution
to save an empire and Great Britain itself from what seemed
certain destruction. In a letter dated 3rd January, 1915, old
Admiral Fisher had written to Churchill: 'In the history of the
world, a junta has never won! You want one man!'

The hour had struck, and beyond a doubt Churchill was the
man, and I have found it impossible to discover any other man
who might have fulfilled his role. As Leopold Amery wrote:
'Churchill, the one man by common consent ruled out from ever
becoming the Prime Minister of any party, was, by equally common consent welcomed as the only possible leader in the hour
of danger.'

The task he undertook with a great surge of spirit which was
swiftly to embrace and infuse the whole nation, could only have
been done by a man knowing it to be his destiny. Success demanded an immense national effort from a people who seemed
to have become disillusioned, lethargic and cynical through the
long years of poverty and unemployment, while those well
enough informed to observe the situations developing in Europe
and the Soviet Union were disturbed and bewildered by the
miserable flounderings of the Chamberlain Government, the
abandonment of Czechoslovakia, and the shame of Munich,
which none the less caused millions to sigh with relief. And
nothing that had happened in the first seven months of war had
aroused the British people from their apathy. Yet in an instant
all this was changed. The limits of the possible had to be extended
over the whole field of national endeavour. In May 1940 very
few well-informed persons with first-class minds could have
genuinely believed in victory, and few in the survival of the

Island. But the people of Britain were not well informed. Most of them thought with their hearts and their emotions, rather than with their minds. Miraculously they reacted to Churchill like the dead coming to life.

'I have nothing to offer,' he said, 'but blood, toil, tears and sweat.' This was a recognisable description of the lot of the common man, and perhaps because of that the people reacted. Perhaps they believed that these were the first honest words they had been offered.

Churchill's great zest for war was infectious. It had impressed the scholarly peace-loving Asquith, and the great public servant, Maurice Hankey, twenty-five years earlier. Churchill had been a man of war from the nursery, yet his vision and concept of war was romantic, and no man loathed more powerfully the squalor, the obscenity and the slaughter. In common with a whole generation of survivors the memory of Passchendaele had bitten very deep. That horrible slaughter and stupidity would not happen again. Above all Churchill was a political animal. Before he was a soldier, before he was anything else, he was a politician, not simply in any narrow domestic sense, but in a world sense. And his country was embarked upon a world war. He had a natural grasp of strategy, arising out of his historical sense, his travels, his visual awareness of Europe and particularly of the Mediterranean. He knew the strategic story and the military story over at least five hundred years, and he knew that tomorrow would arise out of today.

From the outset Churchill was utterly ruthless, quixotic, uncertain of temper, driving all who worked for him and with him to the limits of their endurance. His demands were incessant and imperious, covering almost every field of human endeavour. He ignored the limitations of industry, and the limitations upon the movement of armies, navies and air forces, and therefore upon strategy and tactics, imposed by logistics. Technology and the proliferation of weapons, and the manifold and ever growing needs of troops, had changed the nature of warfare and its tempo. Churchill accepted no limitations until he had to, and then with bad grace. Constantly he extended the bounds of the possible.

Ideas poured from his fertile mind in a ceaseless flow and demanded the immediate attention of dedicated men even when, as was often true, the ideas were impossible. It seems that no rational or reasonable man could have done the job, and Churchill was rarely reasonable or rational. His egocentricity was total, his energy boundless. He was a man with a dimension denied to ordinary men.

Churchill, as I have indicated, saw war in the vast pattern of history. The whole of Europe from the North Cape to the Middle East was his great theatre of conflict and on this stage the *dramatis personae* were nations and empires, resolved upon aggrandisement and power, or upon security, great nations and empires pursuing politics by 'other means'. He had seen the crumbling to ruin of the great empires of the Ottoman Turks, the Romanovs, the Hapsburgs, and the rise of the German Empire. With a foreboding shared by most of his contemporaries on the world stage he had observed the rise of the U.S.S.R. In common with most people in the Western world he had observed this phenomenon in a manner warped by loathing or love or hope or fear, and by a remarkable absence of reliable information.

Churchill was born and grew to manhood in the last dazzling epoch of Empire and of British Imperial power. He served in India as a young subaltern of Hussars when India was still 'the brightest jewel' in the Empress's crown. He was not among those who knew that it was already tarnished. He had served on the North-West Frontier, in the Soudan, in the 'River War', and in the Boer War, which marked the decline of British power and heralded the twentieth century. He was very much aware of the Russo-Japanese war and its implications, and because of these things Britain was at last awakening to her extreme danger. Churchill was present at the birth of that awakening, and was very fully aware of it.

Refusing the hard grind of scholarship or of soldiering, a law unto himself, his exuberant mind and spirit unable to accept disciplines and restraints imposed by others, ranged freely over the great panorama of the human story. His mind was profoundly stirred by his great ancestor, Marlborough, but he was also deeply aware of his American ancestry, and that in him were two bloods, each so powerful that his maternal grandfather, Leonard Jerome, had doubted whether two such strains could be reconciled in one body. Perhaps the English strain in the last resort would be the most powerful. He had a remarkable respect, almost an awe, of his father, Lord Randolph Churchill, and he knew at an early age that politics would be his battleground.

In the First World War Churchill had played a vital part, and by his enormous zest, his invincible optimism, and his fearlessness of responsibility, had made a great contribution to victory, to which the sober and meticulous Maurice Hankey had paid glowing tribute, linking him with Balfour, Asquith and Lloyd George as one of the four men whose foresight and courage had saved Britain in the first half of the twentieth century.

Long before the Second World War Churchill's chronicles rivalled, if they did not surpass, the achievement of Thucydides as a reporter, even if he could not match the Greek in detachment.

The course of the First World War had impressed Churchill profoundly. He knew that strategy and politics at the highest levels constantly overlap, and had written: 'The distinction between politics and strategy diminishes as the point of view is raised. At the summit true politics and strategy are one. The manoeuvre which brings an ally into the field is as serviceable as that which wins a great battle.'[1]

'There is a region,' Lloyd George wrote, 'where the soldier claims to be paramount and where the interference of the statesman seems to him to be an impertinence.' Passchendaele had been such a 'region', and Lloyd George had fought the military commanders, Haig and Robertson, convinced 'that it would fail for reasons which I gave in great detail to the Cabinet and to Haig and Robertson before the offensive commenced'. The combined Allied offensive in Champagne and Artois was also, in Lloyd George's view, a costly and fatal mistake. 'The strategical as well as tactical error of judgment then perpetrated by the army commanders prolonged the war by two years. Should the Asquith coalition have exerted its overruling authority and vetoed that offensive?'

These events had influenced Churchill deeply, and helped to condition him for the great task he would face two decades in the future. His idea of Britain's role, and its means and methods were already clear in his mind when he wrote *The World Crisis, 1911–1914*.

'The mighty enemy had delivered his onslaught. It was our turn now. The initiative had passed to Britain—the Great Amphibian. The time and means were at our command. It was for us to say where we would strike and when . . .'

In 1940 the time and means were not at our command, but they would be unless disaster overtook the country. 'The Great Amphibian', developing Combined Operations forces, would strive to keep the enemy 'on the jump all over the vast enemy

[1]Churchill, *The World Crisis* (1915).

held coast line from the North Cape to the Eastern Mediterranean'. This was the basis of Churchill's strategy and tactics.
Moreover it was the pursuit of the 'art of the possible', the natural
strategy and tactics for an island and sea power, neither able nor
willing to deploy large ground forces against great land powers
like Germany. It would, in due course, infuriate not only the
left-wing in Britain, constantly demanding a 'second front' and
unaware of the logistical problems involved, but also his Allies,
who, having vast armies to deploy, tended to regard his strategic
concepts as dispersions of effort. The Americans at last came to
understand that for Churchill, to gain an ally, or to preserve a
neutral, was often as important, if not more important, than the
winning of victory on the battlefield. His motives were always
a mixture of the political and military, and it is difficult for an
Englishman—or indeed for a European, to imagine these two
activities apart.

Lloyd George had observed that Churchill always needed
someone to apply the brakes, to save him from himself and from
his own impetuosity, unlimited ideas, and violent energies. In the
Second World War there was no one man, for this in the nature
of things would have been impossible; but there were the Chiefs
of Staff who, acting with resolution, could and did curb him.
In an effort to cut out delays and, to some extent out-
manoeuvre the Chiefs of Staff, Churchill established direct communication with the Joint Planning Staffs, but the loyalty of the
planning staffs to their military chiefs saved the Chief of the
Imperial General Staff and the Director of Military Operations
from grave embarrassments. But there was no one between
Churchill's fertile mind and the planners, and the time wasted
on pursuing useless ideas was serious. No one with an immensely
fertile and versatile mind could hope to produce more than one
first-class idea in ten. The remaining nine could have been discarded before they reached the planners.

Churchill's vices were inextricably bound up with his virtues.
He caused all his close associates many exasperations and much
wasted time, and it needed real toughness of spirit to stand up
to him. It proved too much for Sir John Dill, C.I.G.S., a man
of great integrity and with a first-class knowledge of strategy.
Yet, in spite of all Churchill's faults he was, in Liddell Hart's
phrase, 'the Great Animator of War'.

... he could create the sense in all who listened to him that he was the mouthpiece of destiny. The controlled wildness of his temperament gave a passion to his oratory which hypnotised criticism and stirred profoundly not only parliament but the nation. He was the first politician England had known whose power rested on the magic symbolism of his own personality and beliefs ... it needed disaster or victory to call it forth.

This passage was written by J. H. Plumb about Chatham.[1] It fits Churchill absolutely, as also do Chatham's words: 'I know that I can save the country and that I alone can.'

As for Churchill, not only he knew, but everyone knew that he was the man.

Leopold Amery, the most romantic Tory of the period, and the only man who might have taken command, perhaps understood more than anyone the long and arduous road Churchill had travelled to meet his destiny. He had known Churchill from schooldays at Harrow, and had observed him throughout his political life. Churchill had had to overcome many physical handicaps. He had imposed a rigid discipline upon himself. He had suffered great loneliness in his childhood and youth. He had been—and remained—a victim of black moods of chronic depression. He had borne all with fortitude and great courage. He had overcome his stammer. He had practised for many hours before a mirror to develop a forceful image as a speaker, thrusting out his jaw to transform his 'baby face' into a formidable mask of aggression. He was an actor, rehearsing always for the great part that awaited him.

In his novel, *Savrola,* he had foreseen his destiny, and never lost sight of it, and all that he did was a preparation for his hour. Churchill's tragedy was in his mixed blood. Had he been wholly an Englishman in the sense that Charles de Gaulle was a Frenchman, he might have won the peace and found a new and noble role for his country as the cornerstone of a new Europe. Instead he wanted to reconcile the irreconcilable in himself and achieve a union of the English-speaking peoples, uniting the U.S.A. and Britain.

[1] J. H. Plumb, *England in the Eighteenth Century,* Penguin.

CHAPTER TWO

The War Leader in the Making

I

CHURCHILL WAS BORN IN BLENHEIM PALACE TWO MONTHS
prematurely. The event precipitated him into the struggle of
life, denying him two months' growth in the shelter of the
womb. The physical results were soon apparent, but the more
profound effects must be incalculable. His skin remained always
a delicate pink and white, his body was almost hairless, and he
found it difficult to bear contact with any but the softest clothing.
Moreover he had the bodily shape described as endomorphic,
recognisable by a large head, and a chest cage smaller than the
abdomen. This vulnerable infant was put at once in the hands
of a wet-nurse. His mother was twenty years of age, involved in
a round of society gaiety and political entertaining as the wife of
the ambitious Lord Randolph Churchill.

'The neglect and lack of interest in him shown by his parents
were remarkable, even judged by the standards of late Victorian
and Edwardian days,' wrote his son Randolph.[1]

The young Churchill was starved of parental affection, and
starved of letters throughout his long lonely days at school.
Instead he had the love and devotion of his nurse, Mrs. Everest.
She was the light of his young life. She sustained him to the
threshold of manhood, and her memory remained with him until
he died.

Until he was seven years old Churchill's world was the
nursery, his imagination stirred by his growing armies of soldiers.
By the time he was fifteen his 'war games' attracted the attention
of his maternal grandfather, Leonard Jerome, and drew grudging
praise even from his father, already sickening from the dreadful

[1]See also Anthony Storr, *Churchill, Four Faces and the Man*, Allen Lane.

scourge which would kill him in a few years. Churchill's skill in handling his troops was marked, and he was already deeply aware of his great ancestor, Marlborough. Perhaps because of his skill in his war games, Lord Randolph finally had him 'crammed' into Sandhurst after several attempts.

Meanwhile Churchill's schooldays had been, in the main, a dark and bitter ordeal. Sent to boarding school at seven years old he was savagely birched by a sadistic headmaster of a type far from uncommon in those days. With his particularly vulnerable body these frequent beatings were grim ordeals. It is not surprising that he avoided games and physical contact.

Rescued from this school at the age of nine Churchill enjoyed the care of two old ladies before going to Harrow School. He was already suffering the moods of black depression which remained with him throughout his life. He had become aggressive and at times recklessly daring, as when he essayed a leap he could not make and fell thirty feet to suffer painful injury. His ambition and his egotism were driving forces, but he would not learn anything he did not wish to learn. He had begun to read very early and loved English almost to the exclusion of all else. His Latin had foundered at his first school with his refusal to regard the vocative case as less than an absurdity. He returned a blank paper in Latin for his entry into Harrow.

At that time Churchill was an awkward and unprepossessing youth with a small and chunky body, freckled face and thin sandy hair. At Sandhurst he was still acutely conscious of his physical shortcomings, and wrote that he was cursed 'with so feeble a body that I can scarcely support the fatigues of the day; but I suppose I shall get stronger during my stay here.'[1]

He was then nineteen years old with a chest measurement of thirty-one inches and a height of five feet, five and a half inches. Yet when he left Sandhurst to join his regiment, the 4th Hussars, he stood up well to the strict riding training imposed by a crack cavalry regiment under a martinet of a colonel. He was no longer a weakling. Polo would give him great pleasure whenever he had the opportunity to play. He had taken up fencing, and was a good swimmer.

In the year 1895 Churchill came of age. His father died, his last years clouded by general paralysis of the insane. Mrs. Everest, his loyal nurse, died also. Although Churchill was still a soldier, and had had considerable experience in warfare in the field, he

[1]Quoted by Storr: op. cit.

knew that the road to power lay through politics, and the army was no more than a stepping-stone which he would contrive to use to his advantage. He had become very much aware of the privileges conferred upon him by his birth and social position. No doors, however exalted, were closed to him. He cultivated the goodwill and liking of the very great, and revealed considerable charm. A. J. Balfour, Lord Esher, Henry Drummond Wolff, were close family friends; Rosebery, Morley, Ripon and Salisbury were also well disposed and accessible. And these were the men filling the key positions in Britain, while Balfour and Esher would be leading architects of the Committee of Imperial Defence, thereby to improve out of recognition Britain's ability to wage war, and to survive two world wars. The Committee of Imperial Defence virtually lifted Britain into the twentieth century after her demoralising experience in the Boer War. Churchill had the good fortune to be present at the birth of this organisation in 1904 and to maintain intimate contact with it and with its key members for the next forty years.

Before serving with his regiment in India Churchill went to New York on his way to the Cuban War, having obtained introductions to the Spanish military authorities. In New York he was fascinated by the world of financial and political tycoons. This was the world in which his grandfather Jerome had made and lost fortunes and survived. But for his powerful sense of destiny Churchill might have been lured to seek his own financial and political fortunes on that stage.

Meanwhile there was Cuba and Churchill hurried off to experience his first 'whiff of grape shot'. Enemy fire at close range passed through the hut he shared with others, and later, riding at the Spanish General's side, he came under direct fire from guerillas. He did not exaggerate this experience, but it was of great importance to his growing up.

In the autumn of 1896 Churchill sailed for India with his regiment, wrenching his right shoulder severely in his impatience to disembark from a skiff heaving against the wharf at Bombay. This does not reveal his enthusiasm to start soldiering. His extravagant mother allowed him £500 a year, insufficient to enable him to maintain the minimum of polo ponies which a young officer of cavalry in India regarded as of the first importance, not only for health and exercise but for his position. For Churchill, the first task was to earn money, indeed to do more than that. Secondly he needed to fill the gaps in his education. The two things would go together. He perceived that his time in India might profit him greatly. His problem would be not to fall foul of his regiment while doing a minimum of regimental duties. This would not endear him to his brother officers, but their good opinion came very low in his priorities.

In the next five years Churchill laid the foundations of a wider education and of his fortunes. There is no blueprint for a man resolved on political power, and for the fulfilment of vague dreams soon to be expressed in his first novel, *Savrola,* which brought him £700, and caused him some embarrassment. For more than a year Churchill dedicated himself to reading and writing. He was his own 'tutor', selecting his own study course with great catholicity. He felt a great hunger for knowledge and fed it with philosophy, sociology, politics, history. His capacity for work was prodigious, and his choice of works eclectic and eccentric. Lecky made an odd mixture with Schopenhauer, Malthus and Darwin. He read Plato, which he hoped, together with a volume by his old Headmaster, Welldon of Harrow, would be sufficient introduction to Socrates. He absorbed Winwood Reade's *Martyrdom of Man* and found time for his favourite, R. L. Stevenson, whose novel *Kidnapped* would be his companion in his captivity in the Boer War. Gibbon and Macaulay were to be lifelong favourites whose influence on his work was great. Later he lamented his failure to acquire a grounding in Latin, and his consequent inability to find a place in either Oxford or Cambridge. He was, I think, fortunate. A more orthodox diet of study might have been of much less use to him.

All this fortified him in his determination to write, but his business was war. He was prepared to bide his time, but not for long. In England he had made his mark with Lord Charles Beresford and used his visits to 'Deepdene' to great advantage. He had not only paved the way for possible service with the Malakand force on the frontier by appealing to Sir Bindon Blood, but had also attracted the attention of the Prince of Wales, soon to become Edward VII. On the voyage to India he had met Colonel Hamilton, an officer serving under Sir William Lockhart, and the meeting would prove useful. Meanwhile Lady Randolph had been active in London on her son's behalf, and no man ever had as good an agent. Not only did she arrange for him to send despatches to the *Daily Telegraph* at £5 per column, but she pursued Lord Wolseley and Lord Roberts for introductions to Sir George White, Commander-in-Chief in India, to help

Churchill to his ambitions. But without Churchill's ruthless drive and resolution none of this would have availed him. The Commander-in-Chief received him frigidly, and was not disposed to be helpful. It remained for Churchill to help himself and he risked disgrace in his military career to achieve his ends.

By 1899 he had been wonderfully successful, having written a story of the Malakand Field Force and a very good book on the River War. He had attached himself to Kitchener in the Soudan, despite that formidable soldier's absolute refusal to help him in any way, even in face of pressures from Lord Salisbury.

Churchill appears to have been impervious to the feelings of others, but it is doubtful that this was so. Often he remarked, half humorously, on the bare civility of those whose likes and dislikes he ignored in the pursuit of his own ends. Particularly was this so when he entered politics after a failure to win a seat in 1899. 'It is melancholy to be forced to record,' he wrote, 'these less amiable aspects of human nature, which by a most curious and indeed unaccountable coincidence have always seemed to present themselves in the wake of my innocent foot-steps, and even sometimes across the path on which I wished to proceed.'

In the late autumn of 1899 he had resolved to go to the Boer War, and was able to arrange a contract with the *Morning Post* to send his Boer War despatches for the then almost 'princely' payment of £250 per month. Once in South Africa he used his military and journalistic advantages in skilful proportion, while his name enabled him to force his way into the company of Lord Roberts and the field commanders.

Churchill's experiences in the Boer War brought him to as true a maturity as he would ever attain. He was appalled by the 'obsolete' condition of the British Army. He saw at first hand the effects of rifle fire directed by Boer marksmen upon slow-moving bunched infantry, and stated that a well-mounted Boer was worth three to five regular British soldiers. He saw the archaic British war-machine blundering from disaster to disaster, and many of the best younger officers drew their conclusions from these events. Time was fast running out, and by the time he returned to England to win a parliamentary seat at Oldham in the 'Khaki election' he was aware of the dangers threatening Britain. The country was without a friend in Europe, or indeed, anywhere else. The war had pitchforked Britain into the twentieth century, and not a moment too soon. The danger was fully realised, and important studies were beginning to bear fruit. These would result in the establishment of the Committee of Imperial Defence due to the drive and energies of A. J. Balfour, Lord Esher and others.

Of these developments Churchill was very much aware. He was studying to write a life of his father, and knew from Lord Randolph's papers of his father's defence studies with Dilke, Havelock-Allan and Beresford, and of his work on the Hartington Commission in 1888. (The Hartington Commission was undoubtedly the first serious effort to develop an organisational pattern for national security.)[1] Even before the Boer War the problems of defence had begun to engage the attention of far-sighted statesmen. Churchill's study of his father was not simply, as Amery remarked, a work of filial piety, it was also a vital factor in his involvement in defence problems and his presence at the birth of the instrument which was to enable Britain to survive. Lord Esher produced the first strategic assessment, and from 1904 onward the Committee of Imperial Defence grew in scope under its Secretaries, George Sydenham Clarke, followed by Admiral Sir Charles Ottley, and finally by Maurice Hankey,[2] a Captain of Royal Marines, whose name was to become almost synonymous with the Committee, and whose influence over more than thirty years in successive administrations was unique. Kitchener had recognised the need for a first-class Secretary at the outset, and had suggested Leopold Amery, but Amery was too much an active politician for such a role. Like Churchill he was absorbed in defence and strategic problems, and was associated with the Committee from its earliest beginnings. In 1940 Churchill and Amery had watched closely the growth of the Committee, its flourishing sub-Committees, of whom they knew the Chairmen intimately, and its ramifications to embrace the life of the nation. For this reason alone these two men could lay claim to being in positions to command and to use to the full the most important instrument of war.

Sir Julian Corbett, the Official Historian, wrote of the vital importance of the Committee in the First World War.

Amongst the many false impressions that prevailed, when after the lapse of a century we found ourselves involved in a great war, not the least erroneous is the belief that we were not

[1] Franklyn Arthur Johnson, *Defence by Committee*, Oxford Univ. Press.
[2] Later Lord Hankey.

prepared for it. Whether the scale on which we prepared was as large as the signs of the times called for, whether we did right to cling to our long tried systems of a small army and a large navy, are questions which will long be debated; but given the scale which we deliberately chose to adopt, there is no doubt that the machinery for setting our forces in action had reached an ordered completeness in detail that has no parallel in our history.[1]

Upon that rock Britain built her readiness for war.

II

Churchill's political success was swift and remarkable. It was also dangerous. While still cutting his political teeth he deeply offended the Tory Party on the issue of Free Trade. He had shown that, like his father, he was his own man. On the other hand his life of Lord Randolph had impressed a wide range of important people, including Rosebery and Morley whose advice he had sought and gained. In 1906 he became Under-Secretary for the Colonies in Campbell-Bannerman's brief liberal administration, and upon Bannerman's death in 1907 he served under Herbert Asquith as President of the Board of Trade, and later Home Secretary. He had fought a losing by-election at Manchester, but had gained a safe Liberal seat at Dundee. He used his experience to the full in all three appointments, constantly broadening his political knowledge, and above all his ideas on world strategy. The influential Lord Esher sought his support as Home Secretary for the appointment of Maurice Hankey as Secretary of the Committee of Imperial Defence, and in 1911 Asquith sent him to the Admiralty as First Lord. It was a marvellous progress, and he had gained powerful support in private and in public. In 1907 he had met Edward Marsh and won his life-long devotion as his personal secretary, and by this he had secured his literary future. At the same time he had won and married Clementine Hozier, and with these two in his camp his home base was secure. On the political front Lloyd George, then Chancellor of the Exchequer, had recognised Churchill's calibre and potential. With Lloyd George's support he was able to lay two keels to Germany's one as the war rapidly approached. Meanwhile he had the friendship of the quiet Asquith with his powerful intellect.

[1]Lord Hankey and Leopold Amery support this view; see Amery, *My Political Life,* vol. II.

Following a fruitful lecture tour in the U.S.A., and with the success of his books he was able to hand his first £10,000 to the safe-keeping of Sir Ernest Cassel, whose financial genius would assure its increase. It was his first security plank. He had visited Greece and Turkey, and embarked with Edward Marsh to Uganda, and on to the headwaters of the White Nile, and thence to Egypt and the Soudan.

At home as First Lord in 1911 he travelled in the Mediterranean, the Adriatic and all the Greek seas, making with his wife a foursome with Asquith and the volatile and irrepressible Margot, and their secretaries. While Asquith filled in the classical backgrounds Churchill estimated strategic and tactical possibilities. A shadow of amusement seems to colour Asquith's liking for this dangerous young politician whose love was clearly war, as Asquith's was clearly peace. Their admiration was mutual.

These were, almost certainly, the happiest years of Churchill's life, a wife and home, a reasonably secure financial background, a high political position in which no man was better placed for the preparations for the war that was unmistakably looming to challenge British supremacy at sea, to change the face of Europe, and perhaps the world. His mother, Lady Randolph, had married George Cornwallis West, and was happily settling into her new life, having in the end done her best with great success to further the interests of her son through the difficult last years of the century. She had seen him safely launched, whatever had been her shortcomings as a mother in her son's childhood. She had, as he wrote, shone for him like the evening star, and—as he did not write—equally remote. He was romantic about beautiful women, and loved their company. He had begun to make friends of his own kind, rather than of his own class. F. E. Smith, later Lord Birkenhead, Bernard Baruch, the American tycoon with stakes in the business of government, and soon Max Aitken, Lord Beaverbrook, acquisitive of news and money. This was the company he liked best, while politically he had an affinity with David Lloyd George whose advice was of infinite value, and whose authority he accepted.

Churchill's great weakness, and his strength, was his devotion to 'Empire' and the Monarchy. Now he had a third love in Parliament itself. He was utterly independent, and said exactly what he thought about anything and everything in and out of season. Naturally he was properly distrusted by good 'party' men. He aroused bitter passions in old-fashioned Tories and

Radical Liberals. Some of his antics, notably in the Sidney Street affair, when he was Home Secretary, had given him a reputation for being unprincipled, irresponsible and above all unreliable and unpredictable. Old Francis Neilson wrote: 'Morley was not the only Cabinet member who had been associated with him, who found him destitute of political morality. To scoff at the principles laid down by Richard Cobden and Henry George was a despicable act of ingratitude.' It is, of course, absurdly unjust, but a great many people are absurdly unjust, especially in politics. In any case, old Morley was a difficult character of a very much older school. Moreover he had a great respect for Churchill in many ways, whatever he may have thought about his 'political morality'.

Whatever anyone thought, Churchill sailed on under full sail, and he had the powerful support both of Asquith and Lloyd George. It is not my purpose to do more than refer to Churchill's part in the First World War. It was a vital part. It was, perhaps, his greatest grounding for the role he was at last to play. He has been accused, wrongly I believe, of all kinds of blunders. He did not consider sufficiently his position as First Lord when he took off for Antwerp in October 1914, but his Antwerp adventure was sound, even though inadequately supported. He was already a 'driving force' in war and recognised as such not only by Asquith, but by the ever vigilant Maurice Hankey, the silent observer of 'the matter of Britain', and the faithful recorder of the minutes of the meetings of the Cabinet. There was a time when Lloyd George remarked about vital meetings, 'Let's ask Hankey what we decided, if anything, yesterday.' He had become indispensable.

The full flavour of Churchill in his prime is in his *World Crisis*. Passage after passage reveals his tremendous zest. From first to last Churchill thinks on his feet, as Asquith said. The book is spoken, not written, and there is Churchill, pacing up and down, waving his cigar, savouring the phrases as they pour out of him. He is, as it were, fighting the war on all fronts, and his trouble was that no job was able fully to contain his energies. He wanted—he always wanted—to carry out every operation from beginning to end, to be the leader in the field as well as the power in the centre of the web of war at home. He had been the moving force behind the defence of Antwerp and the despatch of troops to the Channel ports, all to gain time for the hard pressed Belgian Army. His place, of course, was at the Admiralty, but nothing could hold him back. He had to be in the midst striving to inspire the defence. 'I felt it my duty to see the matter through,' he wrote. 'On the other hand it was not right to leave the Admiralty without an occupant. I therefore telegraphed on the 4th to the Prime Minister offering to take formal military charge of the British forces in Antwerp.'

Asquith could not help being amused by Churchill, but he at once saved him from himself. He would have to return to the Admiralty. Meanwhile he had come within an ace of becoming a soldier. Kitchener wanted to give him the necessary military rank, and on 5th October, 1914, he telegraphed Lord Kitchener: 'Line of the Nethe is intact. Marine Brigade holding important sector north-west of Lierre, has been briskly engaged during the night, with about seventy casualties so far ... General Paris is doing very well ... Later. Infantry attack indicated now appears to be developing ...

Churchill's messages from the 'front' poured out during the day: '4.45 p.m. Attack has been pressed. Marines have stood well ... On their right a regiment has fallen back ... some Germany infantry to west of Lierre are across Nethe.'

In the midst of being First Lord of the Admiralty Churchill was at his job of war reporting. 'I remained in the line on the Lierre road,' he wrote. 'Here about five o'clock Sir Henry Rawlinson joined me.'

No doubt, had it been possible, he would have landed later in Gallipoli, but he did very well with his imagination. All this was giving him the wrong kind of 'image' for a reliable senior minister of government. In the minds of an Edwardian public he was already an exciting adventurer, far removed from the sober and impressive figures of men like Grey, Haldane, Balfour, men remote from the public they served, and the unfortunate Grey remote from the world he was meant to understand. Asquith and Lloyd George, while recognising Churchill's great qualities and concerned to preserve them, knew that it was vital for someone to exercise a restraining hand. Lloyd George was the only man able to do it, but his hour had not yet struck. Asquith had the strength to do so, but he was too civilised, too intellectual and basically too lazy and too enchanted with Churchill, his antics and his zest. Moreover Asquith's grip on affairs was steadily being eroded by his enemies, notably by Beaverbrook and Bonar Law in alliance behind the scenes.

When finally the tragic failure of the assault on the Dardanelles and the disastrous failure in Gallipoli, overtook the British, Churchill became the natural scapegoat. The account should have been laid at many doors, and was due (in Lloyd George's view) in the main to the 'procrastination of Kitchener and Asquith'. The treatment of Churchill was deplorable. 'They had flung him from the masthead, whence he had been directing the fire, down to the lower deck to polish the brass.' The brutality of the fall stunned Churchill. It was a cruel and unjust degradation.

However, Churchill bore the burden, defended his part gallantly, forcefully and with dignity, and left it to 'history'. Briefly, he accepted the Duchy of Lancaster, retaining his seat on the War Council. 'It was on this condition alone,' he wrote, 'that I had found it possible to accept a sinecure office.'

But not for long. Characteristically he went off to serve with the Grenadier Guards on the Western Front. In January 1916 he commanded the 6th Battalion Royal Scots Fusiliers. He led his battalion fearlessly, as one would imagine, but he soon discovered that he was already too old, and too soft, to stand the rigours of active service on the Western Front. At the age of forty-two he could not have become part of the soldier's world. It would never have been possible. He was offered a brigade, but wisely he resisted the temptation to become a general; he was a politician.

Meanwhile Asquith had formed the first coalition government, and had fallen, to be replaced by Lloyd George as head of the second coalition. But there was no place—yet—for Churchill. The opposition to his inclusion in the Cabinet was implacable. The Tories were set against him. 'Is he more dangerous when he is FOR you than when he is against you?' Lloyd George demanded of Bonar Law.

'I would rather have him against us every time,' said Bonar Law. The Morning Post described him as 'a floating kidney in the body politic', and very few had anything to say in his favour or defence. Even Beaverbrook thought that he detected in Churchill the signs of tyranny.

All this temporary disaster, which like everything in Churchill's life added to his experience of war and the running of war, was in fact the result of an idea which could have won the war and saved tens of thousands of lives. Amery had written a powerful, well-reasoned paper, recommending a Balkan strategy. Maurice Hankey also supported a Balkan line. Kitchener and Asquith saw the immense advantages of an attack on 'the

soft underbelly', to bring even at that late hour Turkey,
Bulgaria and Greece into our alliance, and repair the blindness
of Edward Grey. In the event the commanders on the Western
Front would not agree to the transfer of troops. Joffre and Haig
were adamant. French, who had been lukewarm, had been
replaced as Commander-in-Chief of the B.E.F. But there had
been some French support. In the event it had been impossible to
bring the necessary force to bear in time, and when Ian Hamilton
landed his troops it was already too late. In those days the lifeline
might have been established to struggling Russia. A quarter of
a century later the idea held good for different reasons, but again,
and for different reasons, it was not pressed home.

CHAPTER THREE

The Aftermath

IT IS NOT EASY TO THINK CLEARLY IN THE AFTERMATH OF A war that removed the hearts of a continent, made havoc of the relationships and governments of many nations, impoverished half the world, slaughtered millions and changed the face of society and the nature of industry. It is even less simple when a vast land mass on the eastern boundaries of that continent has suffered total revolution, to be rebuilt—or destroyed—by something new, and alien. It is certain that fear and loathing of the regime in Soviet Russia dominated the foreign policies of the western world for generations, and does so still. In that light the views of Thorsten Veblen and Professor Arno J. Mayer merit attention.[1]

Writing of the Versailles Treaty fashioned by leaders, not only dominated by very real and present fears for the future, but almost at the mercy of peoples screaming for revenge against the late enemy, Veblen observed: 'The main consideration was the defeat of Bolshevism at any cost. This was not written into the text of the Treaty, but may rather be said to have been the parchment on which the text was written.'

Professor Mayer supports this thesis. The aim of the victors was 'to build in Europe a solid bastion against the advances of Bolshevism, and in the latter stages of the conference and in its aftermath, this motive came to predominate over every other. By the same token the peace-makers succeeded brilliantly in what they wanted to do.'

Not everyone is adept at reading between the lines of massive

[1] Arno J. Mayer, *Politics and Diplomacy of Peacemaking, Times Literary Supplement,* front essay, 6th June, 1968.

and complex documents, and those who are, do not necessarily reach similar conclusions. But that the Versailles Treaty was a tragic document in its results is certain. Fear of Bolshevism did dominate the Western world, and was an element in the creation of the Third Reich of Adolf Hitler, and the steady march to a second instalment of Armageddon.

Churchill's reaction to the Russian revolution was frightening in a statesman. His support of the White Russian campaign against the Bolsheviks was bitterly pursued at a cost neither Britain nor Churchill could afford, and beyond the point when it was even remotely possible to visualise success. This added to Churchill's unpopularity with the working people of Britain, many of whom believed or profoundly hoped that the new regime in Soviet Russia might be a promise of a new 'world'. Their disillusion was slow and tragic, as the promised 'land fit for heroes to live in' failed to appear in Britain or anywhere else, even on the distant horizon, and they faced twenty years of strikes, appalling unemployment and hunger.

Churchill's personal attitude is important. His violent words revealed a flaw in his character. His rhetoric passed all reasonable bounds. In addition he failed to realise the tragedy of war Russia had suffered. Sweeping aside all the testimony from un-impeachable sources, ignoring the mountains of Russian dead, the millions of civilians desperate with hunger and cold in that vast and tortured land, Churchill announced that Russia 'with victory in her grasp fell upon the earth, devoured alive, like Herod of old, by worms'. But he reserved the full force of his hatred for Lenin and Trotsky, the architects of revolution. 'In the cutting off of the lives of men and women no Asiatic conquerer, not Tamerlane, not Jenghiz Khan can match his fame,' he wrote of Lenin. 'Implacable vengeance, rising from a frozen pity in a tranquil, sensible, matter-of-fact, good-humoured integument! His weapon logic; his mood opportunist. His sym-pathies cold and wide as the Arctic Ocean; his hatreds tight as the hangman's noose. His purpose to save the world; his method to blow it up!'

Such outbursts induced Lord Esher to observe that he became quickly enslaved by his own phrases. The very noise of words enchanted him, and he, at times, permitted himself to be carried upon the tides of his exuberant verbosity. Many deplored his intemperate mode of expression, while sharing many of his fore-bodings. Lloyd George deplored his 'morbid detestation' and described his outbursts as giving 'a ludicrous picture ... made attractive only because of the glittering rhetoric in which it is framed by a great colour artist.' Asquith, Balfour and Hankey, among many others, were disconcerted.

Churchill's reaction to the Soviet regime was not merely personal, it expressed, in a very slightly exaggerated fashion, the feeling that was to sweep the United States and hold that nation in an obsession of fear, crippling strategic thought. Few people could be found, even in the chancellories and war offices of the entire Western world, who were able to take a balanced view of the meaning and import of Soviet Communism. Grand strategy henceforth held a vital flaw. Moreover the triumph of Lenin, as it developed, was to inspire an equally disastrous attitude in those who supported what they believed to be his philosophy and its aims. At the same time a slow and miserable disillusionment awaited the many thousands of the working class who saw, as they thought, the hope of a better world. Thus a dangerous lunacy held the bulk of mankind in its grip, dividing not simply the world but nations.

These things must be remembered if Churchill's attitudes throughout the 1930s are to be understood, for although his violence had abated it was difficult for him to regard an alliance with Soviet Russia as less than distasteful.

It prevented him from seeing clearly the issues involved in the Spanish Civil War; but it did not prevent him embracing Stalin and Soviet Russia when, miraculously, Nazi Germany in the Second World War marched eastward to her doom.

But in the immediate aftermath of Versailles there was much to worry about in the Western world. The United States, having played a leading part in the conference, abandoned the whole business and withdrew into isolation. Churchill commented bitterly:

After immense delays and false hopes that only aggravated her difficulties, Europe was left to scramble out of the world disaster as best she could; and the United States, which had lost but 125,000 lives in the whole struggle, was to settle down upon the basis of receiving through one channel or another four-fifths of the reparations paid by Germany to the countries she had devastated or whose manhood she had slain.[1]

<hr>

[1]Churchill, *The World Crisis: The Aftermath.*

'We have no selfish ends to serve,' President Wilson said. 'We desire no conquest, no dominion. We seek no indemnities for ourselves, no material compensation for the sacrifices we shall freely make. We are but one of the champions of mankind.'[1]

When, like Pilate, President Wilson had washed his hands of the whole affair, his country settled down to absorb its vast booty. It remained for L. S. Amery to underline the situation:

> The United States had emerged . . . with an immensely stimulated production, and now found itself transformed from a debtor to the world's greatest creditor, on commercial account alone, as well as on account of the debts due from its Allies and as the ultimate recipient of the greater part of the heavy war reparations imposed on Germany.[2]

At home in the aftermath of war the challenge was more than the wit of one man could meet. The enormous task of demobilisation, and the absorption of tens of thousands of men back into industry was tackled with skill, ingenuity and energy, but these were not enough. Meanwhile Churchill was deeply involved in support to the White Russians and was chiefly responsible for the sending of 100,000 tons of arms and equipment to Vladivostock, and a total bill of costs which reached £100 million. It was not calculated to enhance Churchill's popularity, and had it been inspired by hatred alone it would have been unforgivable. It was possible to believe that Soviet Communism might have been modified. It could be argued that it was worth trying in the climate of those days.

In 1919 Lloyd George won a sweeping victory and formed his government with Churchill as Minister of War and Air.

For ten years until 1929, Churchill occupied positions in the Cabinet from Colonial Secretary by way of the Ministries of War and Air to the office of Chancellor of the Exchequer. He had survived the fall of governments, fought unsuccessful by-elections, and in 1924 found his seat at Epping ensuring his occupation of a seat in Parliament for the rest of his political life. In the last years of war he had vital experience of industry in the Ministry of Munitions. He had, from his earliest days at the Admiralty revealed a flair for advances in

[1] Wilson's speech, 2nd April, 1917.
[2] L. S. Amery, *My Political Life*, vol. II.

weaponry and had provided backing for the experiments in armour which led to the development of the tank. His mind was wonderfully fertile in that field, and he had few illusions in regard to peace. In an essay, first written in his *World Crisis* and reprinted and developed in his *Thoughts and Adventures* he visualised some of the horrors of future wars.

> Some think that the next war will be fought with electricity. And on this a vista opens out of electrical rays which could paralyse the engines of a motor car, could claw down aeroplanes from the sky . . . Then there are explosives . . . May there not be methods of using explosive energy incomparably more intense than anything heretofore discovered? Might not a bomb no bigger than an orange be found to possess a secret power to destroy a whole block of buildings—nay, to concentrate the force of a thousand tons of cordite and blast a township at a stroke . . .

There is very little that he did not consider in the aftermath of that terrible and utterly devastating war, from poison gas and the development of chemical warfare to something approaching the atom bomb. The whole subject had a fearful fascination for him, and his writings at this time repay reading and re-reading. So also do Lloyd George's recorded thoughts in his *War Memoirs*. L. S. Amery is another of the few whose strategic grasp and humanity demand attention. And, of course, there is Maurice Hankey with his impeccable records of all that was said and done in the highest councils of the nation.

But my subject is Churchill, and how he felt, how he grew into the man who would be ripe to grasp the Supreme Command when the great emergency should overtake the country. 'The story of the human race is war,' he wrote. 'Except for brief and precarious interludes there has never been peace in the world . . .' He notes the steady steps towards Armageddon. 'It was not until the dawn of the twentieth century of the Christian era that War really began to enter into its kingdom as the potential destroyer of the human race.' He reflects on what would have happened if the Great War had gone on into 1919.

> Thousands of aeroplanes would have shattered their [German] cities. Scores of thousands of cannon would have blasted their front. Arrangements were being made to carry simul-

taneously a quarter of a million men, together with all their requirements, continuously forward across country in mechanical vehicles moving ten or fifteen miles each day.

The campaign of 1919 was never fought; but its ideas go marching along.

Perhaps there is a clue to failure to make peace, to achieve peace, in the sudden stoppage of the war to which Churchill draws attention. It 'stopped as suddenly and universally as it had begun'. We did know, at any rate, something of the shape of the next instalment, for that there would be a next instalment there could be little doubt. The heart of Europe seethed with hatred and fear.

Churchill was full of ominous doubts and fears 'as we entered upon a period of exhaustion described as Peace'. It was an entirely new situation. Not only abroad but at home enormous problems demanded settlement. The means of keeping peace were already in ruins, the League of Nations abandoned by one of its principal sponsors at birth had become an emasculated rump. It did its best. Perhaps it would have been better if it had not existed. Perhaps it would have been better if America had never left her vast continent at all. For it was not her war. It was European in its main context, and it was basically a 'civil war'. And it was not finished when the end came. So much was clear. In 1923 France marched into the Ruhr to deprive Germany of the means whereby she might rebuild and meet her huge bill for reparations. At home politicians tinkered with the intricate machinery of war and peace, inextricably inter-mingled.

Churchill was as much at sea as everyone else. When he left the Air Ministry *The Times* commented: 'He leaves the body of British flying well nigh at that last gasp when a military funeral would be all that would be left for it.' At the War Office he had turned the clock back, revealing a mind more in tune with the 'Cavalry Club' than with the young officers of the Royal Tank Corps, who had believed that he would be their powerful ally. Vast numbers of men had to be absorbed into industries while in the course of being adapted from war to peace, and yet, in a sense with one eye on war. None the less the decade of the 1920s was an immensely successful one for Churchill. He wrote his four volumes of *The World Crisis* to consolidate his fortune, and buy him his country home at Chartwell. He had had an appendix operation, and was forced to convalesce through the winter of 1922–23. The death of his great-grand-mother, Lady Londonderry, had brought him a valuable inherit-ance and underlined his security. Henceforth he wrote (because it was in him to do so) and he had begun to paint. Yet his old writing was over. Without his faithful and loyal amanuensis, Edward Marsh, *The World Crisis* must have been delayed, perhaps for many years. Together they had worked on the first volume and completed it in 1921. His books henceforth, with growing armies of research workers, secretaries and Edward Marsh, were, as indeed they had to be, team efforts, but all bearing the unmistakable mark of Churchill.

When Churchill returned again to parliament and accepted with astonishment and joy the office of Chancellor, the Western world was moving steadily towards economic disaster. When he left the Treasury the country was to suffer for a decade from the 'economic consequences of Mr. Churchill' as Maynard Keynes wrote. The condition of the country was unutterably dreary, a series of strikes in the early twenties had culminated in the General Strike of 1926, described by Amery as 'the mildest-mannered revolution that ever tried to coerce a constitutional government'. It gave Churchill the opportunity to enjoy himself editing the *British Gazette* from the offices of the *Morning Post,* and did not enhance his reputation as a democrat or his popularity with the working-classes. The depression was bleak and grey with windows of shops boarded up in industrial towns, and unemployment rising steadily above the one and a half million mark. The malaise was almost worldwide coming to a head with the great Wall Street crash of 1929–30.

In the General Election of 1929 Ramsay MacDonald won a narrow victory for Labour, and brought a momentary spark of hope to the masses not far above starvation level. Lloyd George, the only man in the opinion of his few remaining friends as well as many of his more thoughtful enemies, who might have found a solution to the nation's social ills, was in the wilderness for good, his once powerful Liberal party a mere rump, in ruins. When Baldwin joined a coalition with MacDonald in 1931 the Conservatives were effectively back in power, and Churchill was out for his long sojourn in the 'wilderness'.

Part of Baldwin's idea in joining MacDonald was to exclude Lloyd George and Churchill from office. Churchill, as Amery remarked, had become a 'bad boy' in Baldwin's eyes, mainly owing to his 'die-hard' attitude to India. He was incurably mid-Victorian in many of his attitudes, and had no sympathy for a Commonwealth steadily replacing the old Empire. He was not so much a 'Little Englander' as a 'Great Englander', Amery observed, besides he was a menace to everyone else in Cabinet or Committee, tending always to dominate the proceedings. Both Baldwin and Chamberlain, admiring Churchill's great qualities, wanted to do things in their own ways. The country was in the hands of mediocrities, and the results at home and abroad were deplorable. Elsewhere, notably in Germany and Italy, Nazi and Fascist dictatorships had begun to flourish, preparing to flex their muscles and test the opposition—in France and Britain—if it existed!

As the country stumbled along through the drab 1930s and the morale of the people fell to a very low ebb, the sidelines, or the 'Wilderness', was the best place to be for a politician of Churchill's calibre. He had much to do and much to think about.

II

Throughout the 1930s Churchill was a leader among those pressing for urgency and action in facing up to the disastrous state of British defences, not only the state of the forces, starved of funds not only to rebuild, but even to maintain minimum standards of training. The whole industrial complex upon which the ability of the nation to defend itself must be based had fallen into disuse and obsolescence, largely as a consequence of Churchill's own deeds as Chancellor. The Committee of Imperial Defence was fully aware of the situation, but it was not its business to formulate policy or to instigate action. It provided facts. It kept the record straight.

There is one great flaw in Churchill's claim to prescience and to a clean record. Indeed he was not fully aroused to the nature of Britain's extreme danger until 1936, or even until 1937, when he stated that if his choice lay between Nazi Germany and Soviet Russia he might choose Nazi Germany. His prejudices died hard, but such prejudices should never stand in the way of a statesman's strategic grasp. By 1937 he had at last seen the position in Europe, and had partially allayed his fears of the Soviet bogey that had so bedevilled Western thought since 1917.

The clues to much of the depressing situation in regard to Britain's lack of readiness to meet even the minimum requirements of defence lay in the 'Ten-Year Rule'. Peter Silverman writing in the *R.U.S.I. Journal* in March 1971 drew attention yet again to some of its effects:

> No examination of British Defence Planning during the 1920s and 1930s can be carried on without some knowledge of the infamous 'Ten-Year Rule'. For within this innocuous phrase was contained a policy that placed the British defence services in a financial straight-jacket for twelve years, and which caused the deterioration of the three Services to such an extent that Britain was unable to meet her foreign commitments, or to exert any real influence upon world events...

Briefly, the 'rule' was based upon the premise that there would not be a war for ten years, surely a sane conclusion in the immediate aftermath of the most devastating war in human history! It was discussed in the middle of August 1919 and formulated by the Cabinet in October of that year. Those responsible were Lloyd George, Churchill (Secretary of State for War and Air), Bonar Law, the Lord Privy Seal, Austen Chamberlain, the Chancellor of the Exchequer, and Walter Long, First Lord of the Admiralty. Once formulated the rule was reviewed from time to time, and re-stated for the last time in 1929. The Committee of Imperial Defence was again informed that there could be no major war for ten years, but of course there were many who had other ideas. By 1931 it had become clear to all that the rule was outdated, but the harm had been done, and for the rest of the decade Churchill could devote himself to castigating the government for a state of affairs for which he was as responsible as anyone. Even in 1931, when the rule was rescinded, the Treasury continued to fight the Service estimates and to restrict rearmament. The Chiefs of Staff Committee had been principal movers in getting rid of the rule, but a memorandum to them from the Chancellor, Neville Chamberlain, reminded them sourly that the financial risks faced by Britain were more dangerous than the absence of defences. In fact, the nation had been broke since the end of the war and even in 1931 the entire yield of income tax could not meet the interest on the national debt. Britain's dire financial condition had been the main cause of the whole sorry business. In 1921 the Navy, despite its losses, and growing obsolescence, despite exciting developments in equipment, was granted a mere sixty million pounds, while the Army and Air Force shared seventy-five million pounds between them.

Yet at the end of the war the Army had been forced to maintain half a million men in the Middle East, while a considerable force served uselessly in Russia, and the Army tried to meet its commitments 'in obscure places from the Punjab to South Arabia', undermanned and under-equipped. It did its job as 'policeman and peacekeeper'.

It was the serious financial situation that had forced Lloyd George and then Churchill to take an optimistic view of the future of peace, for in 1919 it would have been impossible for any nation, other than the U.S.A., to make war on anyone. Japan was first among those to realise that her sea power would be unchallenged for many years. Others were not slow to observe, while necessarily slower to act. Britain kept a close watch on German industry, wisely suspicious thanks to the foresight of Eyre Crowe, Esher and Lloyd George. A committee under Desmond Morton had been formed for the job. The Germans were, no doubt, keeping a close watch on Britain. They saw our war industries run down beyond a point of return, our craftsmen losing their skills, our machine tools obsolete, our researches starved of funds. Even military training had to be cut back to a mere embryonic existence.

When the danger began to be realised progress was very slow. The Home Air Defence scheme, approved in 1923, had to be postponed until 1935–36. So also did the work on the defences of Singapore and the naval base. The possibility of purchasing anti-aircraft guns from Germany was even considered.

The 1930s were perhaps the most terrible and miserable decade for a century. Unemployment had begun to eat into the nation's soul, and despair was prevalent in the working-class. Those who lived through those years and observed the 'depressed areas' are never likely to forget them.

The more fortunate clung to idealistic dreams long after the hour of awakening had passed and the alarm bells had rung. In the dreadful climate of that decade—and the one before it had been little better—while almost half-hearted efforts were made to rebuild, it seemed to those in power that there could not be an alternative to appeasement of the dictators in desperate attempts to buy time. In terms of democracy it would have been impossible to get a mandate for rearmament from the electorate, and Baldwin recognised it in his speech of 'appalling frankness' in 1936. 'Supposing,' he said, 'I had gone to the country and said that Germany was rearming, and that we must rearm, does anybody think that this pacific democracy would have rallied to that cry? I cannot think of anything that would have made the loss of the election from my point of view more certain.'

When Mussolini marched into Abyssinia and began to drench the inhabitants with poison gas, for a moment it seemed that Britain would lead the League of Nations into strong measures. For a moment the nation roused, only to slump again into cynicism when it was clear that neither we nor France dared to take decisive action. 'If Britain had used her naval power, closed the Suez Canal, and defeated the Italian navy in a general engagement, she would have had the right to call the tune in Europe.'[1]

But the threat came from Germany. When Hitler marched into the Rhineland it would have been simple to stop him, and it is not enough to blame France. She dared not make an enemy of Italy at this stage, and when Abyssinia was partitioned morale in France and Britain dropped to nothing. Pacifism was rife everywhere, but it was not so much pacifism as despair, despair in government, despair in that promise of a land fit for heroes, which had faded into hopelessness before it had progressed beyond the words. It afflicted almost everyone. Ralph Wigram, one of the brightest stars in the Foreign Office and one of Churchill's private band of admirers and supporters, died of a broken heart after Hitler's seizure of the Rhineland.

Mrs. Wigram wrote to Churchill:

Ralph came back, and sat down in a corner of the room where he had never sat before, and said to me 'War is now *inevitable,* and it will be the most terrible war there has ever been. I don't think I shall see it, but you will. Wait now for bombs on this little house.' I was frightened at his words, and he went on, 'All my work these many years has been no use. I am a failure. I have failed to make the people realise what is at stake. I am not strong enough, I suppose. I have not been able to make them understand. Winston has always, always understood, and he is strong and will go on to the end.'[2]

[1]Churchill, *The Second World War,* vol. I, Readers' Union edition, pp. 158–9.

[2]Letter to Churchill from Mrs. Wigram, quoted in *The Second World War,* vol. I.

'My friend never seemed to recover from the shock,' Churchill wrote. 'He took it too much to heart...Wigram's profound comprehension reacted on his sensitive nature unduly. His untimely death in December 1936 was an irreparable loss to the Foreign Office, and played its part in the miserable decline of our fortunes.'[1]

III

Churchill's political wilderness at Chartwell was a wonderfully inhabited and fruitful place, and there was no danger that he might stagnate. He gathered round him a loosely woven group of experts, advisers and friends, informed in almost every department of foreign, military and domestic affairs, and retained his close connections with the Committee of Imperial Defence and some of its key sub-committees. It may seem curious that he was a member of the Air Defence Research Committee, which was assisted by an Air Ministry technical sub-committee of scientists. He had become a devoted admirer of Professor Lindemann, unhappily to the exclusion of men of the calibre of Tizard, Blackett and others. Much of the schoolboy remained in him and he had a capacity for intense admiration for some of those whose talents were entirely different from his own, and this often clouded his judgment. Moreover he was a slave to his likes and dislikes, as his 'mentor' Lloyd George had never been.

Ramsay MacDonald, Baldwin and Chamberlain in succession not only permitted, but helped him to be a constant thorn in their own flesh, for without the consent of the Prime Ministers of the day some of Churchill's intimate advisers would have been unable to help, and would have been embarrassed to sit in on the discussions. Churchill 'in the wilderness' was, as always, as Harry Hopkins later remarked, at the vortex. From his place on the back benches of the House of Commons he riveted the attention of the government, the nation, and the Dictators, yet with the immeasurable benefit of not being directly involved in the dreary record of appeasement, and slow, reluctant rearmament...

Nevertheless the wilderness role did not please Churchill, even though it was, perhaps, the most fortunate gift ever to befall him. He suffered a great deal from what he called 'black dog', his

[1]Ibid., p. 171.

periods of terrible depression, which he tackled with rare fortitude: he wrote, he painted or he laid bricks, but he did not give in.

These years were 'one of the best things that ever happened
for England', wrote Amery of Churchill's 'exile'. 'For they were
the years in which the strong vintage of his personality matured;
the years in which he wrote the story of his great ancestor,
Marlborough.' That in itself was a marvellous exercise for the
role that awaited him. He wrote much more besides, while his
political activities on the sidelines were as demanding as a seat
in the Cabinet. It seems astonishing that he was already fifty-six
years old in 1930 at the start of his 'exile'. Many would have
despaired, feeling that their hour had passed. His capacity for
work is difficult for ordinary men and women to grasp,
especially, perhaps, for writers. His activities in the whole range
of defence problems, always paramount in his mind, became
overwhelmingly absorbing. In the Commons he led deputations
to the Prime Minister and was the spokesman for a group including Austen Chamberlain, Amery, Boothby, Eden and many
others of great influence in the House and country. Salisbury
was among his prominent supporters and many of the younger
stars in the foreign service regarded him as the hope for England
in the coming holocaust. By the middle of the 1930s all knew
that the holocaust was coming. The Spanish Civil War, used as
a rehearsal stage by the Dictators, underlined the imminence of
European war, and in 1936 when Hitler invaded the Rhineland,
time was growing short. The last steady march to war had
begun. Four days after Hitler's move, on March 13th, Sir Thomas
Inskip, the Attorney-General, a man of moderate abilities, was
appointed deputy Chief of the Committee of Imperial Defence
and Minister for the Co-ordination of Defence. Churchill described the appointment as 'the most remarkable since Caligula
had made his horse Consul'.[1]

For a short time, he was bitterly disappointed until he realised
that it was still too early for his own emergence onto the
stage. So long as there was a chance, in Chamberlain's mind,
of appeasing the Dictators, Churchill would remain out of office.
His appointment to a seat in the Cabinet would have been
sufficient warning to Hitler and Mussolini that England would
fight. It might have given hope to Soviet Russia also of an
alliance with France and Britain before it was too late. For

[1]Unhappily the expression is not original. It was used by Gladstone when
Disraeli recommended his private secretary, Corry, for a peerage.

Churchill had changed his ground. He had disentangled himself from the split attitudes engendered, not only by his nature, but by his dislike and distrust of Soviet Communism. Inasmuch as his dislike was rational he held it at full strength, but much of the emotion had evaporated to permit his strategic thinking to expand and develop. The Spanish Civil War, which had at first clouded his mind, and in which he had been slow to appreciate the importance of the interventions of Germany and Italy, and the rather less blatant and direct aid of Soviet Russia for the Republicans, finally clarified. Politically he might have cried a curse upon both houses, with a bias in favour of General Franco, but the strategic truth, as he saw it, was that Spain, as a Mediterranean power with the British naval base and fortress of Gibraltar in close proximity, must become either an ally or reliable neutral in the coming conflict. Britain must therefore remain on good terms with the final winners in the Civil War. The slightest push might lock General Franco irrevocably in the arms of the dictators.

As Europe moved swiftly towards war the Soviet Foreign Minister, Litvinoff, and the Soviet Ambassador to Britain, Maisky, had done much to soften the Soviet image. Both men wanted peace, and if peace should prove impossible, they wanted security. Maisky had visited Churchill at Chartwell at his own request in 1938, and Churchill had become a leader of the powerful group pressing the government to seek an alliance with the Soviets. Chamberlain's responses remained half-hearted, and it was not surprising that in May 1939 Litvinoff was removed as Soviet Foreign Minister, and his country looked elsewhere for security. She looked, in fact, in the only possible direction open to her if the worst was to be avoided or delayed.

The processes of war were rapidly gathering speed when Chamberlain prepared for his personal appeals to Hitler which at last convinced him that war was unavoidable. Austria had been annexed, Czechoslovakia had followed. The Sudetenland had gone. Poland was the next victim on Hitler's list, and he must have felt that nothing—certainly not his own General Staff—could stop him, least of all Britain's ill-timed and hopeless final guarantee to Poland, and the promise that she would go to war. It would have been impossible for Britain to go to the assistance of Poland, but at least and at last Britain had declared herself.

Churchill's comments were sensible and realistic:

The Soviet Government were convinced by Munich and much else that neither Britain nor France would fight till they were attacked, and would not be much good then. Russia must look after herself.

The dismissal of Litvinoff marked the end of an epoch. It registered the abandonment by the Kremlin of all faith in a security pact with the Western Powers and in the possibility of organising an Eastern Front against Germany.

Physically the preparations for war went very slowly, for Chamberlain was fearful of alarming the public, but behind the scenes the preparations in the field of organisation and in all facets of military thinking and higher military staff training had progressed, and were progressing, magnificently. The Committee of Imperial Defence forged the instrument which would put power into the hands of the chosen leader of the nation, and direct the whole activity of war. It was in being. It worked. There had been continual developments. The Chiefs of Staff Committee, thanks in great measure to Lord Haldane, had flourished, becoming a very clear entity, supported by growing joint planning and joint intelligence sub-committees. 'The Chiefs of Staff Committee,' said the Secretary of State for War, 'is the nearest approach towards a Minister of Defence that has yet been made.' Strengthening the Staff was the Imperial Defence College, established in 1927. It had produced a very high grade of Staff officer, not only in Britain but throughout the Empire. Above all it contributed to the unity of the three services. Students of this development agree with General Ismay 'that the creation of the C.O.S. was by far the most significant inter-war development in Defence'.

In 1936 Hastings Ismay had to say goodbye to his hopes of army command forever to take up an appointment as Deputy Secretary of the C.I.D. under Hankey. Things were beginning to move fast. The joint Planning Committees were strengthened. Churchill's powerful pleas and reasoned papers were having an effect,[1] and Ismay, whose new role demanded his total involvement in all the 'facts' studied the documents with increasing anxiety. It was part of his task 'to lend a hand in preparing the Government reply' to the powerful papers presented by Churchill and a deputation including Lord Salisbury, Sir Austen Chamber-

[1] See Ismay, *Memoirs,* p. 77.

lain, Admiral of the Fleet Sir Roger Keyes, Marshal of the Royal
Air Force, Lord Trenchard and Field-Marshal Lord Milne.

Ismay wrote:

Mr. Churchill's comprehensive and carefully reasoned statement on our shortcomings was particularly impressive. It
ended on an alarming note ... Perhaps the German strength
had been over-estimated? Perhaps there would be time to
put our house in order? But, however much I tried to look
on the bright side, I could not escape the feeling of impending
calamity.

When at last the whole nation hung upon Mr. Chamberlain's
reluctant declaration that we were at war, the sense of relief
was widespread. The Prime Minister's urgent visits to Munich
had brought hope to many, but they had also left a taint of
something like dishonour, even of unreality. Yet these abortive
visits with Hitler had brought home to millions the kind of
challenge the nation had to face.

CHAPTER FOUR

First Lord

I

ON THE MORNING OF 1ST SEPTEMBER, 1939, GERMANY MARCHED into Poland. Complete mobilisation had been ordered throughout Britain, and the whole machinery of war was in motion. In the afternoon Chamberlain invited Churchill to Downing Street. The War Cabinet was about to be formed, and Churchill had reached the antechamber to power. He agreed at once to serve, and expected to hear again from Chamberlain to fix his appointment, and those of his colleagues. On the night of 1st September the British ultimatum had been given to Germany. War, unavoidable since Germany had marched into the Rhineland, was then imminent within a matter of hours. But not quite to Chamberlain. Throughout the 2nd September Churchill—and the nation—waited. Before the day was out Churchill wrote to Chamberlain: 'I really do not know what has happened during the course of this agitated day; though it seems to me that entirely different ideas have ruled from those which you expressed to me when you said "the die was cast".'

In fact Chamberlain still hoped for the miracle of peace!

His hopes were entirely unreal, and he recognised the fact. On the morning of 3rd September a second ultimatum was delivered to Germany, and at 11.15 a.m. that Sunday morning Chamberlain broadcast to the nation. The wail of the air-raid sirens followed his speech. The barrage balloons shone and looked as placid as some fat and somewhat ungainly kine grazing in the perfect blue of that September sky. It was a 'false alarm'; even the war itself began to seem like a false alarm. Except for Poland, where the German blitzkrieg tore the nation to shreds and tatters, leaving a trail of slaughter and destruction; except also

at sea where the passenger liner *Athenia,* outward bound, was
sunk by a U-boat. But activity was great, especially in the Middle
East where British oil was at once at risk, and the road to
India must be preserved.

On the afternoon of the 3rd Churchill became First Lord
of the Admiralty. 'From the morning of the 4th I laid my
hands upon the naval affair.' He had spent a large part of the
night of the 3rd meeting the Sea Lords. He was back in his
old seat, the one he had vacated so unhappily twenty-five years
earlier, and now delighted that the Admiralty had sent a signal
to all ships and men, 'Winston is back'. Yet everyone had not
always thought so well of him. When he had left the Admiralty
in 1915, Admiral Beatty, one of the most dashing and
'Churchillian' of naval commanders, wrote: 'The Navy breathes
freer now it is rid of the succubus of Churchill.'

In the years between the wars Churchill was vilified by the
Army and Air Force for his conduct in peace. He pleased none.
The 'Ten-Year Rule', and his policy as Chancellor had run
down the armament industry until it had virtually ceased to
exist. His Permanent Under-Secretary at the Treasury commented: 'We converted ourselves to military impotence.' This,
was one of 'the economic consequences of Mr. Churchill'.

His comparative political isolation throughout the 'wilderness
years' was due in great measure to his responsibility for the
military unpreparedness he so urgently attacked; to the grave
suspicions of him nursed by the trades unions; and to the lack
of support for him in the political parties, or in the country.
He was his own man, and this was part of the price. 'To his
imperious spirit,' wrote A. G. Gardiner, 'a party is only an
instrument.' Leo Amery saw him as a 'Mid-Victorian, steeped
in the politics of his father's period'. His judgment was suspect
even to his friends and admirers, and he was hopeless to argue
with. Again as Amery said, he flung rhetorical phrases at you,
and all you could do was to fling back counter-phrases. Lord
Esher had summed him up perfectly: 'He handles great subjects
in rhythmical language and becomes quickly enslaved by his own
phrases. He deceives himself into the belief that he takes broad
views, when his mind is fixed upon one comparatively small
aspect of the question.' That was one of the difficulties in discussing war problems with him. Liddell Hart, one of the 'focus'
group at Chartwell, had found that he ceased to pay attention
the moment his mind fixed on some small part of a problem
which fascinated him.

Yet as Arthur Ponsonby wrote to Edward Marsh in 1930: 'He is so far and away the most talented man in political life . . . but this does not prevent me from feeling politically that he is a great danger, largely because of his love of crises and faulty judgment. He once said to me years ago: "I like things to happen, and if they don't happen I like to make them happen."'

This last phrase out of Churchill's own mouth is the best clue to his triumphs and to his disasters in war and peace. He was pre-eminently a man of action, and in spite of all that can be said, the comment of the Official Historian, welcoming his appointment to the Admiralty and to the War Cabinet, is valid:

'Mr. Churchill's past tenure of so many great offices, his long study of war in all its aspects, his prescient warnings during the years just past, his independence of mind, his driving power and his eloquence, all set him in a class apart, and until he succeeded to the highest post his proper place in the team was not obvious.'

The only place for Mr. Churchill in any team was in command, and few doubted he would occupy that place which, politically, must have remained forever out of his reach. Meanwhile he had carried the Service Ministers into the War Cabinet, so that all three Services were represented by their Chiefs at the highest level. Lord Chatfield, Minister for Co-ordination of Defence, and Lord Hankey, Minister Without Portfolio, were already members. The combined experience of these men in the organisation and management of a nation at war was unrivalled.

The fear that Germany could and would strike an immediate and devastating blow from the air 'was widespread among the Government and the public, and the gross exaggeration of the threat was one of the factors in the decision to allow Czecho-slovakia to fall under the control of Hitler'.[1] Great preparations had been made for the worst, and in one memorandum 750,000 beds were made ready for expected bombing casualties. In Churchill's memoirs, *The Second World War,* vol. I, the figure is amended to 250,000.

The fear was unwarranted, but it remained of the first importance. The natural corollary was that the enemy could be defeated by sustained bombing, and while many in high places regarded this conclusion as extremely doubtful, a bombing policy was adopted and pursued far beyond the bitter end. The Official Historians of the Strategic Air Offensive commented: 'Such ideas

[1] *The Strategic Air Offensive Against Germany,* vol. I.

were . . . aberrations inspired by excessive optimism or excessive depression. In essence they were a reaction against the horrible conditions of trench warfare and no less against the hopeless odds of the campaign which ended at Dunkirk.'[1]

These were certainly foremost among the considerations that swayed Churchill to support the massive bombing programme of the Chief of Bomber Command, and to accept the statistical fallacies of Professor Lindemann, and consistently to reject the advice of Sir Henry Tizard and P. M. S. Blackett.

Meanwhile a sense of anticlimax gripped the nation as the worst not only failed to happen, but nothing seemed to happen. The nation was not yet fully mobilised for war, and there was no sign of that massive and all embracing effort that alone could ensure survival. On land, as in the air, people quickly accepted what Chamberlain called the Twilight War, and which soon came to be known as the Phony War. The resulting apathy was a very poor state of mind—it might have proved disastrous—for a nation needing every minute of every hour of this unlooked-for respite if the worst omissions of the past were to be made good. The drive of leadership was lacking, and with that, the inspiration which alone might prepare the country to meet the greatest ordeal in its history was also lacking.

Throughout the whole of Britain, even over much of the coastline, the war seemed almost to have been forgotten, and tens of thousands of would-be volunteers, both young and old, were soon discouraged by the lack of organisations to welcome them, or to know what to do with them. The plans were made for the rapid expansion of the Services, of the great heavy and light industries upon which they and the nation must depend, but it took time, and in the early days the immense efforts behind the scenes were not apparent to the great majority.

In those twilight months before the real awareness of war burst upon Britain those who had lived through the terrible decades of the Twenties and Thirties, and observed the miseries of the working people and the extreme prejudices of the well-to-do middle classes, would not doubt that if Britain had been overrun, and suffered the fate in store for Belgium and France, Holland, Denmark and Norway, quislings and collaborators would have abounded. Admiration for the Dictators, and their ability, not only to run trains on time, but to control the 'proletariat' was freely expressed. It would need a traumatic

[1]Ibid.

experience of the first magnitude to arouse the country. The Channel, perhaps for the last time, saved Britain, and probably Europe.

II'

There was no Twilight War for the Navy and the Admiralty was a hive of activity. Churchill's driving force and powerful personality was at once felt by 'all hands' from the Sea Lords to the naval ratings at sea, from the planning staffs, already bearing the brunt of Churchill's incessant inspiration and demands, to the cipher clerks and typists. He had become a far more formidable figure than the comparatively young man of a quarter of a century earlier. Age had not mellowed him, nor, it seemed, abated his astounding energy. While others laboured at all hours of the days and nights Churchill shielded himself and conserved his energy. As his wife said of him: 'He's a Pasha!' and no one in contact with him was likely to forget it. He was as fresh and demanding through many long nights as he could be by day. It was no miracle.

The Navy was at war. The Battle of the Atlantic had been joined instantly. It would rage throughout the entire war, and the enemy would not begin to lose for three and a half years. At times it was touch and go. Few would have imagined in the first days the enormous tonnages of shipping destined to be sunk month after month, year in year out, nor the immense tonnages built and always building, all with crews, the living replacing the dead, all maintaining a wonderful standard of devotion. The Atlantic was the main battleground. On it the life of the Island depended. And there was, of course, a great deal more to it than that. Without the Navy the great battles destined to rage in the Western Desert could not have been fought, no raids on the long enemy-held coast lines could have been mounted, no invasion of the mainland of Europe contemplated.

In the first days and months of the war Churchill was the man to give this great organisation and fighting force impetus. Enemy 'pocket battleships' and U-boats had sailed for the Atlantic before the end of August and were awaiting their prey alert and unseen. They had lost no time in sinking the s.s. *Athenia* in the first hours, but as yet the U-boat fleet was small. It would grow alarmingly until in March 1943 it seemed that the sinkings of British and Allied shipping would far outpace building, and the Island was at least as gravely threatened as it had been in 1917. By 7th September, 1939 the first ocean convoys were introduced. Magnetic mines added to the dangers.

Churchill, whatever the demands of defence, was a man dedicated to offensive action, however hard pressed. Before the outbreak of war he had conferred often with General Ironside, a huge warrior figure, himself a man of action, and soon to be Chief of the Imperial General Staff in succession to General Lord Gort, V.C., who had taken command of the British Expeditionary Force in France. Plans were advanced to increase the Army from its five divisions to fifty-five divisions, while the Royal Air Force pressed ahead vastly to increase the size of its fighter and bomber forces and the training of pilots, navigators, bomb aimers and gunners, together with the ground staff of mechanics and highly trained personnel to keep the squadrons in the air.

Ironside had toured Poland just before the outbreak of war, and reported to Churchill favourably. The awakening was rude and devastating. On 17th September Soviet Russia had marched into Poland from the east to ensure the security of her north-western frontiers against her very temporary 'ally' Nazi Germany. Twenty-seven days after the Nazi blitzkreig Warsaw fell, and the tragic Polish nation embarked upon a new phase of her brave and terrible history. The military survivors, taking refuge in Britain, added to British military strength. There were to be many such survivors, a most valuable force in the aggregate, some bringing with them overseas territories and considerable wealth.

Perhaps the speed of the Polish disaster should have warned Britain of what might be in store, but it did not. Churchill's exalted view of the glory and present power of French arms remained unimpaired, and Ironside, shrewd and experienced as he was, in a military world which had ceased to exist, retained his confidence. The Maginot Line seemed to delude everyone but the enemy.

But in the Admiralty Churchill was showing his temper and the kind of commander he was and would be. In the First World War he had used naval designers and engineers in the development of the first tanks. He used what he could wherever he might find it. With Ironside he discussed his ideas for a huge 'mole' to cut a wide swathe through the earth at speed and provide a trench along which armour and infantry might advance.

It was named 'Cultivator'[1] and orders were given for a limited production. It was abandoned. At the same time his mind had focussed on the Baltic, a vital sea and refuge for German naval forces, while enabling them to defend iron-ore shipments from the Swedish port of Lulea on the Gulf of Bothnia. Churchill's first plan—known as 'Plan Catherine'—was to introduce British warships into the Baltic, and to reinforce their armour for the purpose by designing and manufacturing huge 'blisters'. 'D.N.C. thinks it would be possible to hoist an "R" (a battleship of the *Royal Sovereign class*) 9 ft., thus enabling a certain channel where the depth is only 26 ft. to be passed.'[2] If this could be achieved Churchill thought that command of the Baltic could be gained.

The importance of these two early schemes is that they reveal the remarkable fertility of Churchill's mind. He caused an immense amount of work on the part of the planning staffs, to designers, to engineering shops, and this work grew and multiplied from beginning to end. Some of it was useful. Very rarely an idea like the 'Mulberry'[3] was magnificent, and of incalculable service, but the wastage of the most rare and skilled manpower was a high price to pay, above all for the 'planners', many of whose war lives were spent in incessant and too often, abortive toil.

Yet Churchill's personal frustrations as First Lord of the Admiralty were very great. Predictably he would make a decisive attempt to make an end of such frustrations if and when real power was his. In September 1939 that day was still a long way off, but never, I believe, out of Churchill's sights. On 29th September, 1939, he had suggested strongly that the Norwegian leads should be mined with the precise intention of blocking German shipments of iron ore from the Swedish mines of Gällivare. This desire led to the attempts to seize the ports of Narvik and Trondheim, destined to end in futility. The whole Norwegian affair is somewhat typical of the difficulties in mounting any attack, or any new enterprise. Some of these difficulties were unavoidable, the problems of maintenance and supply,

[1]Churchill, *The Second World War,* vol. II, appendix O: 'I believed that a machine could be made which would cut a groove in the earth sufficiently deep and broad through which assaulting infantry and presently assaulting tanks could advance in comparative safety ...'

[2]D.N.C. = Director Naval Construction. For 'Plan Catherine' see Churchill, op. cit. appendix G.

[3]Artificial harbours finally used off Normandy, 1944. Remains may still be seen on and off beaches, Arromanches.

soon to be known as 'logistics' and comprising the entire needs of a force from ammunition to bootlaces. These depend upon transport and demand highly skilled loading of ships or aircraft, and particular attention to priorities, remembering that usually the last in means the first out. These things and the assembly and transport of the force, the provision of supporting arms, of naval and air support if necessary, of the provision of landing craft if an assault from the sea is contemplated, are common to all operations and to all powers, dictatorships or democracies. The speed with which such operations are carried out is always vital. The fatal factor in Britain, especially in the early days, was decision. At the time of the Norwegian proposal the Finnish war was in progress. What or what not to do about it engaged the War Cabinet in discussion for sixty days. In the end nothing was done because it was next to impossible to do anything. It involved not only having the troops properly equipped and trained for such a task, but also the neutrality of Sweden and the permission to reach Finland through Swedish territory. The problem of Norwegian neutrality was also involved with the mining problem of her coast and of her territorial integrity, and added to the probability of provoking Germany to act.

The proposal to mine the Norwegian leads was made by Churchill on 29th September, 1939. On 8th April, 1940 authority was finally given to the Admiralty. Outlining the course of events in the committees involved and in the War Cabinet, Churchill commented: 'Now after all this vain boggling, hesitation, changes of policy, arguments between good and worthy people unending, we had at last reached the simple point on which action had been demanded seven months before. But in war seven months is a long time.'[1]

The mounting of the expedition to attack Narvik and Trondheim suffered similar delays. On 15th January, 1940, Churchill wrote to a colleague after a depressing Cabinet meeting: 'My disquiet was due mainly to the awful difficulties which our machinery of war-conduct presents to positive action.' The letter goes on to detail some of the problems and arguments involved, the departments consulted, the Joint Planning Committee, the Chiefs of Staff Committee. 'All this makes me feel that under the present arrangements we shall be reduced to waiting upon the terrible attacks of the enemy . . .'[2]

[1] Churchill, *The Second World War,* vol. II, Readers' Union ed., p. 464.
[2] Ibid., pp. 443–4.

But these delays, serious as they were, were not the cause of the failure of the Norwegian expedition. The basic cause of failure was that Britain did not possess the troops, trained and equipped for such an expedition, nor did she have the means of providing essential air cover, or even of enough anti-aircraft defence. Shortages of most of the demands of war were still acute, and the troops in France and in the Middle East had to come first. Secondly, planning was piecemeal partly because the object and even the objective was constantly changing. Finally the command situation in Norway was deplorable. It is a very long story. It may be followed briefly in the official history, *Grand Strategy*, Vol. ii. Chapter VI, and there is a good description of events in Maund's *Assault from the Sea*. The Official Historian quotes almost a page of the *Manual of Combined Operations, 1938*. It was ignored:

It was laid down in the *Manual of Combined Operations* 'that for the effective working of the system of joint command [such as was first prescribed for the Narvik expedition] the commanders must be suited both by temperament and experience to co-operate with each other. They must not only be able to enjoy each other's confidence and to work as a team but each commander should also have a broad knowledge of the capabilities and limitations of the other Services.' This condition was unfortunately not fulfilled at Narvik.[1]

Indeed it wasn't.

Two men more temperamentally unsuited to each other than Admiral Lord Cork and Orrery and General P. J. Mackesy would have been hard to find. Moreover they had never met. Lord Cork, who enjoyed Churchill's confidence was given his orders by the Admiralty, and he also attended a key meeting of the Co-ordination Committee on the 10th April. General Mackesy had no such advantages. He was sent orders by General Ironside, Chief of the Imperial General Staff. His 'object' would be to turn the enemy out of the Narvik area. He was ordered to establish his force at Harstad, and assess the situation. According to Churchill he was ordered to advance to Gällivare, the Swedish ore mines. Sticking, however, to Narvik, General Mackesy was to take it if he could. Ironside's personal message to him read in part: 'Latest information is that there are 3,000

[1]*Grand Strategy*, vol. II, p. 141.

Germans in Narvik. They must have been knocked about by naval action ... You may have a chance of taking advantage of naval action and you should do so if you can. Boldness is required.'

Lord Cork's 'orders' according to his Despatch[1] stated that his 'impression on leaving London was quite clear that it was desired by His Majesty's Government to turn the enemy out of Narvik at the earliest possible moment'. He had no written orders. He reported by cipher direct to the First Lord of the Admiralty; General Mackesy reported to the C.I.G.S. There was no combined command, and as Captain Maund, Lord Cork's Chief of Staff, pointed out, the Army Commander should have been the senior:

> It was an operation where the predominant partner was the Army and where the Navy, as in most landing operations, had to serve the Army. In these circumstances the senior commander should have been the Army Commander. Instead, an Admiral of the Fleet, over sixty years of age, was appointed to work with a young Major-General. Next the instructions given to the two commanders were not the same and finally they had neither planned nor made the passage together in the same ship. It would have been a miracle, personalities apart, if such a scheme of command had worked harmoniously.[2]

In the upshot, Major-General Mackesy, a soldier of distinction who had greatly impressed in his running of the Staff College at Quetta, and who produced his untrained troops with the greatest skills on the shores of Rombaks Fiord within three or four miles of Narvik and to the rear, from which it was simple to take the town, was sacrificed. He was the first man of distinction and great promise to be Churchill's victim. He refused a hopeless assault from the sea in open boats on Narvik, which was defiladed by machine guns and out of reach of naval gunfire. In military opinion such an attempt would have been 'sheer bloody murder'.

Perhaps the most depressing part of the whole sorry affair was the German invasion and occupation of the ports and key points between 'dawn and dusk' on 9th April. It was a perfectly planned operation, carefully prepared, not least with the pro-Nazi groups in Norway led by Vidkun Quisling. This had stimu-

[1] L. E. H. Maund, *Assault from the Sea.*
[2] *Grand Strategy*, vol. II.

lated the British to even greater efforts. A direct assault on Trondheim having been discarded, flanking assaults were mounted to the north of the port at Namsos and to the south at Andalsnes. The only soldier to enhance his reputation was General Paget. His fighting withdrawal of the Andalsnes force was brilliantly and successfully carried out, and the force returned safely to Britain in the first week of May. Paget had been sent out on 25th April to do the job.

Churchill was undismayed. Narvik had become an increasing obsession. He wanted it taken at any price, even though it would have to be abandoned almost at once. Ironside found him at times very nearly impossible to deal with. On 22nd April Ironside wrote in his diary:

> Winston very much interested in the Narvik affair. He wanted to divert troops there from all over the place. He is so like a child in many ways. He tires of a thing, and then wants to hear no more of it. He was made to divert the Brigade from Narvik to Namsos and would hear of no reason. Now he is bored with the Namsos operation and is all for Narvik again. It is most extraordinary how mercurial he is.[1]

General Ismay, already at that date detailed as Churchill's principal military aide and his representative with the Chiefs of Staff Committee to the war's end, made similar observations years later. Churchill did not change. 'Men like Winston never think of the tail (of any army),' Ironside further observed sadly, 'they push so gaily into new adventures.' He never did think reasonably of the tail, and no one ever made him.

Churchill had disliked the decision to evacuate the troops from the Trondheim areas 'and began to mumble about the British being allowed to disperse in the mountains to help the Norwegians carry on guerilla warfare. That it was better to condemn the force ashore to fight to the end. I could not find any military reason for doing this. It was all political.'[2]

Yet Churchill was showing signs of being 'a little weighed down by the cares of being solely responsible for Narvik. He wants it taken and yet doesn't dare to give any direct order to Cork.'

Finally Narvik was taken on 28th May. On 22nd May the Chiefs of Staff had recommended evacuation as soon as it was

[1] The Ironside Diaries.
[2] Ibid.

captured. Evacuation was successful on the night of 7th June. By that time, the avalanche of German military power had destroyed France, Belgium and Holland, and Norway was forgotten. It had done something. German Naval losses had been severe, giving Britain an urgently needed relief at sea, especially at Dunkirk. Even the military lessons, too many and perhaps too obvious to detail here, were slowly learned.

Churchill perhaps should have the penultimate, if not the last word, on this affair in which he bore so much blame. He had put almost intolerable pressure on the unfortunate General Mackesy. A stiff cable had been sent to Mackesy, urged by Churchill upon the Military Co-ordination Committee, of which he had become Chairman. Mackesy did not reply. He went on with the course he was convinced was correct. Churchill knew that the assault he demanded would have to be made from open boats under machine-gun fire. 'The responsibility for a bloody repulse would fall exclusively on the home authorities, and very directly upon me.' He went on to lay the blame for the failure of the Narvik enterprise upon General Mackesy, even to impugn the General's courage. According to all the testimony this is most unjust. General Auchinleck had been sent out to Narvik to tie the loose ends and wind up the sorry business. He thought highly of Mackesy, and of what he had achieved. Yet Mackesy was sacrificed.

Churchill's responsibility was great, but his was not the power, and the final responsibility must be with the Prime Minister. Without Churchill's drive, energy and remarkable powers of persuasion it is possible, even probable, that the Norwegian expedition would never have been mounted. He dominated the Committees. He dominated the Chiefs of Staff. Very few stood out against him for long enough, either then or very often later. He bulldozed his way through to win his way, and succeeded perhaps partly because men did not wish to seem defeatist by opposing him to the end. Yet the plain fact is that Britain had not the power to mount and to sustain the assaults on the Norwegian coastline. And even without the power a fearful mess was made of it. Ships were not tactically loaded; commanders were often separated from their troops, and arrived at different ports. There seemed to be no idea in Whitehall of the geography of Norway, of the weather conditions, of the deep snow. The Admiralty seemed to have the idea that the tiny port of Harstad, at which Mackesy's force landed and assembled, was a kind of Southampton. In fact its harbour and wharf could accommodate one moderate-sized ship. At times a dozen vessels were forced to wait outside in dangerous waters.

For the enormous list of 'botcheries' as Lloyd George called them, Churchill was very much to blame. Lloyd George knew it, and yet called upon Churchill not to make himself into an 'air-raid shelter' in an attempt to protect the Government. Amery knew that Churchill was to blame, and feared that because of it Churchill might not be chosen when Amery delivered his terrific 'Phillipic', as Harold Macmillan called it, to bring down the Government, and free the nation from the incubus of Chamberlain. For in his stubborn clinging to power he had become an incubus.

Churchill himself thought it was astounding that he should survive the Norwegian fiasco unscathed. He survived, as he was to do in the future, not because men were bemused by him or blind to his tremendous faults and dangers, but because, knowing those faults and seeing those dangers, there was no one else, and at last no one better. In those early days of May while France and the Netherlands came to ruin, and the storm raged in the British House of Commons, only Amery among politicians knew as much about war as Churchill, and was a better strategist. But Amery lacked the personality and flair to set a nation on fire. And it had come to that.

The official final view of the Norwegian affair is brief: 'because we had no airfield we could not mount the air strength to secure one; because we had no proper base we could not assemble the men and material to capture one; because we had no consistently held objectives not one of our objectives had been achieved.'[1]

It was Churchill's 'Antwerp' if not his 'Dardanelles'.

It should have been a final lesson to Churchill, but it was not. He was a victim of his excessive exuberance, too often mistaking words for deeds. His statements in regard to the Norway expedition rebounded upon him. Hitler's invasion of Norway, he had said, was a blunder comparable with Napoleon's invasion of Spain. The advantages of communications were with us, which was palpably absurb. He would sink every ship in the Skagerrak. Thus when things were going wrong he demanded an impossible success and blamed his commanders for failures. When he could not blame them, as was the case with Auchinleck

[1]*Grand Strategy,* vol. II.

and Paget, it is almost certain that he harboured resentments. The failure of the Norwegian expedition was inherent. Germany had been alerted to British intentions as far back as September 1939. First by the British attempts to persuade Norway into the war; secondly by mining the Norwegian leads and the obvious intention to block shipments of iron ore to Germany. The final alert followed the sinking of the pocket battleship *Graf Spee,* off Montevideo in the River Plate. At once Churchill alerted naval forces to hunt the *Graf Spee*'s supply ship, the *Altmark,* finally run down in Norwegian territorial waters.

'As soon as the news arrived of the end of the *Spee,*' Churchill wrote, 'I was impatient to bring our widely scattered hunting groups home. The *Spee*'s auxiliary, the *Altmark,* was however still afloat, and it was believed that she had on board the crews of the nine ships which had been sunk by the raider.'[1]

On 14th February the *Altmark* was sighted in Norwegian waters. At once Churchill gave orders to capture the ship and release the prisoners. The ship was run down in Josing fiord. Two British destroyers were informed by Norwegian boats that the *Altmark* was unarmed and had been cleared to return to Germany by way of Norwegian waters, whereupon the British destroyers withdrew. Churchill at once intervened and ordered action. Captain Vian, in command of the destroyer, *Cossack,* at once acted, 299 British prisoners were released after a short sharp 'pirate' fight between the British boarding party and the enemy. This, of course, was a boost to British morale, but it gave the enemy a final alert. 'Whatever the justification,' wrote Liddell Hart, 'it showed our hand.'[2]

Unhappily the Norwegian blunder provided Churchill with the first of his military victims in Major-General Mackesy. He was retired from the army as soon as he reached England.

Eight years later [wrote Piers Mackesy] when Churchill's memoirs appeared, Mackesy found that his conduct was criticised in a manner unparalleled elsewhere in the work. The narrative of the events at Narvik was cast in a framework of factual inaccuracy, of careful innuendo, and of inconsistencies which can only be explained by the author's profound emotional involvement in the operation.[3]

[1]Churchill, *The Second World War,* vol. I, Readers' Union ed., p. 423.
[2]Lecture delivered by Liddell Hart in 1944.
[3]*Royal United Services Journal,* December, 1970. Factual inaccuracies stated.

III

Throughout the months of Churchill's stewardship as 1st Lord his responsibilities had grown, while power remained in the hands of the Prime Minister. It was an unsatisfactory situation, for responsibility without power is far more frustrating than power without responsibility (as enjoyed by the press lords) but less dangerous. General Ismay, destined to play a very important part in Churchill's running of the war and exercise of Supreme Command, was summoned to Downing Street by Chamberlain at the end of April.

> He told me [wrote Ismay] that it had been decided that in future Mr. Churchill would not only take the Chair at all meetings of the Ministerial Co-ordination Committee at which the Prime Minister himself did not preside, but would also be responsible *on behalf of that Committee* for giving guidance and direction to the Chiefs of Staff Committee. Mr. Churchill was to be assisted by a suitable 'Central Staff' under a staff officer, who would be an additional member of the Chiefs of Staff Committee. The officer in question was to be myself![1]

Ismay felt uneasy about these arrangements and said so, but Chamberlain had made up his mind, and that was the end—or the beginning—of it. Ismay was, nevertheless, delighted at the chance to serve Churchill, whom he greatly admired, while doubting the value of the new idea. He saw clearly that Churchill's responsibilities would greatly increase but that he would be able to give the Chiefs of Staff Committee 'only such guidance and direction as the Military Co-ordination Committee approved'.

But Churchill dominated the Committee as he was apt to dominate all committees in which he played a part, even including the War Cabinet. Meanwhile Ismay became an additional member of the Chiefs of Staff Committee, and virtually Churchill's representative. Churchill brushed aside all Ismay's doubts and fears of the new development, but without dispelling them. He already had Ismay's central staff lined up, Oliver Lyttelton for supply, Desmond Morton, the behind-the-scenes

[1] Lord Ismay, *Memoirs*, pp. 112–3.

political adviser, especially in the foreign field, and Lindemann, the scientist almost viciously opposed to Sir Henry Tizard and Professor Blackett. And there were others about to become part of Churchill's personal team. The network of his friendships, relationships, and ties of various kinds, was wide and influential. He was a natural member of what had been a ruling class for a very long time. It interwove like a great family. He knew he could rely absolutely on men like Alexander Cadogan of the Foreign Office and a powerful Chairman of one of the Committees of the C.I.D.

Ismay left Churchill feeling very strongly that the new arrangement would not work, but as he noted, events were moving very fast and it would never be put to the test. It was, however, of great value to Churchill for his personal (yet official) staff was now truly in being and ready to be with him at all hours at the very heart of his administration.

While the German Armies consolidated their hold on Denmark and Norway, submerged Holland, and struck at the heart of Belgium and France, and it was clear that Chamberlain must fall, Brendan Bracken, Churchill's devoted younger friend, and one whom Churchill regarded with affection, was sounding out political opinion. The Labour party would not work with Chamberlain at any price, but they would work with Churchill. Clement Davies, the Liberal leader, and Amery the dedicated Conservative, both embraced Churchill's cause and swayed Clement Attlee, the Labour leader, in his favour. There were only two possible candidates at the end when Churchill stood with Lord Halifax at Chamberlain's side confronting the Labour leaders, Attlee and Greenwood. It was known that Churchill would not serve under Halifax, and it is improbable that Halifax truly wanted the job of Prime Minister and war leader. Churchill waited calmly for the brief confrontation to reach its inevitable conclusion. At six o'clock on that evening of 10th May, 1940 he presented himself to the King, and returned at once to the House of Commons to promise blood, toil, tears and sweat. He promised also victory, not only in words, but in the minds and hearts of men and women about to be awakened by the tragedy and triumph of Dunkirk. That was the grim and terrible music of war to which Churchill provided the magnificent words.

PART TWO

War Lord

CHAPTER FIVE

The Power and the Glory

I

WITH THE GERMAN ARMIES SWAMPING THE NETHERLANDS AND sweeping through Belgium, soon to overwhelm France and force the British Army back into the sea, Churchill took command of Britain with enormous zest and the mien of a conqueror 'Thus then,' he wrote, 'on the night of the 10th May at the outset of this mighty battle, I acquired the chief power in the State, which henceforth I wielded in ever growing measure for five years and three months of world war.'

Churchill was a warrior, a natural fighter needing the stimulus of danger, of challenge, of violent argument, but he had become a politician because that is the way to power. The road to glory is not easily defined. But it is impossible to be a statesman and a politician in a democracy, and to be a general controlling armies on many battlefields at the same time. Churchill tried. It was not simply that he had to be a 'Generalissimo' directing strategy, nor even a Supreme Commander telling his generals what to do. He wanted to direct tactics on the battlefield, to be, as John Connell wrote, 'a super-general'.[1]

'Prime Ministers need luck as well as generals,' commented General Sir John Kennedy, Director of Military Operations. 'Prime Ministers who usurp the role of Commanders-in-Chief need a double dose of it.'

Luck is not a word appropriate to Churchill, the man of destiny. He was a law unto himself. He survived all the reverses Britain suffered, often by his untimely actions, because his un-defeatable spirit and ruthless energy enabled Britain to survive

[1]John Connell, *Wavell, Scholar and Soldier.*

unavoidable disasters. His was the triumph. He was an egomaniac and megalomaniac on a scale perhaps impossible for an ordinary man to grasp and to understand. He was no ordinary man, but an enigma, an almost irresistible force; those who served him and their country resisted to the limits of their endurance, often with success, and always with great courage. But although Churchill was a tycoon—even a tyrant—he was not a dictator. He had a remarkable, and strictly personal, reverence for parliament and for the monarchy. He saw himself always as the servant of parliament, and a loyal servant of the Crown. He used all his remarkable gifts to sway parliament, but he did not abuse his privilege. There lay the source of his power. He won the support, in spite of their misgivings, of War Cabinet, Chiefs of Staff, parliament and people.

From the outset he intruded menacingly into the entire business of war, which was the entire business of the nation, bludgeoning his Chiefs of Staff and his commanders in the field in a way unmatched in the history of warfare. The great burden of his violent character and personality was borne by his generals. As time went by men of great experience became increasingly uneasy, wondering how they might induce him to share the load he insisted upon bearing himself, but very few wished to get rid of him. There was no one to replace him. He was unique in his time and place. He prevailed in the teeth of all criticism because he was the engine, the dynamo, the great driving-force, the inspiration of a nation. From the first hour his immediate tonic effect upon the British people was almost miraculous. The nation awoke suddenly from its long inertia to face the realities of war, and within a month to the reality of a crippling defeat, transformed by 'a miracle of deliverance' into a kind of victory. A total of 338,325 troops of the British Expeditionary Force, together with 139,097 allied soldiers, landed almost weaponless from little ships on the shores of England. For the first time in centuries Britain and all that she stood for, was not merely in danger of defeat, but of invasion and occupation by an alien power.

This great event gripped the imagination of the people, and many believed that the confrontation with catastrophe would have been enough in itself to stir the whole people to furious energy, but it was Churchill who stirred the imagination and brought 'Dunkirk' into every home. If these were not heroic days they certainly sounded—and felt—as if they were. In his great speech in the House of Commons on 4th June he warned that wars are not won by 'evacuations'. The losses of British destroyers had been severe, but the Navy and Air Force had met the enemy challenge, and held it in the sight of a minor host of ordinary people.

'Can you conceive,' said Churchill, 'a greater objective for the Germans in the air to make evacuation from these beaches impossible, and to sink all these ships which were displayed, almost to the extent of thousands?'

This 'victory' in defeat boded well for the security of Britain, and Churchill's speech was calculated to inspire, and at the same time to emphasise the extreme gravity of Britain's predicament and the long haul ahead.

> Even though large tracts of Europe and many old and famous States have fallen or may fall into the grip of the Gestapo and all the odious apparatus of Nazi rule, we shall not flag or fail. We shall go on to the end. We shall fight in France, we shall fight on the seas and oceans, we shall fight with growing confidence and growing strength in the air, we shall defend our island, whatever the cost may be.

Churchill ended his speech on a restrained note, deeply impressive:

> I have myself, full confidence that if all do their duty, if nothing is neglected, and if the best arrangements are made, as they are being made, we shall prove ourselves once again able to defend our island home, to ride out the storm of war, and to outlive the menace of tyranny, if necessary for years, if necessary alone. At any rate that is what we are going to try to do. This is the resolve of His Majesty's Government—every man of them.[1]

If Churchill's contribution to victory had been confined to words alone, none could question his superb and unique achievement. Churchill's words arose out of his total involvement, his complete identification with Britain, out of the feeling that he generated that wherever he was there lay the struggle also, that he was at the heart of the matter. He was one and indivisible and all attempts to persuade him to share his burden were doomed to failure. Served by his intimate circle and in almost daily

[1] Churchill, *The Second World War*, vol. II, Readers' Union ed., pp. 108–9.

and nightly session with the Chiefs of Staff, he was peculiarly alone. Perhaps Brendan Bracken was the only man who evoked his affection. But all were fascinated by him, and all accepted the incessant challenge of his demands upon them, some opposing him even in his most violent outbursts, as resolute as he was himself, but always loyal.

Behind the scenes of his public life, his private life was inviolable and usually calm. His wife, while not the 'power behind Churchill' was an abundant source of strength and stability. They were a team, inseparable, not in war or peace, but in life.

In sober terms Churchill had reminded parliament and people that the French were still fighting, but few could have indulged a hope that the Germans might be halted. The French high command was rotten, and in the last days the British Army had been forced to take care of itself, and in so doing had given a small glimpse of what might have been. Two battalions of British armour had forced the enemy to halt at Arras. It was a military feat of great significance. It had sown fears in the enemy command, inducing, if not compelling, a halt at the eleventh hour.

'For a short time,' said von Rundstedt, the German Commander-in-Chief, 'it was feared that the panzer divisions would be cut off before the infantry divisions could come up to support them.'

On the following morning Hitler issued his order to halt when the road to the Channel was wide open, if not the through road to England. 'It may well be asked,' wrote Liddell Hart, 'whether two battalions have ever had such a tremendous effect in history as the 4th and 7th R.T.R. achieved by their action at Arras.' Even so Churchill had blundered by urging the Army to 'furious unrelenting assault', when the only hope of holding the enemy lay in defending the waterlines. At the same time Churchill called upon the Calais garrison to fight to the death.

At this stage, General Lord Gort, commanding the British Expeditionary Forces, short of ammunition and support, directed the retreat to Dunkirk and the beaches with great skill and courage. Gort, whatever his shortcomings, and they were, I think, exaggerated, suffered from an inefficient and even absurd command situation. The British formed part of the French Army Group 1, but took orders direct from General Georges, commanding the north-eastern front. Orders, when there were any, were slow and confused. 'In fact,' wrote Montgomery, com-

manding the 3rd British Infantry division, 'there was no co-
ordination between the operations of the Belgians, the B.E.F. and
the First French Army, the Commanders of these armies had no
means of direct communication except by personal visits.'[1]

Thus, when it became clear to Gort that a disaster was imminent and inescapable, he saw his duty very clearly. He had
to save the British Army. 'It was because he saw very clearly,
if only for a limited distance, that we all got away at Dunkirk,'
wrote Montgomery. There was no time for anyone, even
Churchill, to intrude purposefully into the immediate business
on the battlefield. Those in command did what they had to do.
In the last days Montgomery took over the command of 1st Corps
from General Brooke, while General Alexander took over the
2nd Corps and commanded the rearguard.

The command situation at home and abroad was adjusting
to the urgencies of war. General Ironside had never been at ease
in the chair of Chief of the Imperial General Staff, and on 27th
May he relinquished the position with relief, to take over command of the Home Forces, about to become—if there were any
'home forces'—perhaps the most important command in the
British Army, including Senior Naval and Air Staff in its Headquarters. Invasion, it was believed, was imminent, and whether
it might become a reality or not depended upon the unknown
factor of what was in the enemy mind, and what, in particular,
was in the mind of Hitler. In fact there were no enemy plans
for invasion of England at that stage; but if such an invasion
were to be attempted its success or failure must depend upon the
ability of the British Navy and Air Force to stop it in the Channel
and in the air over Britain. It would be necessary for the German
Air Force to defeat and destroy the British Air Force together
with the aircraft industry. Even then it would be necessary to
build and to assemble a host of troop-carrying invasion craft to
land and maintain substantial forces in Britain in the face of
the growing strength of British Home Forces. All this must take
time. Moreover it was uncertain whether the defeat and occupation of Britain was an enemy aim.

Very clear awareness of these and many other factors may
have been the inspiration for Churchill's statement in early
September 1940 that 'the Navy can lose us the war, but only
the Air Force can win it.' The first part of the statement was
correct, especially in regard to the 'Battle of the Atlantic' which

[1] Montgomery, *Memoirs*.

grew in intensity from the first hours of the war. The second part of the statement was wrong in emphasis and unfortunate. It was taken as a slight upon the Army and partly inspired Churchill's decision to back Bomber Command's bombing policy, pursued with ruthless energy by Air Marshal Portal and by Air Vice-Marshal Harris (Bomber Harris). It also assuaged his restless desire for action and to hit back at the enemy without delay and with the only weapon to hand. This policy absorbed some fifty per cent of Britain's industrial resources and starved both the Navy and Army of support aircraft, of fighters, reconnaissance and transport.

War is a choice of options, and emphasis on the role of the bomber was an illustration of this truth. It was almost certainly a bad choice. Major-General Sir John Kennedy, Director of Military Operations, wrote: 'Mr. Churchill was, of course, responsible for deciding the allocation of manpower and industrial production of the three Services. We in the General Staff were quite sure that the decisions he gave at this time were dangerously wrong.'[1]

Churchill also issued a directive in which he assumed that the 'Army would never play a primary part in the defeat of the enemy'.

Unfortunately the bombing policy of the Air Staff became a private matter between Portal and Churchill, and was not controlled by the Chiefs of Staff. Thus the Chiefs of Staff were never able to co-ordinate the three Services and true combined operations were gravely handicapped. The 'evil genius' behind the scenes in this regard was Professor Lindemann, whose statistical charts and graphs, based on false premises and invariably misleading and wrong in their conclusions, fascinated Churchill.

Nevertheless the bombing policy was alien to Churchill's nature as a warrior and to his conscience as a man of great humanity. Desmond Morton, perhaps the most intimate of his personal assistants, insisted that Churchill never liked it and became increasingly uneasy about it. Nor, said Morton, did Churchill like 'Bomber Harris'.[2]

In the very early stages it was believed that economic factors would decide the issue, and that the economic blockade of Germany, and therefore of all conquered Europe, must be pursued by all available means with the utmost rigour. Strangely the

[1]John Kennedy, *The Business of War*, p. 97.
[2]Private correspondence with the author.

Chiefs of Staff tended to accept this in the first year, while the Ministry of Economic Warfare believed that the Army would be the instrument of victory.

II

While important policy discussions and decisions were demanding urgent attention the battle for France was moving swiftly into its last phase. It would be followed almost certainly by the battle for Britain. Meanwhile there were still British troops fighting with the 10th French Army, and there was still a very faint hope that some sort of defence might be established to halt the triumphant enemy. Perhaps a small enclave or redoubt might be established in Normandy. In these conditions General Brooke had the thankless task of leading a 'little B.E.F.' to France by way of Cherbourg. This was the route chosen by Edward III and the Black Prince in 1346 which led to the remarkable victory near Abbeville at Crécy. History would not repeat itself, nor was there any hope that it might be so. It was a brave and quixotic gesture, but it had to be made while the French continued in the fight and the British units involved might be saved.

By the time General Brooke's force began to disembark, and 157 Brigade with the 52nd Lowland Division in the van moved at speed in an attempt to get into the battle, the French 10th Army was caving in, and 51st Highland Division was cut off with four French divisions before it could get away from Le Havre.

In the few dangerous days that 157 Brigade went forward and back, wondering what Scotland might feel if two Scottish divisions should be lost at the very end in France, it retreated skilfully back to Cherbourg. Its journey had not been in vain. On 15th June the 'little B.E.F.' was on its way home again together with strong elements of the 1st Armoured Division.

Perhaps wisely very little was known about this brief adventure. Honour had been served, and in those last days—thanks largely to Churchill's emissary, General Spears—General de Gaulle, in growing danger from the demoralised French government, was flown out of France before any French officials realised what was happening.

Thus, as France went down to utter defeat, France in the person of Charles de Gaulle came to Britain. Very few people at that time understood the possible significance of de Gaulle, and perhaps his best recommendation was that the French Government condemned him to death. On 30th May he had attacked the enemy at Abbeville with the 4th French Armoured Division, but without success. De Gaulle was one of the very few who knew that if French armour had been properly organised, and if the offensive spirit had not been lacking, the enemy might have been matched. As the long months of the 'phony war' had dragged on German strength had grown, but for a very long time their very few trained divisions facing the Allies on the western front would have been unable to withstand a determined attack. In the upshot it is difficult to avoid the conclusion that the French high command, seemingly incapable of thinking in terms of attack, and with their powerful armour parcelled out over a wide front incapable of concentration, had hoped that a stalemant might continue indefinitely.

III

The complete surrender of France in the last half of June put Britain in immediate mortal danger, and confronted her with agonising problems of great urgency. At the heart of the matter lay the impending 'Battle of Britain', the attempt of the powerful German Air Force to destroy Britain's fighter strength, and to soften her up and make invasion possible by land forces. At the same time the balance of power at sea had been drastically changed, not only by Italy's entry into the war on 10th June, challenging Britain's naval power in the Mediterranean, but also by the ambiguous position of the French fleet. It was also painfully clear that the Battle for the Atlantic would be the key to British survival if the Island held out against the enemy.

At this time Churchill showed himself Britain's leader beyond all doubt, and ready to make decisions of great boldness. The French disaster had been difficult for him to understand and to digest, and his feelings, if not his illusions, were shared by some of his intimate circle, notably by Major-General Spears and Desmond Morton. Both of these men had met Churchill in France in the First World War when he had briefly commanded a battalion on the western front, and later when he had visited Haig's H.Q. as Minister of Munitions. Churchill had at once recognised their quality and they enjoyed a unique place in his mind and in his confidence. They were more than fifteen years his juniors. Both had been brave soldiers; both spoke French with complete fluency.

Major-General Spears had been the first to recognise the qualities of the young French General de Gaulle, and they had become friends before the collapse of France. In the last days de Gaulle had tried to help M. Paul Reynaud to hold France together, and to preserve her dignity. It had been hopeless. Senior commanders like Weygand were ready to accept German surrender terms and to become servants of a new French Government under the old First World War hero, Marshal Pétain. Admiral Darlan, commanding the powerful French Navy, while pledging his honour not to permit the French fleet to fall into enemy hands, was equally determined not to sail it out of harm's way, or to fight with Britain. Darlan had the power to provide the strength and the rallying point for the preservation of France, to establish a government in exile based on France's vast African empire, and to fight the German enemy until such time as the tide should turn. But Darlan was an Anglophobe, and he chose defeated France.

In the middle of June while there seemed a chance that the French would resist German surrender terms, Churchill had offered France union with Britain. The heart had gone out of France, and there was no one capable of inspiring the French people. M. Reynaud had done his best.

On the 16th June, Churchill recorded:

M. Reynaud informed us that he was beaten and handed in his resignation. Combination of Marshal Pétain and General Weygand (who were living in another world and imagined they would sit round a green table discussing armistice in the old manner) had proved too much for weak members of Government, on whom they worked by waving the spectre of revolution.[1]

On that day, 16th June, M. Monnet, a member of the French Economic Mission, and General de Gaulle, were received by Churchill in the Cabinet room. These men were clearly passionately devoted to France, and would continue to preserve the spirit and heart of France to the end, or to a new beginning. Monnet, as Churchill noted, 'wished to save as much as possible from what seemed to him the wreck of the world'.

De Gaulle was a man of different quality, but very few would have perceived it, or if they did, would have realised at that

[1]Churchill, *The Second World War*, vol. II, Readers' Union ed., p. 183.

time the unquenchable spirit of the man, that without arrogance—or with a faith so profound and integral in him that humility of such an order might seem to be arrogance, or madness—knew that he was the physical and spiritual vessel which was France. Possibly Desmond Morton, in whose mind the idea of union with France, had generated, glimpsed in de Gaulle remarkable spiritual strength.

In that interview with Churchill, while Monnet pleaded in vain for Britain to commit precious fighter squadrons to France, to defend the undefendable, and thus to prejudice Britain's imminent struggle for her own survival, de Gaulle remained silent. Only when the interview was over with Churchill's rejection of Monnet's hopeless plea, and both visitors were on their feet, did de Gaulle as it were, reveal himself. Taking a step towards Churchill and addressing him directly in a kind of personal isolation, he said simply, 'I think you are right.'

Churchill was deeply impressed. 'Under an impassive imperturbable demeanour he seemed to me to have a remarkable capacity for feeling pain,' Churchill wrote. 'I preserved an impression, in contact with this very tall phlegmatic man: "Here is the Constable of France".'

It was the instant recognition of one great romantic for another; yet there was little or nothing of the small boy in de Gaulle that was in the essence of Churchill, and nothing of the impishness or waywardness. De Gaulle possessed and was possessed by the bleak austerity of a saint, a knight in shining armour, with nothing in him of the adventurer always restless in Churchill and longing to get out. In both men there was a sense of glory.

It was a wonderful thing that in the hour of disaster overwhelming France and so closely threatening Britain two such men should come together in the absolute conviction that they would preserve their countries.

For two or three weeks British hopes remained that the French would establish a strong government in Britain or Africa, but it was not to be. The new French Government of Marshal Pétain had swiftly tightened the noose round those who strove to escape. General Noguès in Tunisia adhered to defeated France, arresting those who had sought his help, and while the peoples of the vast territories of French Equatorial Africa showed unmistakable signs of restlessness French officials accepted the writ of the 'legitimate' Government of Vichy France.

Safely in England the young General de Gaulle was alone, establishing himself and his headquarters with the minimum of staff and fuss, and with the help of General Spears and Desmond Morton. Thereafter Spears headed the official British 'mission' to de Gaulle, while Desmond Morton was a potent ally behind the scenes. Slowly, painfully slowly, dribs and drabs of support trickled in from French soldiers, seamen and airmen.

IV

The fall of France confronted Britain with agonising problems of great urgency. It was a time for the kind of bold decisions perhaps only a Churchill could have made, and for which only Churchill could have won agreement from Chiefs of Staff and War Cabinet. And it seems to me that Churchill was seldom wrong in those days of decision. He was most dangerous in his days of indecision when, having forced grudging and often weary acquiescence in his ideas, after shifting his ground, trying first one way and then another, he would find that he had argued himself into doubt. By then it was often too late to halt the march of events he had set in motion. Perhaps his greatest weakness was that he was incapable of true discussion. In the First World War Lloyd George had rebuked him on one occasion with unusual acerbity: 'You will see the point when you begin to understand that conversation is not a monologue.' But Churchill never did understand. His physician commented that when Churchill was 'batting' everyone else was 'fielding'. He did the talking, and if ever he came up against someone as forceful as himself, as he had done with General Fuller before the war, he could not tolerate it. There is one rather endearing and revealing remark of his: 'All I wanted was compliance with my wishes after reasonable discussion.'

For years his wife had reminded him, as no one else could, of his great fault. No doubt she had taken some of the edge off his violence. Undoubtedly her influence worked profoundly for his benefit, and for the benefit of England. Yet his great virtues and great vices were inseparable. His incessant prodding of almost everyone in almost every sphere of Britain's struggle, his diabolical versatility and the violence of his expression, caused immense time wasting, and was too much for many men of talent, dedication and scholarship. Even then, in the first weeks of Churchill's Supreme Command, some were feeling the strain.

General Sir John Dill, who had followed General Ironside in the seat of the Chief of the Imperial General Staff, was soon showing signs of strain, not because of his weakness, but because his keen mind and integrity compelled him to reason.

Others, more durable, seldom argued, they simply said 'No' and went on saying 'No' until Churchill would change his ground, and finally abandon it, wondering what all the trouble had been about.

But in the days of dire emergency and instant challenge when there was no time to assess all possible factors governing decisions, few said 'No'. The decision to attempt to sink or decisively to cripple the powerful French fleet if it should prove impossible to persuade the French Government, the admirals, captains and commanders of French vessels, to sail their ships out of reach of the enemy, or to disarm them in neutral ports, was Churchill's. It was a brave decision, and despite all the criticism levelled against it I believe that it was not only bold but right. It was also tragic. Only Admiral Cunningham commanding the British fleet at Alexandria succeeded in persuading his French opposite number, Admiral Godefroy, to disarm his ships. It demanded qualities of great tact, patience, resolution and fortitude on the part of the British admiral, who refused to be pushed into instant action, and won the confidence and ultimate support of the French admiral.

The French ships in British ports were seized without great difficulty but the main strength at Mers el Kebir was only crippled after brief but violent action.

Those who still harboured some hopes of Marshal Pétain's Government stated that the British action had flung Vichy France into the Nazi embrace. Vichy France was in the Nazi embrace already and the early lack of support for General de Gaulle seemed to confirm the defeatist sentiments of an overwhelming proportion of the French people.

As it was de Gaulle had not been consulted, but despite his immediate feelings of intense 'pain and anger' at the British action, he swiftly understood it. Having weighed the pros and cons he wrote: '...it must be recognised that, faced by the capitulation of the Bordeaux authorities and the prospect of future flinchings on their part, England might well fear that the enemy would one day manage to gain control of our fleet. In that case Britain would have been mortally menaced.'[1]

[1] De Gaulle, *The Call to Honour*, p. 97.

It was a prospect too terrible to contemplate. 'The life of the state and the salvation of our cause were at stake,' Churchill wrote. It was a 'hateful' decision. 'It was Greek Tragedy.' Indeed the anguish of the British admirals involved was as great as any man's, save perhaps only de Gaulle's, 'who was magnificent in his demeanour'.[1]

On July 8th de Gaulle was permitted to broadcast from the B.B.C. He said what he had to say freely. No pressures were brought to bear upon what he might or might not say. 'The British Government,' he wrote, 'was clever enough and elegant enough, to let me use the B.B.C. microphone . . . however disagreeable for the British the terms of my statement may have been.'[2]

He was already the authentic voice of 'Free France'. He was France.

V

With Britain 'mortally menaced' on all sides, and with the German assault from the air probing the defences in the early stages of the Battle of Britain, there were no signs anywhere of defeatism. Long and short term plans were pursued as though the nation was embarked on a course of victory. At home, Air Marshal Sir Hugh Dowding, Air Officer Commanding-in-Chief, Fighter Command, had husbanded his forces with skill and was ready to fight the Battle for Britain's life. At sea the Navy had won successes to cause restrained rejoicing, but the real enemy lurked beneath the waves and not on top of them. The Battle of the Atlantic would be a struggle of attrition. In the Middle East General Sir Archibald Wavell had caused a giant base to rise out of the desert sands, and was preparing undismayed, to defend Egypt, Abadan oil, and much more besides, against forces outnumbering his slender armies by ten to one. India was already providing troops and preparing to meet whatever war might bring. The dominions and colonial territories were already bringing all their strengths to bear, not only for their own salvation but for the survival of the 'Mother Country'. Faced with boundless calls on her resources Britain supported General de Gaulle in his attempts to win the vast territories of France's African empire to his side. The peoples and Governors of Chad

[1]Churchill, *The Second World War*, vol. II, Readers' Union ed., p. 198.
[2]De Gaulle, *The Call to Honour*, p. 97.

and the Cameroons gave clear indications of support for Free France, and there in equatorial Africa, if not in the north, de Gaulle might establish a power base.

An immediate target for Britain and for de Gaulle was Dakar, the French naval base and port of Senegal, French West Africa, strategically well placed to menace and to harry British shipping in the South Atlantic. For de Gaulle it could be the key to gaining the support of French West Africa. Bold measures were justified, and de Gaulle, aided by Spears and Desmond Morton, produced a plan. This was at once approved in principle by Churchill and the Chiefs of Staff. There followed a succession of changes and modifications arising out of doubts about the best means of attaining the object. It was not a question of an all-out assault in strength, but of assessing the will of Dakar to resist. De Gaulle was opposed to the idea of Frenchmen fighting Frenchmen, while Britain hoped to succeed without bloodshed, or with very little.

In the event, when the expedition sailed at the end of August it was doomed to dismal failure, and it would be tedious to follow the series of errors of which perhaps the principal and fundamental error was the virtual inability of de Gaulle, or of the British, to grasp the bleak fact that a majority of Frenchmen remained loyal to the duly appointed Government of France. The authorities at Dakar had been in two minds, but the garrison had been unexpectedly reinforced by a powerful French naval force permitted to sail peacefully out of Toulon and through the Straits of Gibraltar to the Atlantic. It had been observed, of course, but owing to a delayed signal to Gibraltar from the Admiralty, believed to have been caused by an air-raid on Whitehall, the French warships had slipped through to join the crippled battleship, *Richelieu,* at Dakar. It was very soon apparent that there would be no peaceful landing, and in the face of the shore batteries and powerful guns of the *Richelieu* and the French naval force, the only course was to retire.

In the upshot a torrent of abuse, from which Churchill was not immune, fell upon de Gaulle both in England and America, and there was some loss of prestige. The United States maintained an attitude of pettiness and spite towards de Gaulle to the bitter end. Churchill and de Gaulle bore it all with outward equanimity. 'Mr. Churchill,' de Gaulle wrote, 'although he himself was being strongly harassed, did not disown me any more than I disowned him.'[1]

In the House of Commons Churchill stated that all that had happened 'had only strengthened His Majesty's Government in the confidence they extended to General de Gaulle'. There was in fact very little cause for gloom. The attempt at Dakar had strengthened the resolution of the Free French everywhere. An entry into French West Africa was swiftly achieved by way of Duala, and the Cameroons and the route through to Fort Lamy and thence to Chad was open. Meanwhile the French warships were bottled up at Dakar to prevent any attempt they might make to the north or the south. Rapidly French Equatorial Africa was in de Gaulle's hands. At the same time Britain was establishing an overland route for light reinforcements and supplies from Takoradi on the Gold Coast through to Cairo.

Reinforcements and supplies for the Middle-East Command had become a matter of extreme urgency, and had to be met, for the most part, by using the long haul round the Cape. Italy's declaration of war on 10th June immediately challenged British sea power in the central and western Mediterranean. At the same time Italy began to mount operations against Egypt in overwhelming strength from Libya and Italian East Africa. On paper the odds seemed absurd. The Italian declaration of war had fully justified the British action against the French fleet at Oran, at Alexandria and in British ports, while the despatch of French warships to Dakar justified British fears of the German ability to influence the French Vichy Government, despite the surrender terms and the assurances of Admiral Darlan.

The pattern of war was beginning to take shape with the Middle East the battlefield. The Free French were developing into very useful allies, and the Army, destined to take the Free French from Lake Chad to Paris by way of the Sahara, North Africa and Normandy, had established a base. In Cairo General Wavell, surveying his vast command and the complex threats against him on all sides, was undismayed by the Italian menace, and so were his generals. Outnumbered by at least ten to one they had the utmost confidence in victory. The security of British oil supplies and of the Nile Delta depended on the defence of Egypt and the Soudan, Iraq, Palestine, Aden and Kenya. Perhaps no more formidable task had confronted a British general with such slender resources in the history of war.

While these great challenges were engaging the urgent atten-

[1] De Gaulle, *The Call to Honour*, p. 134.

tion of those on and off the field, of Churchill, the Chiefs of Staff, the War Cabinet and numerous committees, the Battle of Britain was fought in the skies over the Island, so that almost all those who dwelt in the land were spectators of their own fight for survival.

It was a time when unreason was triumphant, and Britain constantly achieved not only the illogical but the impossible.

By the middle of September, thanks to the tactical genius of Air Marshal Sir Hugh Dowding, and the courage and dedication of the fighter pilots, the battle was won. 'The foresight of Air Marshal Dowding deserves high praise,' Churchill wrote. 'We must regard the generalship here shown as an example of genius in the art of war.'[1] Nevertheless within a few months Dowding was pushed into retirement. Probably his dogged intervention to save his fighters from being squandered in the final phase of the Battle of France had angered Churchill. He could not tolerate opposition, especially if it won.

A month later Admiral Cunningham, commanding the British Mediterranean fleet, brought about a master-stroke to cripple the Italian fleet in Taranto harbour. This operation, conceived and carried out with great boldness and high courage, allied to brilliant timing, was achieved by twenty-one Swordfish aircraft flown from the carrier, *Illustrious*. The date was the 11th November, 1940. The results eased the dangerous naval situation in the western Mediterranean, and opened a new chapter in naval history.

> The Italians, in those brief blinding minutes, had their naval superiority destroyed and their morale shaken beyond measure [wrote Ernle Bradford]. Taranto was an action as significant in its way as Drake's at Cadiz in 1587. Although battleships would continue to be used in the Mediterranean and the Pacific Ocean for the rest of the war, their passing was heralded that night when the torpedo-carrying aircraft altered the balance of power at sea in a few minutes.[2]

By the end of October the security of Britain was almost assured, and a position had been reached when it was possible to say with truth that even if a road to victory against the immense forces opposing the country could not be seen, Britain

[1] Churchill, *The Second World War*, vol. II, Readers' Union ed., p. 267.
[2] Ernle Bradford, *The Mediterranean*, Hodder and Stoughton.

should not be beaten, and those plans for a retreat to Canada in the worst possible case, and the sailing of the Royal Navy across the Atlantic, could be torn up, and dismissed entirely from the mind. Not that Churchill, I believe, had ever truly imagined himself being forced to carry them out.

Great exertions had been devoted to the expansion of the Royal Air Force, and especially of Bomber Command, under the driving energies of Lord Beaverbrook as Minister of Aircraft Production. Throughout the winter, although the 'Battle of Britain' was won, the enemy concentrated on bomber attacks on centres of industry, on ports, and particularly on London. These were to continue for nearly seven months with intensity, causing widespread damage, but without dangerously hampering essential production. In spite of the comparative enemy failure in the air Churchill was firm in his view that only the bomber could bring victory, or soften up the enemy and even the odds. 'Our one hope, so far as could be seen at present, of overcoming the immense military strength of Germany lay in the power of the bomber to paralyse her economy. The Air Force and its action on the largest scale must therefore claim the first place over the Navy or the Army.'[1]

Meanwhile urgent steps had been taken to establish a Combined Operations force to harry the enemy wherever it might be possible, and to compel the attention of alert enemy forces over the immense coastlines of the territories he occupied.

It was already clear that, whatever mistakes and misjudgments might be made, and had already been made, Britain had never been better served on land, sea and in the air. The admirals, air marshals, and generals could stand beside the best of their forebears, and, more important, beside the best of their opponents. The great priority was to put the materials of war into their hands. It was not 'a war of masses of men hurling masses of shells at each other' Churchill observed. 'It is by devising new weapons, and above all, by scientific leadership, that we shall best cope with the enemy's superior strength.'[2]

Perhaps the truly astonishing aspect of Churchill's leadership is that with the vast range of problems with which he, his Chiefs of Staff, the War Cabinet, the numerous important committees, and ministries, had to deal daily and nightly, together with his personal concentration on drawing the United States

[1] *Grand Strategy*, vol. II.
[2] Churchill, *The Second World War*, vol. III.

into the war, and the gaining of allies or the securing of neutrality wherever it might be possible, his major preoccupation was 'leadership in the field'. He surveyed his war maps in 'The Hole' under his offices in Whitehall, fighting the war personally, and sending out floods of orders, memoranda and directives often couched in the language of 'Operations Orders' to his generals. This was his greatest and abiding weakness, reflecting his deep longing to lead men into action. If he had been able to abjure his ambition to be a 'super-general' his record would provide little with which to quibble. Few aspects of war at home or abroad escaped his vigilance and attention, invariably with good results, but on the battlefields it was different. He had not progressed in that field since the end of the nineteenth century, and could not grasp what the administration of a vast area like the Middle-East Command entailed. He nagged ceaselessly.

Confronting his war maps Churchill squared up like a prize fighter, longing to swing a left hook to the head, the North Cape, while tearing at the 'underbelly' in the Mediterranean. It was his abiding dream. In the main his longings could not be translated into action. The strategy of the nation was his business, but the tactics of commanders in the field was not. As First Lord in 1914–1915 he had longed to seize Bordeaux with his left and to assault the Dardanelles with his right—he was the same man.

His immense versatility was staggering, his energies almost miraculous, for even when his bodily energies were strictly curtailed, not only by his age, but by the various illnesses that beset him, and the emotional strains to which he was subjected, his mental energies remained unabated. His activities and intrusions into the whole business of war, except for his intrusions in the field of battle, were often salutary and stimulating. But he was like a virtuoso conductor of an orchestra, unable to resist, without abandoning his baton, dashing down from his rostrum to seize the drum sticks from the drummer, the flute from the flautist, the violin or bass, even the triangle and to pursue his players with a flood of instructions and suggestions while they needed absolute concentration on their instruments.

It was when he seized the batons of other great conductors serving Britain, that his behaviour became intolerable. When the orchestra seemed to be losing its place Churchill blamed the very conductor whose baton he had seized.

CHAPTER SIX

The Supreme Command

I

IMMEDIATELY UPON CHURCHILL'S BECOMING PRIME MINISTER AND Minister of Defence, the Supreme Commander of Britain and all its resources, the machinery of war and government had moved into top gear. It maintained its driving energy through the relentless, restless energy of the 'Old Man' at the top. In sickness and in health the pressures exerted by the 'Old Man' continued unabated, the flow of ideas and messages, of sharp questionings and criticisms, of directives, orders, demands, incitements, going out in spate even from his sick-beds. His grip upon the machinery of war was total, and to oppose him demanded moral courage and great reserves of stamina and nervous energy. He preserved himself whatever the cost to those who strove to serve him and the nation, and all those high officials and important men under his direct command conformed to his timings. He slept or rested often in the middle of the day but when he aroused himself all had to labour with him, or simply listen to him, through the nights, propping open their eyes and ears as best they might, unable and unwilling to match him in his great consumption of alcohol, or to stem the flood of words. He was fifteen, twenty, even thirty years older than most of his 'lieutenants'. He made his own rules.

Churchill's personal entourage, the inner heart of his head-quarters, was immediately installed. They were men who had been with him as advisers and helpers in the 'wilderness years'. They were in a sense his intimates and friends, experts in various fields, and dedicated to carrying out his wishes.

General Ismay, Churchill's personal representative on the Chiefs of Staff Committee, was a key figure and would remain so from beginning to end, a man of equable temperament and absolute integrity. Ismay was head of the military wing of the War Cabinet Secretariat, and with his able lieutenants, Colonels Hollis and Jacob, formed the inner staff of the Ministry of Defence.

Churchill, as Prime Minister and Minister of Defence, took over the direction of the Chiefs of Staff Committee whenever he had a mind to, and arranged for himself immediate access to the Joint Planning Staff. Only the loyalty of the planners to their military chiefs prevented Churchill from studying vital documents ahead of his own Chiefs of Staff. Moreover, by virtue of his office Churchill was also chairman of the two Defence Committees, covering operations and supply. Thus he was in truth and in fact the Supreme Commander of the nation and its armed forces. It became swiftly apparent that he was not only resolved upon formulating grand strategy and the strategy of the armies on the battlefield, but of attempting to dictate tactics, thus usurping the roles of his commanders in the field. Yet he was not a dictator. He had to answer to the War Cabinet and to parliament, and it would be the task of the Chief of the Imperial General Staff, General Sir John Dill, to confront Churchill and attempt to ensure the smooth and practical running of the military machine.

By the time Churchill demanded the attendance of his personal and senior staffs most of them had already done a full day's work, while he was completely refreshed by his rest periods. To meet his demands often meant travelling in difficult conditions to Chequers or Ditchley, houses for the use of the Prime Minister in Buckinghamshire and Oxfordshire.

President Roosevelt's personal emissary to Churchill, Harry Hopkins, described these night meetings at first hand. 'Churchill,' he wrote, 'always seemed to be at his command post on the precarious beachhead and the guns were continually blazing in his conversation; wherever he was there was the battlefront.'

It was the complete reverse of the kind of tranquillity always surrounding Roosevelt, and since Hopkins was not on the receiving end of Churchill's 'blazing guns' he was intrigued, startled and amused. The Prime Minister

was getting full steam up along about ten o'clock in the evening; often after his harassed staff had struggled to bed at 2 or 3 a.m. they would be routed out an hour or more later with an entirely new project for which a plan must be drawn up immediately . . . Churchill's consumption of alcohol . . . could be described as unique, for it continued at quite regular intervals through most of his waking hours without visible effect on his health or on his mental processes . . . His principal aides—General Sir Hastings Ismay, Professor F. A. Lindemann, Commander Charles Thompson, Sir Desmond Morton, J. M. Martin and Bracken—made no attempt to keep up with his consumption of champagne, whisky and brandy . . . and they had to summon reserves of energy to be able to keep up with him in work.[1]

Churchill's principal aides were seldom directly involved, and the great burden of this behaviour fell upon the Chief of Staff, the Director of Military Operations and the planning staffs involved in whatever plan, or set of plans, he was resolved upon forcing through. Most of Churchill's plans had to be resisted in the face of violent invective and accusations of defeatism. Desmond Morton, who was perhaps closer to Churchill than anyone else, said that nothing could be discarded without fierce argument and proof of its impracticability. He wrote:

Even then he was not done. He would set his brain to work out further suggestions as to the general way (never in detail) how this might be overcome, and the staff officer would then have to work out a lot more facts and figures in which W. was quite uninterested, being interested only in the conclusion. If this last was hopelessly unfavourable to his plan, he might easily produce another, and yet another set of ideas to which no one could give an immediate answer.[2]

For the Chief of Staff, the Director of Military Operations and the Planning Staffs it was a very grave matter, and General Kennedy, the D.M.O., wondered whether it might not be possible to establish some sort of 'ghost staff' but it would have been as impossible to hoodwink Churchill, as it was impossible to argue with him. He would often appear to listen carefully to the daily discussions, but his mind would invariably pick on some point in a careful exposition, and focus on that. He rarely

[1] Robert Sherwood (ed.), *The White House Papers of Harry Hopkins,* vol. I, p. 242.
[2] Personal letter from Sir Desmond Morton to the author.

saw any problem whole, and it was difficult for soldiers and scholars to stick to their guns when they were absolutely certain of the wrong-headedness of many of Churchill's ideas. And even when his ideas were good they were often impossible. He refused to understand administration and the limitations imposed by logistics and transport. In his mind, too often, the armed forces were made up almost entirely of fighting troops. Of course he knew as well as any man that this was not so, but he denied it constantly, and often ignored it in his arguments.

Ismay wrote of Churchill:

He is a mass of contradictions. He is either on the crest of the wave, or in a trough; either highly laudatory, or bitterly condemnatory; either in an angelic temper, or a hell of a rage; when he isn't fast asleep he's a volcano. There are no half measures in his make up. He is a child of nature with moods as variable as an April day.

Perhaps most difficult to bear were his 'tantrums' when crossed, when he would slump in his chair, his chin sunk on his chest, lips pouting like a baby. As someone remarked, he had contrived to pass from childhood to second childhood without maturity intervening. 'He is like a child that has set his mind on some forbidden toy,' wrote Sir John Kennedy. 'It is no good explaining that it will cut his fingers or burn him. The more you explain, the more fixed he becomes in his idea . . .' Yet he was immensely formidable, a man of power, ready to destroy those who stood in his way.

General Dill bore the brunt of Churchill's tirades, but very soon he began to show signs of great weariness and strain. In 1940–41 nothing could be squandered, nothing could be irresponsibly committed to any venture unless absolutely vital to the security of the nation, and it was General Dill's job to preserve Britain's slender resources, and to build up the nation's strength for the future. It demanded eternal vigilance and dedicated courage. Dill was a man of reason and of great military ability, but was not equipped to deal constantly with unreason and to withstand the kind of violence Churchill brought to bear as a matter of course. Moreover Churchill did not like Dill, and with Churchill that was always fatal.

General Sir Bernard Paget, whose task it was to work ceaselessly on the intricate plans for the return to Europe, and to build up and train an army for the purpose, had no patience with Churchill, and said so, daring to dismiss the graphs and diagrams Professor Lindemann prepared for his chief as rubbish. Certainly they were invariably misleading and of little use, but they gave Churchill the kind of pleasure a picture-book gives to a child.

> Often I wondered during the war where Churchill got some of his more outrageous strategic ideas from [Paget wrote]. He much preferred to seek and take advice from people like Cherwell [Lindemann], Harris, Wingate . . . than of the C. of S. Fortunately for us, unlike Hitler, he did not in the last resort go against the advice of the C. of S.[1]

Certainly in the last resort if the Chiefs of Staff stood their ground with unshakable determination, they prevailed, but often they were bludgeoned into actions against their better judgment.

'The reader must not forget that I never wielded autocratic powers, and always had to move with and focus political and professional opinions,' Churchill wrote in apologetic mood. It was true—but only just true.

II

General Sir Archibald Wavell arrived in London from the Middle East on 8th August at Churchill's request. 'I felt an acute need of talking over the serious events impending in the Libyan desert with General Wavell himself,' Churchill wrote. 'I had not met this distinguished officer, on whom so much was resting . . .'

One of the official histories covering the war in the Mediterranean and Middle East, takes as its text a quotation from Cicero's *De Officiis*: 'An army is of little value in the field unless there are wise counsels at home.' Few could imagine that, with Churchill at the helm, there were wise counsels at home for the commanders in the field, and the Official Historians, although guarded and restrained in their references to this aspect of Churchill's attempts at 'super-generalship' do not entertain such untenable beliefs. Major-General Sir John Kennedy, the

[1]Personal correspondence.

Director of Military Operations, is the most outspoken critic of Churchill's continuous attempts at direct command.

The first meeting of Churchill with Wavell filled General Dill, and other close observers, with grave fears. Two more dissimilar or more incompatible men would be difficult to imagine. Wavell was the Commander-in-Chief of the vast territories of the Middle-East Command, which embraced nine countries, many of them remarkable for the devious methods and conflicting motives and loyalties of their governments, and thick with intrigue. The area covered was some 2,000 by 1,700 miles of territory. Moreover Wavell's responsibilities were far wider than this commitment, including constant attention to the situation in Greece, Turkey, and the Balkans, and the defence of Malta and Cyprus. In short, Wavell was not simply a military commander, but an administrator and statesman. The defence of Egypt and the Nile Delta, and the safeguarding of Abadan oil were among his priorities, and their importance loomed very large in Churchill's mind.

In August 1940 the Middle East Command was short of almost everything, of fighting troops, of aircraft, of armour, artillery and equipment of all kinds. The creation of the great base in the desert to support the operations absorbed great quantities of men, outnumbering fighting troops by ten to one. It was a fact of life to which Churchill did not take kindly. The official history spells out the problem clearly:

> . . . an underdeveloped region which becomes an important theatre of war becomes also a bottomless pit. Setting up the base and armed forces in the Middle East was like gradually transplanting a complete modern society with all its complicated needs. Almost every activity known in ordinary life was being carried out there by someone in uniform.[1]

Wavell at once gave Churchill a lucid appreciation of the whole situation, of the numerous threats developing to the north, south and west, of his dispositions, and of his intentions. The meeting of Churchill with his greatest general was distressing in the extreme, and one who was present said that the temperature lowered at once and could not be revived. Churchill was exuberant, rhetorical, weaving words; Wavell was quiet, reticent, a dedicated soldier, a master of his command and its

[1] I.S.O. Playfair, *The Mediterranean and the Middle East,* vol. III, p. 372.

problems. He made it crystal clear that he took his own decisions, and no man could take them for him. He had already had a foretaste of Churchill's constant proddings, which he had borne with equanimity, while his fellow commanders at sea and in the air, Admiral Cunningham and Air Marshal Longmore, showed resentment, regarding Churchill's interference as a slight upon their integrity, their loyalty, and their patriotism. They were as concerned to fight and to defeat the enemy as Churchill was. They knew their business, and resented tactical instructions in matters which were their direct concern as questioning not only their ability, but their courage.

As for Wavell, 'He would not—indeed he could not—surrender his own integrity and independence of judgment; and this was, in fact, what Churchill demanded, quite unconsciously but inexorably.'[1]

It would have been impossible to explain this to Churchill. Like Wavell he was simply being himself, the same man, a quarter of a century on, who had left the Admiralty to take command at Antwerp, and prepared for the first time but not for the last to give up everything to be a general. His longing—his need— to command was a part of him. He could not be otherwise.

The part Churchill wished Wavell to play was simply 'to be foremost among my commanders in the field'. Wavell was not, nor ever could be, Churchill's general. He was a dedicated servant of his country, of the Crown.

Except for one night at Chequers Wavell stayed with his friend, General Dill, the C.I.G.S. in London, and became aware that this would add to Churchill's dislike and distrust. There was nothing Wavell and Dill could do about it, except their duty. Churchill's dislike and distrust were purely personal. While the two most senior generals in the British Army worked and talked and exhaustively answered Churchill's constant flood of demands, the Battle of Britain was reaching its climax in the sky over London, and the Prime Minister and Britain were in their great hour of glory to be made imperishable in Churchill's great phrase: 'Never in the field of human conflict was so much owed by so many to so few.'

There would be glory, too, in the Western Desert when the plans carefully laid in the utmost secrecy by Wavell and his generals culminated in General Richard O'Connor's amazing

[1] Connell, *Wavell, Scholar and Soldier*, p. 243.

triumph in the total defeat of the Italian Army in Africa. But that tide, halted by Churchill at Beda Fomm, would not be taken at the flood to lead on, almost surely, to Tripoli, and even beyond.

Meanwhile Churchill had wisely appointed a Middle-East Committee with Anthony Eden, the Foreign Secretary, as Chairman, L. S. Amery (India Office) and Lord Lloyd. These men were all well versed in Middle-Eastern affairs. They were at once impressed by the grave shortages suffered by the whole Middle-East Command. The need for aircraft was very great, but while the bombing of Germany grew in intensity, building up to the first of the 1,000 bomber raids mounted against the cathedral city of Cologne, the armies overseas, the fleets on the seas, the soldiers, sailors and airmen, would be gravely hampered in their struggles. Nevertheless ships and armour were soon on the way to reinforce the Mediterranean and Middle East.

Through all the week from 8th to 15th August Churchill seemed resolved to argue comparative trivialities with Wavell. The General answered all his questions with 'closely reasoned answers', but the feeling between the two men worsened. It was not a conflict of wills, but a basic incompatibility, which would have been unimportant if Churchill had confined himself to his role of Prime Minister and Minister of Defence, and had not been utterly resolved to direct the war single-handed. It was not simply a matter of standing up to him—which was difficult—but of preventing the enormous wastage of time he imposed, especially on Planning Staffs. Dill did oppose Churchill bravely, but with little effect. Brooke, his successor, established a *modus vivendi,* but nothing checked the flow of impractical schemes and ideas with which planning staffs were forced to deal. Sir John Kennedy records that Brooke, having reduced the draft of a minute to the Prime Minister by nine tenths, remarked: 'The more you tell that man about the war, the more you hinder the winning of it.'

But it was not enough for Dill, or for Brooke after him, simply to oppose Churchill's wildest schemes, and somehow to conserve and build up British resources. Somehow Churchill should have been prevented from direct and constant interference with his commanders in the field, and this was not achieved. Even Lords Chatfield and Hankey, men of very wide experience in the waging of war, and of Churchill himself, were unable to persuade him to share some of the load he insisted upon bearing himself. The choice was Churchill 'warts 'n all' or no Churchill, and no one, not even his severest critics, was prepared to do without him. That, perhaps, is a measure of his extraordinary stature.

The root of Churchill's trouble was the curious blend of past and present which, coupled with his romantic nature, his genuine love and admiration of the heroic, and together with a sense of Britain no longer based upon present realities, led him constantly to demand the impossible, and to suggest schemes, often strategically sound in themselves, but quite impossible to carry out.

'I found that Winston's tactical ideas had to some extent crystallised at the South-African War,' Wavell wrote, 'just as his ideas on India's political problems, as I discovered later, had not advanced much from his impression as a subaltern in the Nineties.'[1]

Undoubtedly this was part of the truth, but it was far more complicated than that. Churchill's tactical views went back to Rorke's Drift, Isandlwhana, Omdurman, and by way of the Boer War to the First World War, to the Second World War. He carried it all in his memory, and it coloured his imagination. He knew as much as, if not more than, any man about the realities of the situation in 1940 to 1945. He knew the shortages in manpower and equipment. He knew all about the inevitable growth of the 'tail of an army', of the enormous problems of transport and maintenance of growing armies of machines. And yet he thought constantly in terms of an heroic past. He was convinced that men should, and would prefer to fight to the death rather than live to fight another day. He was genuinely appalled that his great commanders had made plans for 'the worst possible case', although he had done the same himself. Any commander who had failed to make such plans would have been guilty of gross and inexcusable negligence. Yet when Churchill learned of Wavell's 'worst possible case' plans in the event of the loss of Egypt and the Nile Delta, he regarded them as defeatist. Major-General Kennedy, the D.M.O., speculated on what Churchill's reaction might have been had he known that Wavell had plans for even worse disaster, plans to fight on from an African base, even if the British Isles should be lost. These plans were evidence of an unconquerable spirit and resolve. Fortunately Churchill did not know. His concentration upon the defence of Egypt and the Delta was becoming steadily more

[1] John Connell, *Wavell, Scholar and Soldier*, p. 256.

irrational. Soon he would raise it from the fifth place in the defence priorities to second place. He produced a Directive without consultation with the Chiefs of Staff which stated that 'the loss of Egypt and the Middle East would be a disaster of the first magnitude to Great Britain, second only to successful invasion and final conquest'.

Major-General Kennedy and Sir John Dill disagreed with this absolutely. It was wrong. 'It is quite wrong,' wrote Kennedy, 'to say that the life of Great Britain depends on the successful defence of Egypt. It is also quite wrong,' Kennedy continued, 'to say that British forces, land, sea and air, would not wish to survive the evacuation of the Middle East. If they did not survive it we should have insufficient forces left with which to carry on the war successfully.'

Nothing could have been more defeatist than Churchill's insistence that troops would rather die heroically than give ground. His attitude to the Middle East was becoming increasingly ominous, and expressed in the week that Wavell was in London by his reaction to a brave and skilful British withdrawal from Somaliland. On the eve of his departure for London Wavell had ordered General Godwin Austen, then on his way to Kenya to take command of a division, to proceed at once to Berbera to take command of the small garrison in British Somaliland, and to do the best he could against the overwhelming strength of the Italians. Godwin Austen, handling his small force with great skill and courage, avoided envelopment and disaster. It was at once apparent that the only sane course was to evacuate British Somaliland, and General Wilson, Wavell's second-in-command, immediately ordered this course. It was a difficult operation, demanding steadfast courage on the part of the officers and men.

When Churchill heard of Godwin Austen's success and the comparatively light casualties the British garrison had sustained, he demanded General Godwin Austen's dismissal, and called for a full court of enquiry to be set up. Wavell refused absolutely to reprimand his general, and was in fact very pleased with his achievement. Godwin Austen had fought a bold rearguard action, inflicting 1,800 casualties (admitted by the enemy) while suffering 260 to his own troops, of whom only thirty-eight were killed.

On 15th August, back in his command, Wavell received a 'red-hot cable' from Churchill demanding retribution. Wavell cabled back that the troops had fought very well, and ended with a remark that 'a big butcher's bill' was not necessarily evidence of good tactics. Whereupon Churchill blew up, the full force of his rage falling upon the unfortunate Dill, 'who invariably bore the brunt of Churchill's fury'.

The situation was grave, and both Dill and Wavell knew that they would not survive for very long. There was too great a contrast in temperaments, in character, in attitudes between Churchill and these two generals, scholarly men, whose lives had been devoted to the mastery of their craft. Churchill had always wanted to be a general without going through the long grind. Why, with all his brilliance could he not skip all that and arrive at the end by other means? His attitude to the army and its generals had always been ambivalent. He seemed to take pleasure in insulting the army to the point where Dill could barely contain his anger, and would complain bitterly to General Kennedy. Fortunately Kennedy was a tough and brilliant Director of Military Operations, sustaining his chief through many ordeals, and ready at all times to confront Churchill with the unvarnished truth, whether he liked it or not. It was not enough simply to stand up to Churchill. He was the same man he had been in those far-off days in the Admiralty, but now there was no Asquith, and no Lloyd George. And there was the inexorable pressure of time, of age and sickness. He had waited so long for this great chance, and nothing should stop him.

John Connell wrote: 'Churchill used every weapon of agressive debate—mordant sarcasm, prosecuting counsel's bullying, extravagant rhetorical flourishes, urchin abuse, Ciceronian irony and sledgehammer brutality—and Dill had to bear it all and suppress his anger and anguish.'[1]

The restraint of Dill and Wavell added to the Prime Minister's fury. He could not understand that they did not retaliate. He was convinced that Wavell would have his 'revenge', ultimately attacking him in words. Later he questioned Dill about Wavell's ability as a writer. What was Wavell writing? Was he writing anything? Yes, he's a fine writer, Dill told him, and then drily, 'He's writing poetry'.

What a pity it was, Kennedy thought, that Churchill 'did not devote his energies to the things he could do so well—like pushing on the organisation of our resources and industrial production, negotiating with the U.S.A. and so forth'. It was a great and grave pity, for in the end victory in the field must depend upon these things, upon the wise choice of options. To

[1] John Connell, *Wavell, Scholar and Soldier*, p. 256.

cheer Dill up after the terrible storms of Churchill's wrath, Kennedy suggested constant prodding of Churchill in his handling of the urgent matters that were his direct concern. Suppose he, Churchill, had been incessantly harried and prodded and insulted about his dealings with Spain, Turkey, the Balkans, Singapore, and above all the need to bring U.S.A. into the war. At least it made Dill laugh to think about it. But Churchill was 'Our Baby Dictator' as Cadogan called him. Baby Dictators are as formidable as the adult variety—if such there be.

On 16th August Churchill issued a Directive for the conduct of the campaign in the Middle East that was virtually an Operation Order, and no part of Churchill's business. By it, in effect, the Prime Minister and Minister of Defence proclaimed himself Commander-in-Chief of the Armies in the field. The document gravely disturbed Sir John Dill, astonished Sir John Kennedy, and left no doubt in anyone's mind of Churchill's vision of himself. Even the Official Historians would permit themselves to comment: 'So detailed a directive from a Minister to a commander in a distant theatre was to say the least unusual.' It was clear that Wavell's days were numbered. He knew at once from the Directive that the Prime Minister did not trust him to run his own show. 'Detailed tactical instructions were given, down to the forward and rear distributions of battalions.'[1] The Directive included 'meticulous and minutely detailed orders' for Wavell's employment of his forces, and these things having been done, 'the Army of the Delta will finally defeat the Italian "invasion"'. Churchill had omitted Q.E.D.

Wavell, of course, had his own ideas and would continue on his course, but he replied in a conciliatory manner. He needed equipment, especially armour and aircraft, with great urgency, and was determined to get it. He did not need instructions on how to command his forces. His generals, Wilson, his second-in-command, Sir Richard O'Connor, commanding the Western Desert Force, and Dorman Smith, his brilliant young deputy Chief of Staff, were immediately at hand. All had worked with Wavell since the early 1930s and were in the vanguard of military theory and practice. There were more like them, and but for the resolute obstruction of the pundits in the War Office and the persistence of the 'Cavalry Club' mentality, Rommel and Guderian might have met their match in France. Even Churchill, one of the progenitors of the tank in the First World

[1]*Grand Strategy*, vol. II, p. 130.

War, had been tainted with this brush. But now Churchill responded boldly to the need in the Middle East with magnificent urgency. It needed courage to send an armoured division out of the country while the invasion threat was at its height. Moreover he defied powerful advice and had the armour routed through the Mediterranean, with all its hazards, and saving precious time. All was safely delivered.

Meanwhile, in complete secrecy, Wavell and his generals had planned the defeat of the Italian Armies in their own fashion. At the end of the year Wavell gave Churchill the victory he had longed for, but only to see its final fruits left on the tree, ripe for the plucking. By that time 'Greek Tragedy' was building up, not only over Greece, but over British naval and military forces in the Middle East and the eastern Mediterranean. It was also Churchill's tragedy, and its consequences, which included the arrival of Rommel and the German Afrika Corps in North Africa, changed the course of the war.

III

Inevitably it is unjust to concentrate on a particular facet of Churchill's leadership. He was a giant of a man, a tycoon, happy in the company of his cronies, Birkenhead, Beaverbrook and Baruch, but he was also a romantic whose boyhood heroes had not faded with the years. D'Artagnan was not dimmed, nor were Clive and Dalhousie. He had added Lawrence of Arabia (that prince among men), and would soon find it hard to resist the panache of Orde Wingate (the Clive of Burma!). In spite of his immense duties and total involvement in the entire war effort he found time to read C. S. Forester and the adventures of Hornblower. Moreover he delighted in the cinema, however banal, and wept whenever he saw the Emma Hamilton film, even, to Sir Alexander Cadogan's astonishment, at the fifth time of viewing. He loved also to weave romances himself, dressed in his grey 'romper-suit', and 'to ramble on' sometimes for as long as two hours to his captive midnight audiences. It was not all and always invective, abuse, rhetoric directed at his Chief of Staff and the generals in the field. There were not only lighter moments, but valuable 'conferences' covering many areas in which Churchill was not emotionally involved. Meeting the doyen of the female secretarial staff outside the Foreign Office, Cadogan was delighted when she described Churchill's constant night gatherings as the 'Midnight Follies'. She had worked at No. 10 since the days of Lloyd George, but Churchill's days and nights in 'office' were peculiarly his own. Perhaps only a woman would have produced, casually, such a description. In Cadogan's view it was wonderfully apt. For his part he disliked wasting time, and was often bored by Churchill's flights of fancy and incurable liking for the sound of his own voice, and his interminable monologues. 'It is quite shattering to me,' Cadogan commented, 'the love to talk some people have.' On that occasion the sight of Churchill in a new romper-suit struck Cadogan as very odd indeed, and he was hard put to it to keep a straight face. 'He [Churchill] talked from 9.30 till 12, round and round and across.'[1]

Yet Cadogan, who had viewed the choice of Churchill as Prime Minister with misgiving, became devoted to him, at least partly under his enormous spell. Halifax had told Cadogan: 'Always stand up to him. He hates doormats. If you begin to give way he will simply wipe his feet upon you.'[2] There was never a danger of that, for Cadogan would storm back at Churchill if need be. Unfortunately Cadogan held British generals in great contempt. Churchill must have been aware of it, but although he raged and stormed at the British Army and its generals he did not share Cadogan's contempt. He was jealous of Wavell, and even more jealous of Auchinleck when the time came, for these men were where he would have liked to have been, but he had chosen another road, and the choice was irrevocable. It frustrated Churchill that the Army, unlike the other arms of the Services, could not go into immediate and decisive action. It was not the Army's role to save Britain from defeat—unless invasion came—but to be the spearhead and the final instrument of victory—when that came.

Meanwhile the Navy was fighting the terrible battle of attrition in the Atlantic, and Churchill lived with it every day, and even through many nights when he studied the charts of the Atlantic battle and the positions of all the little 'beetles' representing U-boats. He knew the tragic figures as they came in, the huge losses of ships and men, at the worst exceeding the capacity of combined British and American resources to build. And men could not be built.

In the air, the Royal Air Force fighters had won the vital

[1] *Cadogan Diaries.*
[1] Ibid., p. 301.

battle, and improved Britain's position with the neutrals and possible allies, but the growing fleets of bombers, and their crews, were being expended in pursuit of a will-o'-the-wisp. Few shared Churchill's early belief that victory could be won that way. It was one of the dangerous illusions fed by Professor Lindemann. Churchill's liking for Lindemann had nearly proved disastrous before the war, when Churchill had nominated his protégé as a member of the Tizard Committee, dedicated to solving the riddles of radar. Lindemann had threatened by his hatred of Tizard, and the constant violence and irrationality of his behaviour, his pursuit of 'gadgetry', to disrupt the committee. But for the spontaneous decisions of P. M. S. Blackett and A. V. Hill to resign when they would not tolerate any more of the violence directed against Tizard, there would not have been radar, and Britain might well have lost the war.

Fortunately the committee had been at once reconstituted with E. V. Appleton replacing Lindemann, and all was well by the time Churchill came to power, taking Lindemann with him to 10, Downing Street, to use his position to sack Tizard at once. Thereafter Lindemann busied himself producing elaborate graphs of production, and producing figures to prove that bombing would be ten times more effective than it in fact was.

Meanwhile Tizard and Blackett were sent into the wilderness for questioning Lindemann's grossly misleading bombing figures, and insisting that 'two and two made four'. They were labelled defeatist, but they had invented radar. Henceforth Lindemann held undisputed sway in all scientific matters, directing 'Churchill's toyshop', producing innumerable gadgets to delight Churchill, of which a few only, like the limpet mine, were useful.

'Judged by the simple criterion of getting what he wanted, Lindemann was the most successful politician of the age,' wrote C. P. Snow.[1]

Lindemann was, in fact, a man after Churchill's own heart. General Sir John Dill and Wavell were not. He did not understand people of absolute integrity, to whom ambition was secondary to service. Nor could he understand men who would not hit back at him. These things, as Cadogan and Morton pointed out, were unintelligible to Churchill.

In the autumn of 1940, when it was clear that Britain had weathered the first storms, and the worst dangers had begun to recede, all Churchill's restlessness, his determination to hit the

[1] *Science and Government.*

enemy everywhere, filled his close advisers with alarm. His mind was becoming more and more focussed upon the Greek seas and the eastern Mediterranean. A score of names echoed in his mind from long ago, and the planning staffs were constantly forced to plan operations beyond Britain's power.

It boded ill for Sir John Dill whose duty was to oppose Churchill's wild ideas at all costs, and to attempt to defend Wavell's position in the Middle East.

CHAPTER SEVEN

Greek Tragedy

I

THE TITLE OF THIS CHAPTER DOES NOT REFER SIMPLY TO THE tragedy enacted in Greece in the early months of 1941, to the disaster to British troops and naval and air forces involved, or to the tragic missed opportunities brought about in the campaign in the Western Desert, or to the disastrous results of those missed opportunities. Nor does it refer specifically to the loss of the British Empire and the dominance of the United States from 1942 onwards. These few early months of 1941 were the tragedy of Churchill. It was a tragedy inherent in his attitudes deriving even from the 'nursery', apparent in the Dardanelles and Gallipoli disasters in the First World War, and to a far lesser degree even in the Norwegian fiasco of 1940. In none of these disasters was he in command. His influence was powerful, but he was far from all-powerful. His responsibility for both events was very great, but the blame, especially for the tragic blunders in the Dardanelles and in Gallipoli lies at many doors.

But the disaster to British arms in Greece and Crete, and the consequent disasters in the Middle East until the first week in July 1942, were Churchill's. 'I believe,' he wrote, 'I had as much direct control over the conduct of the war as any public man had in any country at this time.'[1]

Yet in the midst of the build-up for disaster in Greece, and in spite of Churchill's continuous and horribly disturbing attempts to enforce his will and his tactics upon the Commander-in-Chief in the Middle East, Wavell and his generals achieved the complete liquidation of the Italian empire in Africa and relieved all possible landward threats to Southern Africa. Wavell's campaign in East

[1]Churchill, *The Second World War*, vol. II, Readers' Union ed., p. 485.

Africa was brilliant in its tactical conception and handling, and as devastating in its way as the victory achieved by General O'Connor in the Western Desert, culminating at Beda Fomm. Churchill had misjudged Wavell's campaign in East Africa from the beginning, 'and had directed at it a fusilade of criticism and would-be interference which, if it had had its full desired effect, would have removed all chance of victory,' wrote John Connell.[1]

Churchill's directives of early February, which could not be denied, did in fact put an end to O'Connor's almost certain conquest of Tripoli after Beda Fomm, and must have had the probably decisive result of letting Rommel and the Afrika Corps loose in the desert. Indeed, there are many who believe that Churchill lost 'The British Empire' in those tragic days.

The essentials of this story begin at Beda Fomm on 7th February. Four days later, on February 11th: 'The Defence Committee had taken important decisions. The advance in Libya was to be halted at Benghazi and our efforts there limited to the creation of a secure flank for Egypt. All of Wavell's forces that could be spared would be transferred to Europe, and to Greece rather than to Turkey.'[2] In fact, in the opinion of General Sir John Dill and of Sir John Kennedy no troops could be spared. Greece had refused and continued to refuse British offers of troops on 11th February. 'In the General Staff we thought we were well out of it, but Churchill now returned to the charge,' wrote Kennedy.[3] A day earlier Wavell had telegraphed: 'The extent of Italian defeat at Benghazi seems to me to make it possible that Tripoli might yield to small force if despatched without delay.' On that day, 10th February, Wavell had not heard the news from O'Connor of the remarkable success of British arms at Beda Fomm. It would be all in vain. On 11th February Dill, the C.I.G.S., and Anthony Eden, Foreign Minister, had been instructed to leave for Egypt, Turkey and Greece. Later on that day Dill had made a fruitless attempt to change Churchill's mind. Apart from anything else he believed his place was at home with the Chiefs of Staff, and so was Eden's, for it was clear that Churchill would be left without his principal advisers and the only men who might—it is a very small 'might'—have brought their influence to bear on decisions. Dill told Kennedy:

[1] *Wavell, Scholar and Soldier,* p. 358.
[2] *Grand Strategy,* vol. II, p. 439.
[3] *The Business of War,* p. 74.

I gave it as my view [to Churchill] that all troops in the Middle East are fully employed and that none are available for Greece. The Prime Minister lost his temper with me. I could see the blood coming up his great neck and his eyes began to flash. He said, 'What you need out there is a court-martial and a firing squad. Wavell has 300,000 men, etc. etc.' I should have said: Whom do you want to shoot, exactly? But did not think of it till afterwards.[1]

On the day that Eden and Dill began their flight to Cairo, Brigadier Dorman Smith, later Major-General Dorman Smith, and Wavell's representative with O'Connor, reached Wavell's headquarters. Dorman Smith was recognised by Wavell and later by Auchinleck, as he had been much earlier by military thinkers of the calibre of General Fuller and Captain Liddell Hart, as perhaps the greatest 'Staff' mind of his time. I am able to relate the sequence of events after Beda Fomm in his own words:

On the afternoon of February 7th '41, O'Connor and I discussed what should be the proper course of further action. O'Connor was no longer free to act independently, he had come under Wilson's[2] command, but he was out of touch with Wilson who was making for Barce. We agreed that the pursuit should be pressed towards Tripoli. O'Connor told me to go to Barce, contact Wilson and express O'Connor's views. I stopped the night 7th/8th in Benghazi and met Wilson when he arrived in Barce about noon on 8th. Wilson agreed with O'Connor and we prepared an appropriate message to Wavell. But there was no communication system ready. So Wilson told me to go on the 9th to the nearest point of communication at Tobruk, a long run for a lone car over demolished roads and through unoccupied territory. I got to Tobruk on the evening of the 9th (having spent the night 8th/9th at Barce because the major demolitions had still to be repaired). From Tobruk I sent the message to Wavell. Wavell got that message on the 9th; the next morning he must have telegraphed the C.I.G.S. seeking agreement on an advance to Sirte. I left Tobruk early on 10th and reached Cairo at midnight 10th, a very long run. I saw Wavell about 10 a.m. on 11th February.

[1]Ibid., p. 75.
[2]General Sir Henry Maitland Wilson.

He said, 'Glad to see you,' and waving his hand at his office hung with new maps of Greece, 'You will find me busy with my spring campaign.'[1]

The bitter irony in Wavell on that day, pervading his 'office' hung rather with tragic disappointment than with maps, is perhaps not very difficult to imagine. It was the day on which General Dill had watched 'the blood rising up Churchill's great neck' and when, presumably, Wavell, O'Connor, Dorman Smith and others should be facing a 'firing squad'. None of them knew what was going on in Churchill's mind at that time, and only fragments of all that is known now of Churchill's thinking through the months since Italy had attacked Greece on 28th October, 1940. Greece had at once appealed to Britain for aid. British troops had landed in Crete on 1st November, and air reinforcements, which could not be spared, had been flown to Greece. The Greeks did not wish for more. They managed to throw out the Italians, and fought with skill and courage through a hard winter. The situation after that became confused. Finally British troops left Egypt for Greece on 4th March. and continued to build up. It was utterly useless and unwanted, the Greeks fearing that British 'help' might call down upon them the full vengeance of the enemy.

On 21st April British troops were suffering a 'second Dunkirk' under heavy air attack, while the naval forces suffered severely in their rescue. A month later the tragedy of defeat in Crete wrote the final phase of the whole story.

From the point of view of Wavell and his generals the vital period between 7th February and O'Connor's victory at Beda Fomm, and the 4th March had been lost, and we were never to recover as from 11th February onwards 'events dragged everyone fatalistically' forward to disaster in Greece (and in the Western Desert). Suddenly, too late, Churchill saw the appalling blunder, gazing into 'the strategical abyss' he had opened. On 6th March, only a month after the triumph of O'Connor, Churchill telegraphed Eden in Cairo:

> Difficult for Cabinet to believe that we now have any power to avert fate of Greece unless Turkey and/or Yugoslavia come in, which seems most improbable... We do not see any reason for expecting success, except that of course we attach

[1]Personal correspondence from Dorman Smith to the author.

great weight to opinions of Dill and Wavell . . . We must liberate Greece from feeling bound to reject a German ultimatum . . . Loss of Greece and Balkans by no means a major catastrophe for us provided Turkey remains neutral. We could take Rhodes and consider plans for 'Influx' [descent on Tripoli or Sicily]. We are advised from many quarters that our ignominious ejection from Greece would do us more harm in Spain and Vichy than the fact of submission of Balkans, which with our scanty forces alone we have never been expected to prevent.[1]

It was, of course, too late.

II

It must be vital to an understanding of Churchill's role as 'super-general' to attempt to follow his mind through the months from December 1940 to March 1941. His life and deeds in war and peace up to December 1940 reveal clearly the kind of 'super-general' he was likely to be. His deeds in those grim months reveal the kind of 'super-general' he was. His deeds after March 1941 were less disastrous, but bear the same stamp. But in those months from December 1940 to March 1941 he imposed his will in command upon the Chiefs of Staff, and finally upon Wavell, a man who from the outset of the war had created a base in the desert and had conducted a victorious campaign over vast territories, and whose forces had liberated Abyssinia, driven the Italians out of East Africa, encompassed their defeat in the Western Desert, a feat which opened up wide opportunities. It could have ruled out the need finally to invade Tunisia.

It is difficult to avoid some speculations in 'if' history, and the 'ifs' are manifold, mainly in Churchill's mind. But in this immediate context it is important to remember that in December 1940 Churchill urged upon the Chiefs of Staff the need to attack and seize the island of Pantelleria.[2] In the view of Generals Dill and Kennedy the capture of the island, if successful, 'would bring us no advantage . . . but Churchill had set his mind on Pantelleria', and a 'vast amount of time and energy was wasted upon it'. The project was fortunately abandoned, but the point here is that Churchill had believed it

[1]Churchill, *The Second World War*, vol. III, Readers Union ed., p. 90.
[2]Ibid., vol. II, p. 552. Also: Kennedy, *The Business of War*, p. 63.

both possible and profitable, and therefore it was obvious that
the seizure of Tripoli using the naval forces available and the
Army in the Middle East would be comparatively simple. On
23rd December, 1940 Churchill pointed out in a message to
General Ismay for Chiefs of Staff, with a note for M. Dupuy
(travelling to North Africa):

> Should you see Generals Weygand or Noguès you should
> explain that we now have a large and well-equipped army
> in England, and have considerable spare forces already well
> trained and rapidly improving, apart from what are needed
> to repel invasion.
> The situation in the Middle East is also becoming good.
> If at any time in the near future the French Government
> decide to resume the war in Africa against Italy and Germany
> we would send a strong and well-equipped Expeditionary
> Force to aid the defence of Morocco, Algiers and Tunis.[1]

This message makes it very strange that Churchill refused
even to look at O'Connor's victory, for he was well aware of
O'Connor's progress, and the forces he was ready to offer to
Weygand would have been available to support Tripoli. On
9th February O'Connor would have been on his way to Sirte.
The naval force 'H', *Renown, Malaya, Ark Royal, Sheffield* and
their destroyers could have joined forces with Cunningham's
fleet off Tripoli, and there could not have been German reinforcements for Tripoli. Instead the Greek tragedy let Rommel loose
in the desert at a time when British strength was gravely
depleted, and the 7th Armoured Division, O'Connor's spearhead, withdrawn for urgent refit. It seems to me more than
probable that Churchill's ultimate realisation of what he had
done, although he would have been incapable of admitting it,
or permitting it, to take clear shape in his mind, must account
for his obsession with Rommel, an obsession that led him to
words and deeds unworthy of him.

Again, Churchill's preoccupation with the Balkans, the
Mediterranean and Middle East, blinded him to the growing
menace of Japan, and Britain's defence priorities in Malaya and
Burma, covering India and Australia. The whole area, as he
wrote, was 'in the twilight of his mind'. It was a sad confession.

[1]Churchill, *The Second World War,* vol. II, Readers' Union ed., p. 556,
appendix A.

His cable to the Prime Minister of Australia of 23rd December, 1940, the day on which he had given his memo to General Ismay and directed at General Weygand in particular, reveals the priorities in his mind. Delta Egypt occupied fifth place in the defence priorities of the Chiefs of Staff:

  i. The British Isles.
  ii. Malaya and Burma (covering India and Australia).
  iii. Persian Gulf (and therefore, Iraq, Syria and Persia if possible).
  iv. Gibraltar and Malta, if possible.
  v. Delta Egypt.

Generals Dill and Wavell accepted this order of priority. But soon Churchill insisted that the loss of Delta Egypt would be a major disaster, and moved it to second place in the priorities. Thereby he dragged British strategy towards the loss of the British Empire.[1]

Throughout the first four months of 1941 Churchill became a great and increasing worry to all those directly concerned and in contact with him. His mind ranged over the Mediterranean and the Balkans like a grasshopper, a grasshopper with the sting of a hornet. Every 'outrageous idea' that came into his head added to the great burdens of the Joint Planning Staffs. The distaste of the Chiefs of Staff, of Cadogan at the Foreign Office, even of his personal staff, notably Desmond Morton, were of no avail. It proved impossible to move him away from the Greek adventure which all knew would almost certainly end in disaster, and said so. Morton said that Churchill walked up and down his room muttering 'gallant little Greeks', clearly indulging romantic dreams of a glorious past. On 6th January he became preoccupied with Valona in particular and with the Greeks in general. In a very long memorandum to General Ismay for C.O.S. Committee Churchill wrote:

All accounts go to show that a Greek failure to take Valona will have very bad consequences. It may be possible for General Wavell . . . to establish himself at Benghazi; but it would not be right for the sake of Benghazi to lose the chance of the Greeks taking Valona, and thus to dispirit and anger them, and perhaps make them in the mood for a

[1]See Kennedy, *The Business of War*, pp. 106–9.

separate peace with Italy. Therefore the prospect must be faced that after Tobruk the further westward advance of the Army of the Nile may be seriously cramped. It is quite clear to me that supporting Greece must have priority after the western flank of Egypt has been made secure.[1]

The attitude of Yugoslavia may well be determined by the support we give to Greece and by their fortunes before Valona . . . If Yugoslavia stands firm and is not molested, if the Greeks take Valona and maintain themselves in Albania, if Turkey becomes an active ally, the attitude of Russia may be affected favourably . . .[2]

The Valian counter-offensive of the Greeks into Albania was the very stuff to set the bells ringing dangerously in Churchill's romantic head. He should have known that hopes of taking Valona were receding, and the Greek situation was becoming perilous, for on the same day, 6th January, he received disquieting news from the Foreign Minister: '. . . a mass of information has come to us over the last few days from divers sources, all of which tends to show that Germany is pressing forward her preparations in the Balkans with a view to an ultimate descent upon Greece. The date usually mentioned . . . is the beginning of March.'[3]

Eden was also very worried about Bulgaria, and the German ability to occupy Salonika at great speed once they set their plans in motion.

Eden's message immediately inspired a further memorandum, Prime Minister to General Ismay for C.O.S. Committee, 6th January:

I cannot look beyond Benghazi at the present time, and if Tobruk is taken there will be very few Italian troops, and by no means their best, east of Benghazi . . . [The message is cut here. It may be significant.] Although perhaps by luck and daring we may collect comparatively easily delectable prizes on the Libyan shore, the massive importance of the taking of Valona and keeping the Greek front in being weigh hourly with us.

These preoccupations, mainly with impossible or dangerous

[1]Churchill, *The Second World War,* vol. III, section vi, para. 13.
[2]Ibid., section vi, para. 14.
[3]Ibid., p. 27.

and unprofitable targets, reveal something of the manner in which Churchill's mind worked. The main effect was to waste a great deal of time, involving particularly the Planning Staffs, and harassing the C.I.G.S. and his aides. Every idea had to be taken seriously. A few months later he would reveal, a determination, which proved difficult to defeat, to seize and hold Sicily. The main burden fell upon General Dill, and finally forced his retirement and replacement. Sir John Kennedy wrote:

> When Churchill's projects were finally thrown aside, after the useless expenditure of much labour and energy, he obviously did not realise that he had been saved from disasters. On the contrary, he seemed to think he had been thwarted by men who lacked initiative and courage. At such times as this, we often felt that we would give anything for a less colourful occupant of No. 10.[1]

While some of Churchill's ideas were strategically sound, had they been possible, many others—and Valona is a good example, stemmed from his romantic nature and from his experiences before the First World War when he had become First Lord of the Admiralty, cruising with Asquith on the Admiralty yacht. He sailed the Adriatic, the Aegean and all the Greek seas, and names like Durazzo, Dubrovnik, Valona, Rhodes and the Peloponnese, made music in his mind and memory. The Balkan wars had fired his most violent romantic thoughts. His phrase 'brave little Greeks' dates from the days when they, the Serbs and Bulgars overwhelmed the Turks at Lule Burgas, and again when they stood with the Serbs to defeat the onslaught of the Bulgars. This was very much his world and his 'cockpit'; yet as a Tory he had inherited an affection for the Turks, and especially for such Turks as Enver Bey. This is, of course, merely my personal opinion. It is more important that this business of 'Valona' in particular is a good example of his inability to focus on the heart of any subject, or problem, his mind readily playing with ideas on the periphery of any discussion, and failing to concentrate on the main theme and chance. This failing had caused exasperation to many, and not least to B. H. Liddell Hart, one of his advisers on his 'focus' group at Chartwell. Churchill was the one unable to 'focus'. Had he been able to concentrate on the whole Middle-Eastern theatre he would never have ordered the withdrawal of essential strength

[1] *The Business of War*, p. 174.

and vital reserves from Egypt at a crucial time. If it was politically essential to offer aid to Greece, troops should have been sent from Britain. Moreover, it was a serious blunder to use an Australian and a New Zealand division, even though the Prime Ministers of the two dominions had, reluctantly, given their consent.

It is improbable that Churchill had seen the masterly appreciation of the situation addressed to Sir John Dill by the Secretary of State for India, in a letter dated 1st February, 1941. 'Amery's letter,' wrote Major-General Dorman Smith (O'Gowan) in retirement, when devoting himself to a study of this period, 'is really a brilliant exposé of the futility of intervention from the Middle East into the Balkans and a first-class series of arguments for allowing Wavell to advance on Tripoli.'[1]

Tripoli, Amery pointed out, was the key to any future operations on a serious scale against Sicily, Sardinia or in the Balkans. Amery's appreciation was made a Chiefs of Staff paper, and they had considered the whole problem of Tripoli or Greece before O'Connor's victory at Beda Fomm. Moreover, Amery pointed out, a major campaign in the Balkans would have to be sustained from the United Kingdom.[2]

It is highly improbable that Churchill would have taken the slightest notice of Amery's appreciation, and the Secretary of State for India might have saved his thoughts and efforts for a more productive line of thought. Yet it must be doubtful if any ideas or plans emanating from any source other than Churchill would have any chance of adoption, unless Churchill could have been persuaded that the plans were really his own.

Early on the morning of 6th April the Germans attacked Greece in strength, and it was clear within a day or two that there would be no chance whatever of holding them. Internal difficulties in Greece aggravated by the sudden death of General Metaxas in the early stages of negotiation had led to indecisive leadership. In the event the Greek divisions promised to strengthen the British flank were not available. At the time of the German attack our troops commanded by General Sir Henry Maitland Wilson, withdrawn from his brief governorship of Cyrenaica following O'Connor's victory, were still arriving at Piraeus,

[1] Personal letter from Dorman Smith to the author.
[2] Connell, *Wavell, Scholar and Soldier,* pp. 321–3. 'There is no evidence,' Connell wrote, 'that this document ever received the careful and detailed study, either by the Chiefs of Staff or by the War Cabinet, which it merited.'

and those forward had had no time to become orientated. All that Wilson could do was to make the best of a fighting retreat. This he achieved with skill and fortitude, inflicting severe casualties on the enemy. A total of nearly 60,000 British troops had been disembarked. Nearly 50,000, half of them wounded, were saved by the heroic efforts of the Navy, whose losses were severe. As though to underline the tragedy, the enemy, enjoying complete domination in the air, bombed the port of Piraeus almost out of existence on the night of the opening attack. The predicament of Wilson's troops, with no other escape route open to them except neighbouring beaches, was perilous in the extreme. That they saved what they did, abandoning artillery transport and supplies, reveals the brave but frustrating genius of the British for survival; yet perhaps survival pursued steadfastly and successfully must lead at the last to a kind of victory by the denial of the fruits of victory to the enemy.

On the night of 6th April the s.s. *Clan Fraser*, berthed in Piraeus with 350 tons of T.N.T. in her hold, finally blew up after incessant enemy bombing. Brave and sustained efforts had succeeded in unloading 100 tons. The *Clan Fraser* blazed for two hours, and when she blew up, taking eleven ships with her, the port of Piraeus was destroyed. 'From that fateful night Piraeus virtually ceased to exist as a port,' wrote Anthony Heckstall-Smith and Vice-Admiral H. T. Baillie-Grohman.[1]

In less than three weeks German victory was complete, and the best that can be said about the British part in the tragedy is that honour had been served.

III

While the primary blame for the Greek débâcle, and many of the misfortunes following as a result, must be borne by Churchill, others are not blameless. It is a clear case of political and military issues conflicting and in such cases the politicians dominate the military and make clear military appraisal difficult. No one would deny that the establishment of a Balkan front by the British was infinitely desirable. A successful defence of Greece against the Germans would have provided valuable bases for British aircraft operations against Rumanian oil. In retrospect Churchill wrote that he had never expected success unless

[1] *Greek Tragedy,* 1961.

Yugoslavia and Turkey came in. It was at once evident to those in the Middle East that this would not be so. Wavell had not the slightest faith in the value of Turkish support even had it been forthcoming, and Yugoslavia was on the verge of a political upheaval. These things were obvious to Anthony Eden, Foreign Secretary and Churchill's trusted emissary. Eden's behaviour seems strange almost from the outset, while that of Sir John Dill is peculiar. Wavell, too, cannot escape some censure, although no military appreciation for Greece was ever made.

Sir John Dill had left England convinced that military intervention in Greece would be disastrous, and would also seriously deplete the forces available to Wavell over his Middle East command. Yet he supported the Foreign Secretary, while regretting long before the end that he had done so. Like Wavell he was in a difficult position as a soldier. If it was a political necessity then clearly military support could not be denied by the military commanders. If they had regarded disaster as almost certain should Dill and Wavell have resigned rather than co-operate? It is not an easy question to answer, and I believe that their duty was to state their views unequivocally, and then obey the orders of the British Government. They did not state their views unequivocally, and both gave the impression that in spite of the hazards, known to all concerned, the expedition should go ahead.

The Foreign Secretary must shoulder a major share of the blame. He could have entertained very little hope of the support of Turkey and Yugoslavia, yet he seemed at times enthusiastic about intervention in Greece even when the Greeks themselves were less than keen.

Alex Cadogan's diary comments reflect something of Eden's frame of mind: Friday, 28th February, 'Telegram from A. at Angora, which puzzles me. It is couched in jaunty and self-satisfied terms, talking of the "frankness" and "friendliness" and "realism" of the Turks. The "reality" is that they won't do a damned thing . . . He seems quite happy. What's bitten him?'

On Saturday 1st March Cadogan notes that Churchill has sent a 'sobering telegram' to 'our temperamental Secretary of State', and Cadogan goes on to lament that it's a 'diplomatic and strategic blunder of the first order'.

It was still not too late to call off the expedition. Churchill was having grave doubts, his mind vacillating dangerously, but by the time he gave Eden a clear way out the troops were embarked and it was too late.

Meanwhile the situation in Greece was worsening, and Eden cabled that military arrangements 'which the British had thought to be agreed on 22nd February, had not even begun,'[1] yet he had committed 'us up to the hilt'. On the following day, 7th March, the Cabinet supported the Greek decision (it was too late, in any case, to put things into reverse) and Churchill cabled Eden accordingly.

I do not think Anthony Eden was equal to shouldering responsibility for decisions as momentous as the intervention in Greece, and General Dill's sobering judgment was not evident. His sudden support for the expedition astounded General Kennedy at the War Office. Wavell and the South-African General Smuts in close consultation in Cairo also supported the operation. Yet no one expected it to succeed. '. . . to have fought and suffered in Greece would be less damaging to us than to have left Greece to her fate,'[2] seems to have been the view in Cairo. But perhaps one of the oddest facts about it is that 'no considered estimate was made of how much we were prepared to lose'! Nor was it taken into account how gravely the Middle-East Command must be weakened by a severe drain on resources at a crucial time.

The enemy air assault on the island of Crete on 20th May, which forced the evacuation of the British troops under General Freyberg between 27th–31st May, wrote the last grim paragraph to the Greek débâcle. Yet Crete was of the greatest strategic importance in its own right, and must have been occupied by British troops quite apart from any commitment in Greece. The loss of an island to an enemy without naval support of any kind, and against all the naval power Admiral Cunningham could bring to bear, was a new development in warfare, and a triumph for German paratroops. As late as 25th May Churchill and the Chiefs of Staff were still urging the commanders in the Middle East to hang on, and a message was sent with Churchill's approval that was 'deeply resented' by Cunningham in particular and seemed quite unreal to the men on the spot. Cunningham at once offered his resignation, which was refused. His fleet had lost three cruisers, and six destroyers, while heavy damage had been inflicted on a battleship and an aircraft carrier. Cunningham telegraphed:

[1]*Cadogan Diaries*, p. 361.
[2]*Grand Strategy*, vol. II, p. 447.

I feel that effect of recent operations on personnel is cumu-
lative. Our light craft officers, men and machinery alike are
nearing exhaustion. Since 'Lustre' [Greek Expedition] started,
at the end of February they have been kept running almost
to limit of endurance, and now, when work is redoubled,
they are faced with an air concentration besides which, I am
assured, that in Norway was child's play. It is inadvisable to
drive men beyond a certain point.

Yet they had to be driven further, for on 27th Wavell cabled
that an attempt to prolong the defence (of Crete) would be
useless and dangerous. By 31st May the Navy had lifted 25,000
men out of 32,000 from open beaches and carried them safely to
Egypt. Further heavy naval losses had been sustained.

Grand Strategy states: 'The capture of Crete was a landmark
in the history of war.'[1] Moreover it was comparable with our
failure in Norway, except that this time 'no one desired a change
of leadership'. The fact is that Crete had had to be defended,
and it was not known at the time that the Germans had suffered
so severely that they would not again attempt an airborne attack
on a comparable scale. The German General Student, commander of the XI Air Corps, called Crete, 'the grave of German
parachutists'. The knowledge would have been cold comfort to
Churchill and to the Middle-East Command. It was clear that
Churchill was determined to stir things up, to find scapegoats,
to clear himself of the anger and frustration that had been building
up in him for some months. Greece and Crete were troubles
among many. Events in the Middle East had not stood still.

IV

'The Desert Flank was the peg on which all else hung, and
there was no idea in any quarter of losing or risking that for the
sake of Greece or anything in the Balkans.'[2]

Yet by the decision to mount the expedition to Greece from
the Middle East the Desert Flank was risked, and it should have
been obvious that this was so. The 7th Armoured Division,
the spearhead of O'Connor's advance, had ceased to exist as a
factor 'in the protection of our vital desert flank,' as Churchill
belatedly realised. Only in the absence of any attack by the

[1] *Grand Strategy*, vol. II, p. 513.
[2] Churchill, *The Second World War*, Readers Union ed., p. 161–2.

enemy could the Desert Flank have existed in its advanced positions. At the outset Rommel's arrival in Tripoli was not known, and when it was known its significance was not appreciated, not even by Rommel himself. His purpose was to strengthen the Italians and to help them to hold Tripoli. It was only the success of his patrols, followed by the remarkable success of a limited attack that induced Rommel to grasp the iron while it was hot without waiting for the agreement of the German high command. Middle-East Command was taken by surprise and there was very little that could be done about it. The command situation had been gravely disturbed by the removal of General Wilson from Cyrenaica to command in Greece, and by O'Connor's acceptance of Command in Egypt. Lieutenant-General Sir Philip Neame, V.C., put in command of the Desert Force by Wavell, turned out to be an unfortunate choice, and when O'Connor was rushed to stand at his shoulder it was already too late to halt the enemy. By 4th April the British were in headlong retreat. To make matters worse both Neame and O'Connor were captured by a German reconnaissance group on 7th April.

'In the ruin and retreat of these days,' wrote John Connell, 'there was one important strategic fact: Wavell had Tobruk.'[1] Wavell had flown at once to Tobruk to organise the defence and was heartened by the demeanour of the Australian General Morshead, commanding 9th Australian division. Major-General Lavarack was appointed to the command of all troops in Libya and Cyrenaica, and together Wavell and his generals determined on the defence of Tobruk. It would be held as a fortress.

By his presence Wavell immediately restored confidence in the generals, but his presence was urgently needed in Cairo where Mr. Eden was waiting. The German attack had already gone in against the British and Greek defence in Greece, but there was no doubt where the priority lay. Wavell was absolutely resolved that the Middle East should not suffer further from the involvement in Greece, and Churchill and the Chiefs of Staff were equally resolute. Churchill telegraphed Wavell on 10th April: 'We all cordially endorse your decision to hold Tobruk and will do all in our power to bring you aid.'

It is not perhaps very strange that both Rommel and Churchill developed an obsession about Tobruk. In the middle of April Rommel launched attack after attack in his determination to

[1] *Wavell, Scholar and Soldier*, p. 401.

storm the citadel, but all in vain. The German attack was halted and the immediate danger in the desert had passed, but all the great gains—or most of them—of Wavell and O'Connor's great advance were lost.

Strangely in these very grim days Churchill became, as Connell wrote: 'magnanimous, constructive and helpful. He was suddenly at his best.' He was almost certainly aware that he had harried Wavell unmercifully, and that he would do so again, but in the meantime the whole command from Churchill downwards was working in accord. On 22nd April Churchill telegraphed to Wavell: 'I have been working hard for you in the last few days, and you will, I am sure, be glad to know that we are sending 307 of our best tanks through the Mediterranean, hoping they will reach you around May 10 . . .'

Churchill had done this against the will of Home Forces and the Chief of Staff, and was almost certainly right to do so. Nevertheless it was an unhappy sign of Churchill's over-valuation of Egypt. His magnanimous, instructive and helpful mood was over. At Chequers on 27th April he had ranted at General Kennedy, the D.M.O., for suggesting the scale on which the Germans might attack in the Middle East unless their communications could be cut. We might need at least five armoured divisions. Churchill had reacted with fury, shouting: 'Wavell has 400,000 men. If they lose Egypt blood will flow. I will have firing parties to shoot the generals.'

'You need not be afraid they will not fight,' Kennedy answered, 'Of course they will fight. I am only arguing that we should decide the price we are prepared to pay, and can afford to pay, for the defence of the Middle East.'

Churchill did not calm down. The next day he issued a Directive without consulting the Chiefs of Staff. In paragraph 2 the Directive stated: 'The loss of Egypt and the Middle East would be a disaster of the first magnitude to Great Britain, second only to successful invasion and final conquest...' In paragraph 4 Churchill stated: 'The Army of the Nile is to fight with no thought of retreat or withdrawal...'

General Kennedy immediately gave the Chief of Staff his comment:

I do not agree that the loss of Egypt would be a disaster second only to successful invasion. The Middle East does not come second in our priorities. It would be possible to evacuate

the Middle East and still carry on the war successfully, provided that we had not expended so much of our resources
in the Middle East as to prejudice the security of the United
Kingdom, Malaya and the Cape, and consequently our main
sea communication . . .
It is also quite wrong to say the British forces would not
wish to survive the evacuation of the Middle East. If they
did not survive it we should have insufficient forces left with
which to carry on the war successfully.[1]

Kennedy also criticised the Directive for again attempting
to interfere 'with the conduct of the campaign by commanders-
in-chief on the spot'! But of course, Churchill was striving to
interfere almost daily with the conduct of the campaign by his
constant flow of demanding messages. A watered-down version
of these criticisms was handed to Churchill by the Chiefs of
Staff a week later, but it had no effect upon him. He stuck to
his priorities while Dill, and his successor, General Brooke,
Wavell and his successor, Auchinleck, disagreed absolutely. But
for them Churchill would have put Egypt and the Nile in grave
jeopardy, or lost it entirely together with Malaya.

It was a terrible time for Wavell, resisting Churchill's
furious telegrams while handling the disastrous Greek campaign
and evacuation, followed by the disaster in Crete. At the same
time, apart from the potent menace in the Western Desert serious
situations were developing in Syria and Iraq, demanding instant
attention. He was also conducting operations in East Africa.
For all these tasks over an immense area he had insufficient troops,
and was very short of the transport to move those he was able
to scrape up. Moreover the shortage of aircraft was acute, and
for this Air Chief Marshal Longmore was the first of Churchill's
victims, a miserable injustice. The land, sea and air command
in the Middle East had worked in great harmony, and all those
concerned had worked near miracles with acute shortages and
difficult maintenance facilities.

Churchill never understood, nor wished to understand the
problems of administration, maintenance and supply in such an
area. He had no idea what it meant to keep aircraft in the air,
or armour and infantry in the field. If all these things were
present on paper, or even in fact, then they were operational
from the moment of arrival. He disregarded the need for training

[1]Kennedy, *The Business of War*, p. 111.

and acclimatisation, and would continue to disregard these vital factors until the end, long after it mattered very much what he thought. But throughout the year 1941 and the first half of 1942 it mattered very much indeed, and no one at home could stem the flood of his directives, suggestions, vituperations and constant attempts to interfere in the field. It wore out commanders far more than the strains and complexities of their campaigns.

In spite of the support of the Chief of Air Staff, Air Chief Marshal Longmore was recalled to London, and quietly removed from his command. The official history comments:

> Longmore's task had been an exceedingly difficult one... Longmore had never had anything approaching the resources required for these (concurrent and conflicting) demands, and much of what he had was of little fighting value... He was unfortunate in being relieved of his command just when the days of acute shortage were drawing to a close.[1]

Longmore's treatment was in the pattern of those to follow, as commanders were removed when things were improving and after they had held on through many months of dangerous scarcity. Wavell, I believe, had no doubt that he would be the next to go, for the burden of Churchill was becoming hard to bear on top of the intricate problems of his command. He was fighting on five fronts. He had to shoulder the responsibility for the evacuation of British forces from Greece and Crete while faced with urgent threats in Syria, involving the Free French and Vichy France, and in Iraq, where a *coup d'état* by the pro-German Raschid Ali at once threatened the British air base at Habbaniya. Both these Arab countries were fertile fields for German exploitation and infiltration, and both countries were vital to British security. Iraq carried the oil pipe-lines to Haifa and Lebanese Tripoli, and was our land route to the Persian Gulf, while the port of Basra was becoming more and more important as a supply port.

Wavell had to move swiftly, for if the Germans had been quick to act they might have forestalled us. Somehow Wavell scraped up a mixed bag of troops in Palestine and relieved the dangerous situation at Habbaniya. It had been surrounded by 9,000 Iraquis with fifty guns, but on 7th May the Iraquis withdrew, and India command had sent a powerful force to Basra.

[1] *Grand Strategy*, vol. II.

Five days later German aircraft began to land in Syria, and
again, following careful negotiations with de Gaulle and the
Free French General Catroux, Wavell contrived to invade,
occupying Damascus on 21st June. On that day Churchill sacked
him. Meanwhile on 16th May the Duke of Aosta surrendered
at Amba Alagi.

Wavell's magnificent achievement in the Middle East is
unsurpassed in British military history. His shortages of troops
and supplies forced him into improvisations of unique brilliance
and conception. Moreover he had built the Middle-East Command. Of his achievement in East Africa, Robert Woollcombe
wrote: 'Wavell conquered East Africa on two fronts with an
economy and flexibility of force that ought to rank as a feat of
spontaneous exploitation unsurpassed in war.'[1]

But for Churchill these things were as nothing compared with
the threat in the Western Desert created by his own strategic
errors, and in the Western Desert success was a long way off.
Persuaded by Churchill into premature action Wavell permitted
General Beresford Peirse to attack through the Halfaya Gap
on Sollum. Peirse, a corps commander, based the plan on a
superiority he did not possess. It was doomed to failure from
before the beginning, and was defeated by Rommel with speed
and skill. Churchill's fury was boundless, and he blamed everyone
but himself.

The armour available to Peirse had not had time to train,
and it was not the equal in speed or firepower to the armour
deployed by the enemy. Nevertheless the British generalship
was very poor. The loss of General O'Connor bore very heavily
on Wavell. He alone of the commanders in the desert might
have proved himself an army commander of the stature to hold
and defeat Rommel. He alone might have handled the armour
available in a manner to deny victory to the enemy, even
though German armour and firepower were superior. Army
commanders of quality are very rare indeed, and those commanding Britain's armies with great skill throughout the Second
World War on all fronts may be numbered on less than the
fingers of one hand. At that early stage in the desert none had
experience of such a task, and it would be a very long time
before an adequate general emerged, overwhelmingly armed,
and was available for the job. Many of those who were tried
and found wanting had done extremely well in the handling

[1] *The Campaigns of Wavell, 1939–1943.*

of comparatively small groups, and of divisions. It is a bitter irony that the only two men able at that time to command armies were in fact Commanders-in-Chief, and could not be spared from their great tasks.

Wavell blamed no one but himself for the failure of the premature attack, code named 'Battle Axe'. Churchill had awaited the news in a curious mood for him. He had gone down to his home at Chartwell, alone and wanting solitude. When he had the news of failure and the destruction of much of the armour he had sent out so boldly, 'I wandered about the valley disconsolately for some hours,' he wrote.[1]

According to John Connell, Sir John Dill had written to General Auchinleck, Commander-in-Chief in India, in regard to his replacement of General Wavell in the Middle East on 21st May. He had also written to Wavell on that date. But Wavell was not removed from his command until 21st June, and Churchill wrote that he took the decision in the last ten days of June.

'At home we had the feeling that Wavell was a tired man. It might well be said that we had ridden a willing horse to death . . . The fact remains that after "Battle Axe" I came to the conclusion that there should be a change.'[2]

There is no suggestion anywhere that Churchill attached the slightest blame to himself. Liddell Hart wrote of this period: 'Churchill had reverted to his old fault of seeing and attempting too many things at the same time.' That characteristic had particularly marked the first phase of Churchill's 'super-general-ship,. 'The image of Rommel now filled Churchill's eye to the exclusion of all else,' and for that obsession 'Britain paid a heavy penalty—the forfeit of her positions in the Far East.'[3] He had done this in spite of Sir John Dill's constant warnings, and the warnings of his Chiefs of Staff, by moving Egypt into second place in the priorities. As a result Singapore, in particular, had been neglected.

Sir John Dill was soon to be dismissed, and it is probable that both Wavell and Dill had been doomed from the beginning, from the first meetings in August-September 1940.

The fact is that Churchill bludgeoned his Chief of Staff and

---

[1]Churchill, *The Second World War,* vol. III, Readers' Union ed., pp. 280–1.
[2]Ibid.
[3]Lecture in War Studies: University of London, November, 1960 by Liddell Hart.

his Commander-in-Chief in the Middle East to the limits of endurance. He was incapable of understanding that. For his part, no one bludgeoned him, and he remarked in the midst of Britain's worst trials and tribulations, and when his colleagues were urging upon him the need to take a holiday: 'My life is a perpetual holiday.' And it was true. Without his total involvement he might not have survived.

But there is evidence, unfortunately not in the history books, personal memoirs or diaries, that Churchill had changed very much for the worse in 1941. He wanted to show his power, and by the sacking of a great man of Wavell's stature he felt he could do so. Desmond Morton, who was in close personal contact with Churchill, often in the privacy of his room, said that Churchill prowled up and down, his chin sunk on his chest, and muttering: 'I wanted to show my power'. 'I think that the first time I ever deeply disliked Winston and realised the depths of selfish brutality to which he could sink, was when he told me not only that he was getting rid of Wavell from the Middle East, but why.'[1]

In the same letter Morton wrote:

My analysis (subject to review always) is that Winston heartily disliked any person whose personal character was such that he could not avoid, most unwillingly, feeling respect for that person. Winston's overweening desire to dominate resulted in a feeling of inferiority in regard to anyone who was not in the least afraid of him, and never would be, and in whose character he could not see any flaw. Were there such a flaw, Winston could always attack that flaw and close his eyes to other great qualities.

Naturally any such person must be either a rival or in a position to do Winston some potential harm. But that such a person would never dream of doing Winston harm, never entered his thought-processes. 'If you have power, you use it', would be his unalterable expectation.[2]

[1] Personal correspondence, from Sir Desmond Morton to the author.
[2] Ibid.

CHAPTER EIGHT

Churchill, the Persuader, the Animator, the Statesman

I

IN THE SUMMER OF 1940 WHILE GERMAN ARMOUR BRILLIANTLY led by Guderian and Rommel, dedicated disciples of Britain's great experts on armoured warfare, notably Capt. B. H. Liddell Hart and Major-General J. F. C. Fuller, was overrunning north-western Europe, one of the finest trainers of armoured troops in the British Isles, and probably in the world, was serving as a lance-corporal in the Home Guard in the village of Chipping Campden. He had joined the Local Defence Volunteers, as they were first named, in the middle of March, and at once his dynamic presence had begun to be felt far beyond Chipping Campden. His name was Hobart. He was not ill. He was in his fifties, a dynamo of energy mentally and physically. As Major-General Hobart he had proved himself a great trainer of armoured troops and a leader of genius. His division had been the spearhead of Britain's victories in the Western Desert against the Italians, and his immense contribution was fully recog-nised and appreciated by his commander, General O'Connor. His innovations had proved themselves on the battlefield, and were, wrote Liddell Hart, 'a fresh vindication of the lines on which Hobart had trained the Tank Brigade in 1934–5, and the Mobile Division in Egypt in 1938–39'.[1] That Division had made O'Connor's victories possible. It bore the stamp of Hobart from beginning to end of its great service, as its commanders recognised. And so did all that Hobart trained. But Hobart was an impatient man, scornful of the sloth of some senior generals, whose habits and ideas had been formed in easier times, and were enemies of change. General Gordon Finlayson,

[1]Liddell Hart, *The Tanks,* vol. II, p. 36.

the Adjutant-General, whose headquarters seemed to go into a state of suspended animation at 'siesta time', was one of those resolved to get rid of Hobart, and did not much mind how it was done. His influence was considerable.

Hobart was the victim of the entrenched prejudices and archaic attitudes of those in the military hierarchy who resisted the new gospel of armoured warfare, and lamented the passing of the horse. Thus Hobart had become a victim of the 'horse' and the Cavalry-Club clique. He was also a victim of his own prickly and impatient nature. In common with other dedicated men like General Fuller, who seldom suffered fools gladly, he had made too many enemies in high places, from whom his many friends and admirers had been unable to save him.

General Wilson, Wavell's second-in-command in the Middle East, had been the instrument of Hobart's destruction. His letter to Wavell recommending that Hobart should be removed from his command of 7th Armoured Division is an unpleasant example of personal pique and prejudice. Why Wavell endorsed Wilson's judgment, while recommending Hobart for employment in some other role, remains a mystery. Upon his return to England Hobart fought for his honour as he saw it, seeking in vain to petition the King. He was sacked. It seemed final, unwarranted, unjust and disgraceful, yet typical of the Army at its worst. The march of events, Hobart's friends, and finally Churchill, rescued him. It was not easy.

Immediately upon assuming the leadership of Britain Churchill acted to repair the desperately urgent needs of the country in every department of war. Crash programmes for aircraft and armour were instituted, and often machines went straight into production and service off the drawing-board. Sometimes the results were magnificent, but in the matter of armour quantity had to come before quality. The needs of the Home Forces to meet expected invasion were paramount.

The Army needed not only armour but the men to train and command the new armoured divisions coming into service. In August 1940 Liddell Hart wrote an article in *The Sunday Pictorial* lamenting Britain's wasted brains, especially in armoured warfare. He drew attention to the dismal fact that almost all of those men who had been dedicated to the development and use of armour were not being used in their rightful capacities, notably Generals Pile, Lindsay, Fuller and Hobart.

In August Churchill was seeking a man capable of handling

the whole armour situation. Liddell Hart's article had alerted him to the fact that such a man or men existed. On a visit to the anti-aircraft defences, commanded by General Pile, Churchill asked Pile's views.

'I told him we had a superb trainer of tanks in Hobart,' Pile wrote, 'but he had just been sacked. He asked me to get him to come and see him. I saw Hobart, but he was very difficult; said he could do nothing unless he was first reinstated and said that his honour had been unsatisfied.'[1]

Pile and Liddell Hart used all their abilities to coax Hobart to see Churchill, and at last on 13th October Hobart met Churchill at Chequers.

'Come into the library, General,' Churchill said. 'I want you to tell me about tanks.' Clement Attlee, the deputy Prime Minister was present. 'I remember feeling myself to be unwisely foolhardy,' Hobart wrote, 'when I put our initial need at ten armoured divisions, but all Winston said was "How many tanks?" and when I said ten thousand, nodded his head.'[2]

Immediately Hobart felt sure of Churchill's support, and while still a corporal in the Home Guard, he began to put his ideas down on paper, circulating his proposals to those he knew, or hoped, would be receptive. He wanted an 'Armoured Army' to be trained under a 'General Officer' in command, and the Armoured Army to have a seat on the Army Council. It was an ambitious plan, and attracted support from Generals Pile, Crocker and Tilly among others, notably Major-General Vyvyan Pope, head of the Armoured Fighting Vehicles Directorate in the War Office.

Generals Dill and Alanbrooke were implacably opposed. not so much to the appointment of a Commander Royal Armoured Corps (C.R.A.C.) but to a seat on the Army Council.

Even with Churchill's understanding, liking and sympathy for Hobart there was still a long way to go. The General had confided to Churchill his grievances, and while the Prime Minister regarded these as very real and justified, his first concern was to persuade Hobart back into the command of armour, even if Hobart's wrongs were not righted.

Churchill began patiently with an approach to General Dill, and extracted the promise—perhaps it was. only a half-promise in Dill's mind—that Hobart should have an armoured division.

[1]Mackesy, *Armoured Crusader*, p. 185.
[2]Ibid., p. 186.

Wavell arriving in the Middle East from India to meet Churchill.

Auchinleck.

General Montgomery, Cairo, 1943.

Auchinleck and Wavell, commanding from the Mediterranean to the Bay of Bengal.

Churchill arriving in Tripoli to greet Montgomery.

Churchill travelling in Tripoli; Montgomery in front and Lieut.-General Sir Oliver Leese, G.O.C. 30 Corps, behind.

CHURCHILL AND SMUTS WITH THE WAR COUNCIL AND COMMANDERS. *Left to right, back row*: Air Chief M
Sir Arthur Tedder, A.O.C-in-C; General Sir Alan Brooke, C.I.G.S.; Admiral Harwood, C-in-C M
terranean Fleet; General Sir Claude Auchinleck, C-in-C Middle East; General Sir Archibald Wavell, C
India; Sir Charles Wilson, physician to Churchill; Sir Alexander Cadogan, Foreign Office. *Front*
Field-Marshal Smuts; Winston Churchill; Sir Miles Lampson, British Ambassador; R. G. Casey, Mi
of State, Middle East.

COMBINED CHIEFS OF STAFF CASABLANCA. On the left, power, on the right, experience. *Left (foregro*
Admiral E. J. King, C-in-C U.S. Navy; General G. C. Marshall, Chief of Staff. U.S. Army; Lieut.-Ge
Arnold, commanding U.S. Army Air Force. *Right (foreground)*: Field-Marshal Sir John Dill, British R
sentative, Combined Chiefs of Staff; Air Chief Marshal Sir Charles Portal, Chief of the Air Staff; Ge
Sir Alan Brooke, C.I.G.S.; Admiral of the Fleet Sir Dudley Pound, First Sea Lord and Chief of the Naval

N, ROOSEVELT, CHURCHILL IN TEHERAN (*seated from left to right*).   Allied Chiefs of Staff standing: *third 'eft*, Marshal Voroshilov, Soviet Defence Commissar; General Sir Alan Brooke; Admiral Leahy, Chief of Staff to Roosevelt, *extreme right*.

THE BEGINNING AND THE END: *above*, Churchill, July 1940, touring defenc... North-East Coast: 'We shall fight c... the beaches. . .' *Below*: Churchill wi... de Gaulle, 11th November, 1944.

It was clear that Hobart would be employed as a Retired Officer and that his place on the Army List would not be restored.

On 19th October, 1940 Churchill wrote to Dill:

I was very much pleased last week when you told me you proposed to give an armoured division to Major-General Hobart. I think very highly of this officer, and I am not at all impressed by the prejudices against him in certain quarters. Such prejudices attach frequently to persons of strong personality and original views. In this case General Hobart's original views have been only too tragically borne out. The neglect by the General Staff even to devise proper patterns of tanks before the war has robbed us of all the fruits of this invention. These fruits have been reaped by the enemy, with terrible consequences. We should therefore remember that this was an officer who had the root of the matter in him, and also vision. In my minute last week to you I said I hoped you would propose to me the appointment that day, i.e. Tuesday, but at the latest this week. Will you very kindly make sure that the appointment is made at the earliest moment.

Since making this minute I have carefully read your note to me and the summary of the case for and against General Hobart. We are now at war, fighting for our lives, and we cannot afford to confine Army appointments to persons who have excited no hostile comment in their career. The catalogue of General Hobart's qualities and defects might almost exactly have been attributed to most of the great commanders of British history. Marlborough was very much the conventional soldier, carrying with him the goodwill of the service. Cromwell, Wolfe, Clive, Gordon, and in a different sphere, Lawrence, all had very close resemblance to the characteristics set down as defects. They had other qualities as well, and so I am led to believe had General Hobart. This is a time to try men of force and vision and not to be exclusively confined to those who are judged thoroughly safe by conventional standards. I hope therefore you will not recoil from your proposal to me of a week ago, for I think your instinct in this matter was sound and true.[1]

[1]Churchill, *The Second World War*, vol. II, Readers' Union ed., p. 534, appendix A.

This seems to me to be one of Churchill's most revealing minutes, for it shows clearly his liking for Hobart, and for adventurous spirits, while curbing his impatience with the War Office fear of 'difficult characters', and their seeming lack of realisation of the urgencies of war which allowed no room for paltry prejudices.

A week after receiving Churchill's minute Hobart was invited by telephone to meet the C.I.G.S. at the War Office. Much to the embarrassment of the C.I.G.S. and the sticklers for protocol Hobart wanted to know whether he should present himself for the interview dressed as a civilian, as a lance-corporal in the Home Guard, or as a major-general. 'In the end,' wrote Mackesy, 'the dress of Major-General was decided upon.'

The C.I.G.S. wanted Hobart to accept the role of Commander Royal Armoured Corps, but without a seat on the Army Council. Responsibility without power, Hobart called it. Moreover he thought General Pile or Charles Broad should have the job. There was still much coaxing to be done before Hobart swallowed some of his pride and accepted command of the 11th Armoured Division—and finally formed the astonishing and variegated 79th Armoured, which in the opinions of Eisenhower and Montgomery opened the way into Europe, and (in my opinion) blazed the many trails to victory in Europe. These two were, with the 7th, the three finest armoured divisions in the British Army, and it is difficult to lament that Hobart did not become C.R.A.C., and that a seat on the Army Council was never granted to the holder of the office. Churchill, however, lamented it. Two years later he wrote: 'I am quite sure that if, when I had him transferred from a corporal in the Home Guard to the command of one of the new armoured divisions, I had insisted upon his controlling the whole of the tank developments with a seat on the Army Council, many of the grievous errors from which we have suffered would not have been committed.'[1]

That may be so; yet it is difficult to imagine Hobart in a more useful role than he was to fill as the creator and 'director' of the conglomeration of armoured fighting vehicles, known sometimes as the 'menagerie', the 79th Armoured Division. Its squadrons were parcelled out wherever they were needed most, fought on many fronts but never as a divison. Its 'swimming tanks', its bridging tanks, its flails, flame-throwers, bombards,

[1]Churchill, *The Second World War,* vol. II.

fascines, cleared the way forward on a hundred battlefields. It is not I think (and I'm thinking now, seeing these machines in my mind's eye, that vast panorama spreading north, south and east from Normandy) an exaggeration.

II

Churchill's love of gimmickry and his facility in the creative development of ideas, if not of pure invention, was served not only by Lindemann's activities, but in a wider sense by the growth of Hobart's armour, and also by Combined Operations. Churchill had already looked far ahead and the first tank landing craft was ready for trials due to his foresight. It would be succeeded by the tank landing ship. He had established Combined Operations Headquarters at first under Admiral Keyes, and then under the dynamic Mountbatten. These things were inter-related, and expressions of Churchill's fertile imagination. Lord Louis Mountbatten was a man after Churchill's own heart, readily trying out many strange devices, and providing ideas of his own. Moreover Churchill's liking for Mountbatten was to be of great service in the days to come, when Lord Louis would be appointed to the Supreme Command in South-East Asia. Churchill could not bludgeon Mountbatten as he had bludgeoned Wavell, and was to bludgeon Auchinleck, and Mountbatten's generals could feel secure to devote themselves to the business of war, untroubled by constant interference from home.

In the early days perhaps Churchill's greatest inspiration was in the development of the huge artificial harbours, which were destined to 'sail' (under tow) in several parts to the coast of Normandy. The seed of the idea had grown in his mind since the Gallipoli landings in the First World War.

The creation of these new services, the commando troops operating under Combined Operations Headquarters, and Hobart's armour, was to make increasingly severe demands on manpower of the highest quality. It was never easy to resolve, and it is a point rarely stressed that Britain was able to provide such men while at the same time not depleting the standards of the great mass of troops and naval personnel. From the beginning soldiers had disliked the idea of élite forces, commanders naturally disliking some of their best men being taken away from them for specialised services. Some divisional commanders insisted proudly that there was nothing special troops could do that their men could not do equally well, if not better.[1] But the unescapable fact was that war was developing in many new ways demanding skills of a high order, even from the ordinary infantryman.

From the beginning Combined Operations provided a kind of safety valve for Churchill, enabling him to feel and to know that Britain was harassing the enemy at many and unpredictable points, compelling him to constant vigilance and thereby making a contribution to victory out of all proportion to the size and success of the attacks mounted by small bodies of highly trained men. Without this ability to strike at the enemy from the sea and air Churchill would have harassed his generals even more than he did. He could not help himself. The generals (Army, Navy and Air Force), were instruments of politics, the spearheads of Churchill's statesmanship. Without success in the field Churchill's search for allies, his 'Grand Strategy' would fail. That he drove his generals relentlessly was not so much a sign of his weakness as a Supreme Commander, but of the weakness of Britain in the first years of war. The constant mixture of political-military objects and objectives bedevilled his generals, often deterring them from condemning certain military operations with the brutal frankness they merited. Yet armies are for attaining political ends, or they are mere dangerous toys.

It posed a terrible dilemma for Wavell, Sir John Dill, and for Auchinleck later, for these men understood—perhaps too well—the urgency of the political ends. Greece is the tragic and clearest example. Of course it was desirable to gain Turkey as an ally, to impress upon those fighting in and for the Balkan countries that Britain was a force to be reckoned with. Yet if it could not be done in one way another way must be sought.

And then, of course, it may be more important to attempt the doubtful, even the impossible, than not to try. No one knows. Churchill, in spite of his War Cabinet, his Chiefs of Staff, his advisers, usually had his way. His powers of persuasion were very rare, subtle, at times over-powering. He made his decisions. His generals should have made theirs, for better or for worse. Wavell and Dill should have stated the situation before Greece without equivocation. Had they done so the tragedy might have been averted.[2] This is not to say that a general

---

[1] Notably perhaps General Sir Francis (Gertie) Tuker, whose pride in his India division was fully justified.

[2] Anthony Eden was probably even more to blame in this sphere.

should ever refuse to carry out orders, except on moral issues, and military issues may be moral issues, but it is not his business to interfere with the political and strategic aims of his country.

The Greek tragedy was Churchill's tragedy. In it you feel his rare loneliness, his doubt of his infallibility—for a man taking upon himself the burden of a nation at war must believe himself to be infallible—most of the time. Churchill knew that he had let the Germans into North Africa, that he was 'responsible' for Rommel. It became an obsession. It led to Churchill's worst deeds as a 'super-general'. It also made him human.

III

If Churchill's determination to play the 'super-general' had been all it is improbable that he would have survived for long as the War Leader of the British people; but of course it was far from all. He had a powerful streak of the fighting soldier in him. He thrived on danger. The army had fascinated him from childhood. Few had studied battlefields and battles more assidu-ously. The romantic fighting streak in him needed the leading of troops in battle. He couldn't have been a Lawrence or a Wingate, but he might have been an O'Connor.[1] And had he been in O'Connor's shoes would he have stopped at Beda Fomm? He might have said, in effect, 'I see no signal', and pressed on even though his armour was almost exhausted, and in desperate need of rest, repair, renewal. Probably it would not have stopped Churchill's determination to land troops in Greece, even though reinforcements must have been provided for O'Connor, a division, some armour. Almost certainly the Afrika Corps would have failed to gain a foothold, and no Rommel. All that long struggle in the Western Desert might have been avoided, and the shape of the war fundamentally changed. I wonder if Churchill ever thought about that? It would have been a miserable thought.

The difficulty with attempting to understand Churchill is not simply that he was a man of many parts, but of too many parts, and they make the whole man. That is why it is dangerous to focus on one aspect of Churchill, and why in the midst of focussing upon his 'super-generalship' I have paused not simply to consider his resurrection of Hobart, but his stimulation of the

[1] This statement must be qualified. It is doubtful whether Churchill would at any time have faced the disciplines of the hard road to generalship.

enormous production of varied weapons, his interest in almost everything that went on, the price of bread, rents, even a bizarre prosecution of some woman for witchcraft!

Above all Churchill was a politician, and a statesman. He saw the shape of the world and of nations, always changing in peace or war, never static, never fixed. It was not enough to win battles but to win the great battle for Britain's place in the world, for the kind of world he tried to imagine and to mould, his way. Nothing short of death would have deterred him, or induced him to shed one particle of his power, of the load he bore. His immense involvement kept him alive. He was frequently far from well, and quite often ill, dangerously as the years of war grew, and he reached three score years and ten, the Biblical life-span of man. It is difficult, perhaps impossible to know what effect sickness had upon his conduct of the war, coupled with his drinking and cigar smoking. One thing seems certain to me: that without these things he would have been 'somebody else'.[1]

Churchill's search for allies never faltered, and above all he sought the involvement of the United States. From the outset he wooed President Roosevelt, and before Britain's entire capital assets in the United States, totalling some ten thousand millions of dollars, had been expended on the most urgent necessities, the idea of aid, developing into the concept of 'Lend-Lease' was forming in Roosevelt's mind. The bargain was hard. A deal for the exchange of forty old U.S. destroyers for bases in British sovereign territories, shocked many, including the American Ambassador to Britain, John Winant. The deal does not seem to have shocked Churchill. The forty destroyers, the worse for wear as many of them were, were a symbol as well as an immediate aid in the terrible Battle of the Atlantic.

Slowly but steadily Roosevelt coaxed the American people towards greater involvement, and steadily Churchill coaxed Roosevelt.

On 8th December, 1940, Churchill wrote a long letter to the President. In it he set out what he conceived to be the prospects for the year 1941. The letter ended:

'You may be certain that we shall prove ourselves ready to suffer and sacrifice to the utmost for the cause, and that we glory in being its champions. The rest we leave with con-

[1] See: Lord Moran, *Churchill, The Struggle for Survival.*

fidence to you and to your people, being sure that ways and means will be found which future generations on both sides of the Atlantic will approve and admire.

'If, as I believe, you are convinced, Mr. President, that the defeat of the Nazi and Fascist tyranny is a matter of high consequence to the people of the United States and to the Western hemisphere, you will regard this letter not as an appeal for aid, but as a statement of the minimum action necessary to achieve our common purpose.'[1]

Churchill regarded this letter as probably the most important he ever wrote. He appended a statement of the losses of British and Allied shipping from May to December 1940, showing a total of two and one half million tons. This was a provisional estimate, nearly one million tons less than the final assessment. It clearly revealed the Atlantic as the decisive battlefield of the war, and upon success or failure in the struggle all else must hinge. For two and a half more years the appalling losses were destined to increase, and its loss even in the middle of 1943 could have been mortal to Britain. The awareness lived with Churchill by day and by night. It cast a terrible shadow upon all else.

A month after Roosevelt received the letter he sent his personal emissary, Harry Hopkins, to Churchill. 'Thus I met,' Churchill wrote, 'that extraordinary man, who played, and was to play, a sometimes decisive part in the whole movement of the war.'

Churchill's letter, Hopkins said, had plunged the American President in intense thought. He brooded silently for two days, whereupon in one of his 'fireside chats' to the American people he made it clear that the defence of Britain was the defence also of America, and of democracy. None knew better than Roosevelt how to touch the hearts and arouse the sentiments of Americans, and it may seem strange that two men, Churchill and Roosevelt, both patricians, a now almost extinct class, knew best how to speak to and arouse the common man.

In the mind of Harry Hopkins his main task was to understand the two prima donnas for whom he worked. In this he was successful, although how successful no one will ever know. Roosevelt was no less complex than Churchill, and even more

[1]Churchill, *The Second World War,* vol. I, Readers' Union ed., p. 450 and appendix B.

difficult to know. There was a secret side of him, impenetrable even to his wife, whereas Churchill's wife was his lifelong 'bosom friend', his absolute confidante, his rock and inspiration in good times and bad. In many ways Roosevelt envied Churchill, perhaps taking a rather sour pleasure when Churchill pushed him in his wheelchair, and called himself the President's 'first lieutenant'. It is unlikely that Churchill envied the President or anyone else.

In August 1940 Churchill had sailed to meet Roosevelt at sea off Newfoundland in the first of many conferences. In January 1942, immediately after the Japanese assault on Pearl Harbour had provided the catalyst and brought the United States into the war, Churchill attended the *Arcadia* conference in Washington, and the Combined Chiefs of Staff were formed. Henceforth the Anglo-American alliance was soundly based. Nevertheless it was soon clear that British and American interests and strategies in war and peace would be in conflict. Once the balance of power moved decisively in America's favour in all theatres of war, Churchill's role as the champion of Britain and British interests became vital and conferences became his main battlefields. He needed constantly to convince the Americans of Britain's capability to stand against the enemy, and for this he needed demonstrable successes. In those first two years the Middle East was virtually the only battle ground, the only place where British troops fought the German and Italian enemy. It was his consciousness of weakness and of American potential strength that made Churchill harass his generals in the Middle East, and to demand impossible victories, to insist upon premature attacks. Every set-back in the field seemed to expose his weakness and his dire need.

Perhaps Churchill was not the best champion Britain could have had, although he strove valiantly from beginning to end. It was never possible for him to regard the United States as an alien power, whereas the United States, and Roosevelt in particular, suffered no such difficulty in regard to Britain. Churchill's awareness of the divergences was very clear. He knew that Roosevelt and the American people had no concept of the nature of the British Empire, and were resolved to dismember it. They did not recognise or seem to understand their own brand of financial imperialism, manifest throughout Latin America and the Philippines, and their maintenance of reactionary governments and dictators wherever they had the power.

Churchill's recognition of the situation does not seem to have gone very deep. Perhaps he felt sure that he could convince the Americans of the nature of the British Empire and that, in a sense, it was part of Britain, the very body of the island which was the heart and intelligence behind a concept of colonial development and social growth, the reverse of the static situation the United States sought always to maintain in the parts of their Empire.

It is clear, I think, that Churchill regarded his mixed blood as an asset which would enable him to have a foot in both worlds. This was clearly apparent in the last days of December 1941 when he addressed the Congress of the United States:

'I had never addressed a foreign Parliament before,' he wrote, 'Yet to me, who could trace unbroken descent on my mother's side through five generations from a lieutenant who served in Washington's army, it was possible to feel a blood right to speak . . . I must confess that I felt quite at home, and more sure of myself than I had sometimes been in the House of Commons.'

He broke the ice instantly: 'I cannot help reflecting that if my father had been American and my mother British, instead of the other way round, I might have got here on my own.'[1]

There is not much doubt about it. The American political scene suited his particular brand of fighting nature, and he had felt it very powerfully not only as a youth on his way to the Cuban-Spanish War, but when he had undertaken a lecture tour soon after the Boer War. He had delighted in the atmosphere, often hostile, to the point of view he expressed, and he valued highly the help of two very shrewd U.S. politicians Bourke Cochran and Chauncey Depew, friends of his Jerome family.

It was all a long way back from the Atlantic Conference of 1940 and his address to the United States Congress on the Boxing Day of 1941, but America was his natural home from home. His blood went even deeper into America than his ancestor, the lieutenant in Washington's army, for in Churchill was also the blood of the great Indian tribe of the Iroquois. Yet he was also the very conscious descendant of the great John Churchill, First Duke of Marlborough, as well as of the Spencers. The mixture in his blood was very rich indeed.

Harry Hopkins described Churchill's speech to a joint session of Congress as 'one of his greatest speeches and superbly attuned to the temper of as difficult an audience as he had ever faced'.

[1]Churchill, *The Second World War*, vol. III, Readers' Union ed., pp. 524–5.

It is not surprising. Churchill was still aglow with the United States' sudden and total involvement in the war, not only against Japan but first and foremost against Germany. Deriving from plans made in London at the time of the Battle of Britain the Combined Chiefs of Staff immediately endorsed the strategy that Germany was 'the prime enemy and her defeat is the key to victory.'[1]

On the night of 7th December the Americans, John Winant and Averell Harriman were dining with Churchill at Chequers when the news had come through of the Japanese attack on Pearl Harbour. Churchill's excitement had been immense. 'I went to sleep,' he wrote, 'and slept the sleep of the saved and thankful.'

Immediate relief was natural, but there remained a titanic struggle ahead. In June of the year Germany had attacked Soviet Russia in immense force, and Churchill had at once assured Stalin of all possible British support. At the end of the year against expert opinion and the secret desires of many, Soviet Russia still held. The German assault on Moscow and Leningrad had failed, and the Russians were fighting with renewed strength. If it was still too early to be over-optimistic of German failure rather than of Russian success, it was still clear that Germany had undertaken a gigantic task, from which it might be impossible to extricate herself, even if successful.

Thus Churchill on that Boxing Day was full of assurance. He was addressing an ally and the coaxing was over. 'Here we are together facing a group of mighty foes seeking our ruin; here we are together defending all that to free men is dear.' And he had ended with the words: 'It is not given to us to peer into the mysteries of the future. Still, I avow my faith, sure and inviolate, that in the days to come the British and American peoples will for their own safety and for the good of all walk together side by side in majesty, justice and peace.'[2]

It had been a week of high-level talks, involving Roosevelt, Churchill and the Combined Chiefs of Staff, yet none of this had blinded Churchill to his commitment to Charles de Gaulle and the Free French, to whom the Americans were less than luke-warm, and of whom indeed they were contemptuous. There was anger in the United States at the Free French seizure of the

---

[1]Ibid., p. 525. See also: Sherwood, *The White House Papers,* vol. I, p. 447 et seq.

[2]Churchill, *The Second World War,* vol. III, Readers' Union ed., p. 525.

islands of St. Pierre-Miquelon, and the U.S. administration still wooed the Government of Pétain and Vichy France.

A week after addressing the American Joint Congress, Churchill addressed the Canadian parliament in Ottawa, and left no listener in any doubt of his scorn and contempt for the leaders of Vichy France, and his support and admiration for de Gaulle and the Free French. In particular he supported the seizure by the Free French of the French islands, St. Pierre and Miquelon, in the shelter of the coast of south Newfoundland. This infuriated Cordell Hull, the U.S. Secretary of State, and might have angered Roosevelt had he not had other and more important things to think about.

The New York Herald Tribune commented, and was supported by important sections of the American press throughout the country:

> If there was any longer any question about it, the Prime Minister has certainly blown down all question of St. Pierre—Miquelon and Washington's 'so-called Free French' through the dusty windows of the State Department. To Mr. Churchill there is nothing 'so-called' about the Free French, 'who would not bow their knees'.[1]

According to Hopkins, Cordell Hull's rage mounted to 'hurricane proportions' and he addressed a private memorandum to the President. It was of no avail, but at no time did the U.S. Administration accept the Free French as an ally and accord to them the unequivocal recognition they deserved. Churchill, however, remained de Gaulle's champion to the end, accepting his pride and pretensions with understanding and patience.

It is impossible to say, and doubtless unprofitable to speculate, whether it would have been better or worse for the fate of Britain and Europe had Britain's leader been wholly British and European, a British de Gaulle. It would certainly have been different. All would have depended upon the steadfast courage and stature of the 'man who never was'.

[1] Sherwood, *The White House Papers,* vol. I, p. 460.

PART THREE

The Choice of Options

CHAPTER NINE

The Year of Anti-Climax, 1941-1942

I

CHURCHILL'S PERFORMANCE ON HIS VISIT TO WASHINGTON HAD been masterly and brave, a tribute not only to his strategic vision in the European-Atlantic context, but to his remarkable resilience. In spite of the immediate involvement of the United States following the Japanese attack on Pearl Harbour, and the massive assault of the German Armies on Soviet Russia in June, and their failure to take Moscow or Leningrad, the end of 1941 was in the middle of Britain's and Churchill's worst year of the war. Churchill's resolve almost at all costs to sustain Soviet Russia, coupled with the urgent demands of the Far East, added severely to Britain's burdens. The convoys to Russia by the sea route to Murmansk suffered heavily in ships, men and the precious materials of war. The demands of the Far East had to be met from the reinforcements needed by the Middle East. The Battle of the Atlantic took its heavy toll, while American aid in any substantial way could not be expected to materialise for some months.

In spite of a cautious optimism, success in the Middle East continued to elude our army. Very little had gone right since O'Connor had been halted at Beda Fomm, and the invasion of Greece had let Rommel and the German Afrika Corps into North Africa.

Churchill's elation on hearing the news of Pearl Harbour had been short-lived. Two days later, on the morning of 10th December, he was given the news that the battleships, *Prince of Wales* and *Repulse,* had been sunk off Malaya with heavy loss of life. The Admiral, Tom Phillips, recently Vice-Chief of Naval Staff, had been lost with his ship.

'In all the war I never received a more direct shock,' Churchill wrote. He had pondered alone for a short time, and had then walked from Downing Street to inform the House of Commons. The following day he gave a sombre account to the House of the tragedy and the march of recent events.

'The House was very silent, and seemed to hold its judgment in suspense. I did not seek or expect more.' He knew that he must bear a large part of the blame, if only because without his imaginative and restless vision, his constant demands for action, allied to his great persuasive powers, the two ships might not have been sent to their doom.

There is little doubt that it was a mistake to send the two Capital ships, and a mistake not to recall them when the aircraft carrier, *Indomitable,* was unable to join them. The whole fateful decision had been insecurely based. 'The primary intention had not been to form a fighting force—for which purpose the two battleships were wholly inadequate—but to create a vague, potential menace, which would tend to deter Japan and to embarrass her naval calculations. But this quasi-political application of sea power, perhaps legitimate in itself, had come too late.'[1]

Japanese power and intentions had been grossly under-estimated, or barely estimated at all. The British and American freezing of Japanese assets and their attempts to deny oil to Japan were bound to bring about drastic Japanese action. All that had happened had been virtually invited, and to call the Japanese surprise action against Pearl Harbour 'treacherous' is naïve.

The whole situation in the Far East was not only as Churchill admitted, 'in the twilight of his mind', it was in the twilight even of American minds. For Britain, at least, it was part of a Victorian hangover destined to bring about the collapse, almost without a struggle, of the great British naval base of Singapore and the loss of Malaya, which would in turn render the Nether-lands' East Indies indefensible. At a stroke the Japanese had gained almost complete naval domination of the Pacific, and Australia and New Zealand were at once alarmed for their security; Burma was dangerously threatened, and the tenuous link with Chiang Kai-Shek's China might be broken.

While Churchill had made the Middle East dominant in his strategy, he was fully aware that the Chief of the Imperial General

[1] *Grand Strategy,* vol. III, part I, p. 308.

Staff, Sir John Dill, did not share his views; nor did many others. Nevertheless, in the light of the 'art of the possible' Churchill may have been instinctively right. 'For my part,' he wrote, 'I did not believe that anything that might happen in Malaya could amount to a fifth part of the loss of Egypt, the Suez Canal and the Middle East.' 'He was resigned,' he said, 'to pay whatever forfeits were exacted in Malaya.'[1]

It seems that at that time Churchill could not have had any conception of the forfeits to be exacted. Nevertheless he had sent one of his trusted associates, Alfred Duff Cooper, as Minister of State to the Far East on a mission of enquiry. The Minister's first report, dated 29th October, 1941, began by stating:

'Within this changed and ever changing world of the Pacific the affairs of the British Empire were being conducted at the outbreak of war by machinery which had undergone no important change since the days of Queen Victoria . . .'[2]

Duff Cooper proposed the appointment of a Commissioner-General to ensure smooth co-operation between Britain, the United States, Russia, China and the Netherlands. He must be a man of the highest rank, able to speak on equal terms with all ambassadors, governors, commanders-in-chief, and to be received by the Viceroy of India in India, and in Washington by the President. Even then it might not have been too late, had it been possible to arouse these high personages from their euphoria, and the lethargic habits of an age long since gone. A few stalwarts strove to construct defences on the landward side of Singapore, but only a determined effort by all concerned could have hoped for success.

Churchill, too late, had began to drag this twilight area of his mind into his line of vision. Afterwards he wrote:

I ought to have known. My advisers ought to have known, and I ought to have been told, and I ought to have asked. The reason I had not asked about this matter, amid the thousands of questions I put, was that the possibility of Singapore having no landward defences no more entered my mind than that of a battleship being launched without a bottom.[3]

[1]Churchill, *The Second World War,* vol. III, Readers' Union ed., p. 341.
[2]*Grand Strategy,* vol. III, part I, p. 283(iii)–289.
[3]Churchill, *The Second World War,* vol. IV, Readers' Union ed., p. 55.

In December events rapidly overtook all plans for improving the situation. On the 9th Churchill appointed Duff Cooper to be Resident Cabinet Minister, and on 31st December President Roosevelt, supported by General Marshall, his Chief of Staff, asked for General Wavell to be appointed Supreme Commander, South-West Pacific. The scope of Wavell's command was vague, ill-defined and strategically unsound, Burma could not be separated from India command.

The Prime Minister was complimented by the American choice of a British Commander, and probably somewhat abashed. When Auchinleck had replaced Wavell in the Middle East, Wavell had become Commander-in-Chief India. Churchill had then suggested that the 'weary general' would be able to spend some of his time 'sitting under the Pagoda tree', as though he were some faithful old horse being put out to grass. So much for the quality of the 'twilight'. At least Wavell would be out of the Prime Minister's direct line of fire, but not for long.

As the new year, 1942, dawned, Churchill had begun to lose some of his illusions and was aware of the awesome and impossible task he had to ask Wavell to undertake.

'It was almost certain that he would have to bear a load of defeat in a scene of confusion,' and only the highest sense of duty induced Wavell to accept his burden. To Wavell the nature of this last great challenge seemed in the pattern of his destiny. He was 'required to meet and shoulder the local and military responsibility for the swiftest, most searing and most calamitous succession of defeats that the British Empire had ever sustained'.[1]

Not surprisingly the British Chiefs of Staff viewed Wavell's appointment with suspicion. They felt that a British scapegoat was being deliberately chosen to bear the brunt of the almost certain severe set-backs. Wavell had telegraphed to Dill in Washington that he had been handed 'not just a baby but quadruplets'.

Sir John Dill wrote at once to his successor, General Brooke, in London: 'It would, I think, be fatal to have a British Commander responsible for the disaster coming to the Americans as well as ourselves . . . Never was a soldier given a more difficult task . . . It is of the first importance that we should not be blamed for the bloody noses that are coming to them.'[2]

Apart from this the new C.I.G.S. did not like the arrangements made in Washington to hand over so much of the strategic

[1]Connell, *Wavell, Supreme Commander,* p. 71.
[2]Arthur Bryant, *The Turn of the Tide,* p. 294.

control of the war to 'beginners'. It seemed to General Brooke, lonely and apprehensive at home, awaiting the return of the master who had already alarmed him by 'the most awful outburst of temper' and whose tantrums he had already experienced as C-in-C Home Forces, that the Prime Minister and his colleagues had 'sold their birthright for a plate of porridge'.

This gloomy view expressed Brooke's immediate reaction even though Churchill had won the prize he had set out to win in the American decision that 'the Atlantic and European area was considered to be the decisive theatre'.[1]

Anthony Eden's remark to Cadogan that the Prime Minister had brought back 'lots of jam tomorrow, but not much today' was correct in immediate material terms, but the gains—or losses—could not be so simply expressed. The Prime Minister's fears—if he had fears—and I believe that he had—were not that he had given too much away, but that he might be forced to give too much away in the future. He had, he believed, to take that chance, relying on his persuasive powers with the President to maintain and develop British strategy in the whole of the Mediterranean area. He had, above all, laid the foundations of the Alliance more soundly than could have been expected. In that context it was of profound importance that the establishment of the Combined Chiefs of Staff Committee had been agreed, and that Sir John Dill was already making his mark in Washington, notably with General Marshall, the U.S. Chief of Staff. The choice of Dill for the difficult role of British permanent representative had been inspired. No one was better able to express the British point of view, while at the same time winning the respect of General Marshall. The effects were incalculable, yet Brooke's immediate fears, never again expressed, were justified.

General Dill's first reactions to his new environment were almost those of a visitor from another planet. The lavish scale of living, the absence of any sign of austerity, provoked him to write to General Brooke, 'Never have I seen a country so utterly unprepared for war and so soft.' There was absolutely no sign of anything military, nor did it seem to General Dill, at first, that out of this matrix of pleasure anything military could arise. Even worse, the U.S. Joint Chiefs of Staff seemed to function without any kind of Secretariat, and without anyone even to take the minutes of the meetings. There was no record

[1]*Grand Strategy*, vol. III, part I, p. 345.

kept even of meetings with the President and his Chief of Staff,
Nothing had changed very much since George Washington. It
was rather a shock to anyone accustomed to the Committee of
Imperial Defence and its many ramifications.

Nevertheless it did work, after a fashion, and the creation
of armies, and the ever increasing range of armaments urgently
demanded multiplied with astounding speed to make America
'the arsenal of democracy'.

One source of constant irritation and frustration to the
Americans was the British preparedness for any and all conferences. It would have been unthinkable for the British Chiefs
of Staff, or for Churchill, to come to the conference table
without having plans, and alternative plans, worked out in detail
and ready for lucid presentation. There were also minor problems
of semantics, as Churchill pointed out: 'To the Americans
"tabling a motion" meant putting it away in a drawer and
forgetting it.'

Despite these things, despite antagonism and the fundamental
differences in attitudes to war and strategy, ultimately irreconcilable, the Combined Chiefs of Staff Committee did work,
very much thanks to General Dill and the U.S. Chief of Staff,
General Marshall.

II

Politically and militarily Churchill was the least powerful of
the four Supreme Commanders confronting each other as allies
and enemies upon the vast stage of the Second World War,
which now embraced the world. The pattern was new and
powerful. Britain was, of course, no longer alone fighting for
the survival of the British Isles; she must now fight, not only
against the enemy, but for the preservation from her allies of
much that she held dear, for what might remain of her empire,
for the security of the dominions, and for the future of Europe.

Even at the time of the Atlantic Conference it had been
clear to Churchill that British and U.S. concepts of strategy
seriously diverged, but it was not clear that the concepts of
war itself, or the purposes of war, especially in the context of
European history, had only one piece of common ground: the
defeat of the enemy. 'Unconditional surrender' was the only end
pattern the United States understood. It would be stated at
Casablanca in 1943 with all its tragic implications.

The American Official Historian, writing of the Atlantic Conference, had 'warned the British of certain strong views held in Washington, and had provided unmistakable evidence that the United States was likely to be the controlling partner in any coming alliance.'[1]

The Washington Conference must have made that evident to all, but it did not make evident what this might mean, literally, to the future of the world. The implications were of overwhelming importance in the European theatre of war. Churchill understood very well what Soviet Russian aims must be if they succeeded in driving back the Germans and moving into Eastern Europe: they would stay there. Napoleon had made the conquest of Russia a priority, and Hindenburg had underlined it at Tannenberg, a battle brilliantly described and understood by Churchill.[2] Yet he understood Russian aims in terms of the Czars, and not of the Soviet Union and Stalin. The United States and Roosevelt especially understood even less. In early 1942 all that was a long way off, and might never happen.

American strategy was at once glaringly obvious: to smash the enemy in the shortest possible time by the shortest possible route.

'The Americans took a rigid or black-and-white view of the art of war,' wrote the British Official Historian.[3] 'The resources of their country are very large; they have rarely had to count the cost; and it is natural to them to find the solution to every problem in an overwhelming application of strength—the crash programme, the head-on collision, the quick victory.'

The British historian thought it unlikely that this was clear at the time to the British. It was clear, I believe, to Churchill, and the implications would soon have dawned upon him. Yet, I think, that he failed to realise until too late how inflexible, and how absolutely divorced from political considerations were American military attitudes and strategies. In their thinking politics and war did not mix. They were domestic politicians. In foreign affairs they were ignorant, as their brief history had demonstrated, notably in the Monroe Doctrine, in Latin America and the Caribbean where they had supported dictatorships to maintain the *status quo* and hold millions of peasant peoples in poverty. Their entry into the First World War had not proved

[1] *Grand Strategy*, vol. III, part I, p. 350; quoting Watson p. 409.
[2] Churchill, *The World Crisis*, *The Eastern Front*.
[3] *Grand Strategy*, vol. III, part I, p. 350.

a service to peace, and they would have done well to heed
the warnings of George Washington in his Farewell Address,
19th September, 1796:

> Europe has a set of primary interests which to us have none,
> or a very remote relation. Hence she must be engaged in
> frequent controversies, the causes of which are essentially
> foreign to our concerns. Hence therefore it must be unwise in
> us to implicate ourselves, by artificial ties in the ordinary
> vicissitudes of her politics, or the ordinary combinations and
> collisions of her friendships, or enmities.

The dangers if—and when—the United States imposed her
smash-and-grab strategy in Europe were, I think, clear to
Churchill, but he failed, right to the end, to realise their totality.
Meanwhile he hoped to establish a pattern of strategy, a series
of commitments, difficult to change. It would be a fight against
time, and his first success was in persuading the President to
support joint landings in French North Africa, at first known
as 'Gymnast' and finally as 'Torch'. The immediate American
desire to mount a cross-channel assault in 1942, code-named
'Sledgehammer', was unreal, but it was an aim they continued to
press even when it should have been obvious to them that it was
impossible. They do not appear to have given any thought to
what such an operation would entail, in terms of planning, men,
materials of war, landing craft, air and sea support. Their attitude
was an embarrassment enhanced by the clamouring of sections
of the British left-wing for the opening of a second front in
North-Western Europe to relieve the pressure on Soviet Russia.

In August 1942 the British mounted a cross-channel assault
against Dieppe, involving a Canadian Division with Commando
troops in support. Even this small expedition needed 252 ships,
and strained available air cover to the limits at that range. It
was a disaster, partly because of the inflexibility of the planning,
partly because the object was vague, and the enemy defences
grossly under-estimated. It did represent almost the best we
could hope to do at that time, at that place, and with the
shipping—especially landing craft—available.

Slowly and reluctantly 'Sledgehammer' 1942 became 'Round-
up' 1943, which would become impossible in 1943 if Churchill
succeeded in involving the Americans in North Africa, especially
if his timings went wrong, as they would and did. But for the

impossible 'Sledgehammer' the North-Africa landings might have taken place in mid-summer. But I believe it is fair to say that neither Churchill, nor the British planners, the Chiefs of Staff, and outstandingly the architects and trainers of the Home Forces, ever did less than their best to make a cross-channel assault possible. From the hour of Dunkirk the British had trained indefatigably against the hour of return to the Continent, conceiving specialised weapons for the purpose, constructing such things as artificial harbours, and providing an island base of remarkable magnitude for U.S. forces of all arms, together with training and supply areas and facilities on an immense scale. Nevertheless it is also true that Churchill and his Chief of Staff hoped that it would never happen, or that it would happen at a time when it would be a virtual 'walk-in'.

I write these things here because American suspicions of British intent would be a constant source of irritation and frustration, casting a sour atmosphere over many conferences. They believed that Churchill wanted to 'ditch' the cross-channel assault, and for this reason among others they viewed his Mediterranean and Balkan strategy with acute suspicion, and his longing to mount an expedition against North Norway as a pipe dream. In these attitudes the Americans would find a supporter and an ally in the Soviet dictator, Stalin, who understood Churchill's European 'balance of power' aims very well, while at the same time the Nazi Führer feared a British attack on Norway, and took steps to guard against it.

If Churchill and his staff had anticipated U.S. attitudes on their journey to the first Washington Conference on the battle-ship *Duke of York,* in December 1941, they certainly worked ceaselessly on their plans, and in spite of a warning from the President's adviser, Harry Hopkins, to be careful, they put these plans before the President and the U.S. Joint Chiefs of Staff. Churchill's plans were a remarkable forecast of the course of British strategy in 1942, and probably in 1943.

The Plans should be read in full.[1] Paragraph 11 of the Atlantic and European section reads:

To sum up, the war in the West in 1942 comprises, as its main offensive effort, the occupation and control by Great Britain and the United States of the whole of the North and West African possessions of France, and the further control by

[1]*Grand Strategy,* vol. II, part I, pp. 325–40.

Britain of the whole north African shore from Tunis to Egypt, thus giving, if the naval situation allows, free passage through the Mediterranean to the Levant and the Suez Canal. These great objectives can only be achieved if British and American naval and air superiority in the Atlantic is maintained, if supply-lines continue uninterrupted, and if the British Isles are effectively safeguarded against invasion.

Churchill's plans also 'referred to' rather than 'covered' the naval and military situation in the Pacific, and the campaign for 1943, assuming that the 1942 plans 'should prosper'. If all went well, he thought, it might be possible to win the war by the end of 1943 or 1944. He meant, of course, the European war.

These plans, the Official Historian comments, represented 'a simple application of the rules of warfare', and inspired General Ismay to say of Churchill that 'in his grasp of the broad sweep of strategy—"the overall strategic concept"—as our American friends called it—he stood head and shoulders above his professional advisers.'[1]

That may be so, partly because Churchill was always a master of 'the broad sweep'; moreover, unlike Sir John Dill, L. S. Amery, Wavell and others, Churchill was not a deep thinker nor an imperialist. He was, as Amery observed, a Great Englander, and perhaps that was a sensible and realistic attitude in the midst of the Second World War, when it had become clear that Britain was unable to defend her Empire adequately against a predator like Japan, and with Singapore and much else besides lost somewhere in the *fin de siècle mystique* of the Victorians.

At this time neither Churchill nor his Staff knew which way the United States would jump, either to the Pacific or to the Atlantic. All that was certain was that forces would be available in both theatres. The decision would be, almost certainly, the most momentous in history, although that could not have been foreseen at the time.

Churchill's advisers meanwhile had concentrated upon producing a paper to make the Americans fully aware of the present situation. 'In effect . . . their paper was a reasoned catalogue of the difficulties as they appeared in December 1941, of carrying out such a policy as Mr. Churchill described.'[2]

And there in a nutshell is a major source of Churchill's constant irritation and outbursts against his advisers. Without

[1]Ismay, *Memoirs,* p. 163.   [2]*Grand Strategy,* vol. II.

them Churchill would have tried to achieve the possible by impossible means, or the other way round—which may seem a contradiction in terms, but is a fair comment on Churchill's attempts to conduct the war from day to day. Either Churchill or his advisers on their own might have tried to do too much or too little. Together they did the best they could militarily within the political and military strategy imposed upon them. There was in fact almost no major problem of significance left uncovered.

With the Americans it was very different. They were concerned pragmatically with the crisis in the Pacific and not at that stage with wider problems of strategy. They were prepared only to discuss these things in general terms.

At the time it seemed that Churchill's greatest achievement at the *Arcadia* Conference was to gain the President's faint support for the North-African plan. The President of the United States is also the Commander-in-Chief, able to override his Chiefs of Staff. Churchill, of course, was not in a similar position. The dangers of the U.S. commitment to North Africa were many, but high among them was the matter of timing. June 1942 was the time when the situation would be ripe, when the French in North Africa might welcome, rather than oppose the Allies, but that would depend partly upon British success in the Western Desert.

Perhaps Churchill's greatest mistake was to cast himself as, and call himself, the President's '1st Lieutenant'. He should have been no one's '1st Lieutenant', but the Captain of his own command, his own 'Ship of State'. His English father and American mother were responsible for the ominous split in his loyalties; he could not, as his American grandfather had observed, serve two such powerful masters.

It must not be forgotten that all the observations and conclusions now put forward are subject to 'hindsight'. What could even the best informed have *known* at the time? It was, perhaps, impossible to know, but many had a sense of unease. It was regarded as Churchill's greatest achievement at *Arcadia* that the United States had concluded that Germany was the main enemy, and that the defeat of Germany was the top priority. Not all the U.S. Joint Chiefs of Staff agreed with that decision, notably Admiral King, who fought it to the end and at times came near to persuading General Marshall and the Joint Chiefs of Staff to his views. The balance was always delicate even when the

Americans were deeply committed in Europe as late as the autumn of 1943.

In the final count the American decision to put Germany first may have been a misfortune. The European victory would be an American victory and a Soviet-Russian victory, not a victory for Britain or for Europe.

How did this come about? Churchill's emotional and instant rush to the aid of Soviet Russia in word and deed; his equally emotional reaction to Pearl Harbour and American involvement seem excessive, over hasty, and lacking not only a sense of proportion but also an understanding of British strength. Was Britain so weak that she had to rush into the arms of her new allies, and virtually accept the position of a vassal? Either the United States and the Soviet Union needed Britain as much as she needed them, or the alliance would be fraught with dangers for the weaker partner, unless those dangers were clearly foreseen. There is no need to split hairs.

What does seem clear to me now, and made me uneasy at the time, was the decisive change in Britain's struggle, the struggle that was Britain's alone and must remain so. U.S. and Soviet power had blinded Churchill to the realities of British power, to the strength and devotion of the British people, to the high quality of the armed forces and their achievement. He seemed unaware of the strength of the British Empire, even in decline, in the powerful and magnificent contributions of India, Australia, New Zealand, Canada, South Africa, in the First World War, and now in the Second. Without these Indian and dominion troops it would have been impossible to hold the Middle East, or to make the enormous contribution to the Far East. In both wars dominion troops had been wherever the fighting was fiercest, in Gallipoli, in Greece, Crete and Libya, in Burma, and from New Guinea to the Philippines.

It has not escaped the Australians, in particular, that it is difficult to find a clear recognition of this massive and heroic contribution to British victory in Churchill's great autobiographical works, and personal reportage of the world wars. He was also cavalier, and even insulting in his dealings, and President Roosevelt had been disturbed by the tone of the cables Churchill received from the Australian Prime Minister. The telegrams of 20th February, 1942, Churchill to Curtin, and 23rd February, 1942[1] Curtin to Churchill, are fair examples:

[1]Churchill, *The Second World War,* vol. IV, Readers' Union ed., p. 138.

Churchill to Curtin:

I suppose you realise that your leading division, the head of which is sailing south of Colombo in our scanty British and American shipping, is the only force that can reach Rangoon in time to prevent its loss and the severance of communication with China...if you refuse to allow your troops to stop this gap...a very grave effect will be produced upon the President and the Washington circle...We must have an answer immediately.

On 22nd February Curtin cabled Churchill:[1] 'It was suggested by you that two Australian divisions be transferred [from the Middle East] to the Pacific theatre, and this suggestion was later publicly expanded by you with the statement that no obstacle would be placed in the way.'

The Australian Prime Minister was alarmed and angered by Churchill's tone. He feared that the whole of the Australian Corps might become committed in Burma, and lost. The Greek disaster was fresh in his mind, and the disaster in Malaya. He finished his telegram: 'The movement of our forces to the theatre is not considered a reasonable hazard of war.'

This telegram was followed on 23rd February by another replying to Churchill's of 20th:

In your telegram of 20th February it was clearly implied that the convoy was not proceeding northwards...You have diverted the convoy towards Rangoon and treated our approval as a matter of form. By doing so you have established a physical situation which adds to the dangers, and the responsibility for the consequences rests upon you... Australia's outer defences are quickly vanishing...Now you contemplate using the A.I.F. to save Burma; all, as in Greece, without adequate air support.

Churchill was forced to climb down and the Australian divisions survived to save their country: '...the soldiers were saved, to fight for their own Australia instead of for Churchill, and Chiang and Madam in Burma.'[2]

It seems that Churchill did not appreciate that the self-

[1]Ibid., p. 140.
[2]See J. E. Webb's bitter polemic: Saviour or Wrecker, pp. 44–7.

governing dominions were self-governing. He had not understood the bitterness and even hatred he had caused in Australia following the ANZAC sacrifice in Gallipoli, which was generating anew with the disasters in Greece and Crete. Such minor irritations as his failure to appreciate the generalship of the Australians, Morshead and Blamey, and the disappointment of 9th Australian Division in being denied victory in Tripoli, added to Australian anger.

In December 1940 Churchill had reassured Robert Menzies, the very 'English' Australian—and had played down the Japanese threat. He hoped then to knock Italy out of the war 'very soon', and meanwhile: 'We must try to bear our Eastern anxieties patiently and doggedly until this result is achieved.' Finally he promised Menzies that if Australia was seriously threatened 'we should not hesitate to compromise or sacrifice the Mediterranean position for the sake of our kith and kin.'

These were merely words, reassuring perhaps to Menzies but not to A. W. Fadden, the Australian Prime Minister, and even less to his successor, John Curtin. It did not escape the notice of these dour Australians that Churchill changed the priorities to put the Middle East above the Far East. This must have meant that the Far-Eastern Empire came a poor third after Britain and the Nile Delta.

The contribution to victory of the Indian Army in two world wars is too little known, and I hope it is not out of place to draw attention to it here. India had 573,000 men under arms in 1918.

In July 1939 India had 183,000 men under arms, commanded by 2,978 British and 528 Indian officers. Five years later Indian Army troops were over 2,250,000, commanded by 37,187 British and 13,355 Indian officers. Except for some British officers they were all volunteers:

'There has never been so large a voluntary Army since history began to be written,' wrote Compton Mackenzie in *Eastern Epic*. They fought in almost every theatre of war, in North Africa, in the Western Desert, in Eritrea, Abyssinia, Somaliland, Syria and Iraq; in Burma, Assam, Arakan, Malaya, Java and Hong Kong. They fought also in Italy and Greece and stood guard in Ceylon, Egypt, Persia, Palestine, Cyprus, and on their own North-West Frontier. They also served with occupation troops in Japan.

At 5.30 a.m. 6th November, 1940 Indian troops commanded by Brigadier Slim (later Field-Marshal Slim) were the first to launch an offensive in the Second World War. (There was a British advance into Belgium in May 1940.) They took Gallabat and Metemma in the Soudan after fierce hand-to-hand fighting.

Very few outside Indian Army circles seemed to understand or to appreciate these things, but among the very few were Wavell, Auchinleck and Slim.

Early in 1941, if not before, it was clear that the war was far too big for any one man to command.

III

Churchill returned to Britain from the first Washington Conference to meet a grave and critical House of Commons, and perhaps a certain uneasiness in the country. The main criticism centred upon the supply situation, and the need to appoint a Minister of Supply. This was a matter not greatly in dispute, but there was also a general feeling that would grow, as disaster followed swiftly upon disaster, that Churchill's shoulders, broad as they were, were not broad enough to carry the full burden of war. There should be, many thought—and they included Lords Hankey and Chatfield, who voiced their criticism in the House of Lords—a lightening of Churchill's burden.

The Prime Minister would not consider such a proposition for a moment: 'It is most important that at the summit there should be one mind playing over the whole field . . . I should not of course have remained Prime Minister for one hour if I had been deprived of the office of Minister of Defence.'[1]

Lord Beaverbrook remarked that the proposal was useless anyway, for had a Minister of Defence been appointed he would either have agreed with the Prime Minister or have been removed from office.

It is one thing for 'one mind to be playing over the whole field', but for one mind, and that same mind, to command is another matter. This, to me, is the first hint—it is too slight, perhaps to write 'evidence'—of change in Churchill's leadership. He remains indomitable, but Britain was now no longer alone with 'her back to the wall'. Churchill, of course, was adamant, the country could take him or leave him, all or nothing, and he did not doubt the verdict. 1940, and Churchill's immense service, was very fresh, and would never be forgotten. The country took him. His majority on a vote of confidence in the

[1]Churchill, *The Second World War,* vol. IV, Readers' Union ed., p. 80.

House was devastating, 464–1. That majority 'showed that there was no desire—*at least none that dare express itself*—for a change of leadership.'[1]

Nevertheless criticism was not silenced, and on 24th February Churchill recognised the need to reorganise his Government. His proposals met with general agreement, but he remained under fire at home, and from Australia as a series of disasters followed closely upon each other. The comparatively minor misfortune of the bold escape of the German battle cruisers *Scharnhorst* and *Gneisenau* with the cruiser *Prinz Eugen,* from Brest, to sail up the English Channel on 11th and 12th February in defiance of the British Navy and Air Force, seemed an act almost of contempt. These three powerful German ships joined the *Tirpitz* and powerful enemy naval forces concentrated in north Norway. While it was some relief to the Admiralty the move had some advantages, but not enough. The threat to the British convoys running the gauntlet of the icy seas to Murmansk, bringing relief to the Soviet Union, had become immense, and to the British people the failure to meet the brazen challenge on the very doorstep of England, was cause for grave disquiet.

'The escape of the three ships was a severe blow to British prestige, all the more painful as falling just when the doom of Singapore was imminent,' wrote the official historian.[2]

The day before the break-out Churchill had cabled a message to General Wavell, which Wavell passed on, very slightly modified, to General Percival, G.O.C. Singapore: 'The battle must be fought to the bitter end at all costs... Commanders and senior officers should die with their troops. The honour of the British Empire and of the British Army is at stake.'

But it is not always easy, or even possible, for generals and troops to fight to the last, for 'the last' often comes before death. In Singapore lack of aircraft was the key factor, and the British were almost naked against the Japanese air assault. As usual Churchill also exaggerated the numbers of fighting troops involved.

On 15th February, 1942, General Percival signalled General Wavell: 'Owing to losses from enemy action water petrol food and ammunition practically finished. Unable therefore continue fight any longer. All ranks have done their best and grateful for your help.'

[1]*Grand Strategy,* vol. III, part II, p. 427—my italics.
[2]Ibid.

Percival and his troops were the scapegoats for the sins of their fathers and their fathers' fathers. The Japanese had also dominated the seas.

This calamitous defeat further reduced British prestige throughout the world. The Japanese to their intense surprise had found the airfields, the harbour and large parts of Singapore intact. Fortunately something has been preserved from the tragedy in the records of the Japanese Colonel Tsuji. An unnamed junior British officer was being interrogated:

'Why did you not destroy Singapore?'

'Because we will return again.'

'Don't you believe Britain is beaten in this war?'

'We may be defeated ninety-nine times,' he answered, 'but in the final round we will be all-right—we will win that.'[1]

IV

Severe set-backs to British hopes had also occurred in the Western Desert since the turn of the year, culminating in the fall of Tobruk in June while Churchill was again with President Roosevelt in the United States. 'This was one of the heaviest blows I can recall during the war,' he wrote, but he exaggerated its significance in the dreadful context of that year, and he also exaggerated the defeat of the Eighth Army after two years of fighting in often appalling conditions. He forgot that they had wrested an empire from the Italians.

Churchill immediately asked the President to send as many Sherman tanks as he could spare, and to ship them to the Middle East. The plea is one of the very rare indications that Churchill knew that British armour was outgunned and inferior in many ways to the German armour.

Thus for a second time in five months Churchill returned to Britain to face a vote of censure. In his train down to London from the Clyde he read the news of a Government defeat 'by a sweeping turnover' in a by-election at Maldon. It did not seem to alarm him; he remained absolutely sure of himself.

The vote of censure was moved in the House of Commons by Sir John Wardlaw Milne. It was not, Sir John emphasised, directed against officers in the field:

[1]Quoted by Connell in *Wavell, Supreme Commander,* from the official history, *War Against Japan,* vol. I.

It is a direct attack upon the central direction here in London . . .
the first vital mistake that we made in the war was to combine
the offices of Prime Minister and Minister of Defence . . . I
want a strong and independent man appointing his generals
and his admirals and so on . . . strong enough to demand all
the weapons which are necessary for victory . . . to see that
his generals and admirals and air marshals are allowed to do
their work in their own way and are not interfered with
unduly from above.

It was a forlorn appeal, for where was there such a man? It
remained for Hore-Belisha to sum up boldly: 'How can one
place reliance in judgment that has so repeatedly turned out to be
misguided? That is what the House of Commons has to decide.
Think what is at stake. In a hundred days we lost our empire in
the Far East. What will happen in the next hundred days?'

It was a fair question, and it is perhaps strange that it was
uttered in the very hour when the long ebb tide was about to
turn. In a sense it said, we have ebbed far enough; we shall ebb
no further.

Churchill's reply and peroration were masterly, even though
his scorn for his questioners was unjust. The whole world was
waiting for the verdict on the government and upon himself
as its leader, and it was clear that his position was immensely
powerful: He said:

Every vote counts. If those who have assailed us are reduced
to contemptible proportions and their vote of censure on the
National Government is converted to a vote of censure upon
its authors, make no mistake, a cheer will go up from every
friend of Britain and every faithful servant of our cause, and
the knell of disappointment will ring in the ears of the tyrants
we are striving to overthrow.

The Prime Minister and Minister of Defence won an easy
victory, as he was bound to do, by the overwhelming majority
of 475 to 25. Those last days of June and first days of July 1942
marked the end of Britain's heroic period. The struggle for
survival was over, and so was Churchill's ability to play the
super-general.

CHAPTER TEN

The Struggle of the Eighth Army
1941–1942

I

THROUGHOUT ALL THAT YEAR OF GREAT POLITICAL ACTIVITY AT home and abroad, Churchill had not taken his eyes off the battlefield in the Middle East. It was, he knew, his personal battlefield, upon which his personal political survival as Prime Minister and Minister of Defence of Great Britain might depend. Already, when the second phase of the struggle in the Middle East opened in June 1941, Churchill bore a load of disaster upon his shoulders. Before that fateful year, June to June, was done he might bear a great deal more. Only thus may Churchill's harassing of his Commander-in-Chief and his constant involvement be properly understood.

There was, of course, much more at stake, for while the political future of Britain was being decided in Washington, the military struggle in the Middle East was nevertheless the decisive factor, for upon the outcome must depend, not simply the military present of Britain, but her physical future, for, at the military worst, United States involvement in the Western Theatre would be jeopardised, and perhaps impossible.

It is doubtful whether the implications of a German victory in Egypt, coupled with—as it almost certainly would be—a German drive south through the Caucasus, were ever realised by Churchill. For him the struggle was for prestige, for bargaining power with his American ally, and for victory in the Mediterranean and all that that might mean.

The Commander-in-Chief in the Middle East and his close advisers had few illusions. They knew that in that theatre of war the outcome would be decisive for Britain, that in the Middle East the war could be lost.

Auchinleck, while understanding profoundly the nature of the struggle, was resolved upon victory in the desert, but the instrument of victory, the Eighth Army, was in the making. The British Army, the poor relation of the three services, was striving to drag itself out of the long years of apathy, of old-fashioned thinking, of mental and physical unpreparedness. It faced the most professional, the best-trained and finest-equipped troops in the world. The German and British armies were also the reflection of two vastly different societies, the amateurs versus the professionals, and the amateurs, forged and tempered in battle, must win. Fortunately for the British, the German Afrika Corps round which the German army was built, had an Achilles heel in its Italian component, and of this the British were fully aware.

Generals Sir Archibald Wavell and Sir Claude Auchinleck had changed places in June 1941, Wavell taking over Auchinleck's India Command, and Auchinleck taking over the Middle East. This important move took place as Germany invaded Russia, provoking a welter of emotions, of hopes and fears in British hearts and minds. It could mean almost anything; it could mean an increased threat facing the British in Persia and endangering Abadan oil. It could mean disaster for either of the two great antagonists, but it must mean—for a time anyway—an enormous relief to Britain. These great considerations absorbed and excited Churchill to instant action, but they did not draw his attention away from the Middle East, which for him had narrowed down almost to a personal struggle with the German General, Rommel.

The ordeal Auchinleck would face in the Middle East was very different from that which Wavell had faced so well. 'The whole character of the war in the Middle East was changing,' wrote the Official Historian. 'The initial phase was almost over.'

It is necessary to look briefly at the beginning and end of Wavell in order to understand the beginning and end of Auchinleck. Nothing that happened in the last weeks of Wavell's command may take away the lustre of his liquidation of the Italian empire, of General O'Connor's victories, of his magnificent achievement. He had fought on six fronts involving great distances, and was fighting on five when he was chosen as the scapegoat for the failure of the offensive in the Western Desert, code-named 'Battle Axe', which Churchill had plagued and bludgeoned Wavell to launch prematurely while also involved in Syria. Nevertheless:

... starting from an insecure position in Egypt and Palestine we had gradually extended and confirmed our control over the whole area from Kenya to the Turkish frontier, from the Western Desert to the Persian Gulf. This feat of arms, carried out with small and improvised forces, had been Wavell's achievement. The new task, radically different in kind, was to defend the enormous theatre which he had created against the coming German onslaught.[1]

The virtual sacking of Wavell and the changeover of command in the Middle East compelled General Dill, the C.I.G.S., to face up to the facts of Churchill's 'super-generalship'. Churchill's bitter criticisms of Wavell's generalship did not rid him of his spleen, which could have arisen from his own deep sense of guilt. Churchill had turned on Dill, whose sometimes successful attempts to block his worst blunders drove him to fury. When Wavell's full report reached Whitehall Churchill took the opportunity to circulate it to the Cabinet, adding his own unjust criticisms of Wavell. General Kennedy, the D.M.O., was as horrified as his chief, the C.I.G.S. Dill wrote to the Prime Minister a quietly worded protest: 'I feel you must know how shocked I am that you should make such an attack on General Wavell.'

The problem was what, if anything, could be done to curb Churchill?

It is not a simple question to answer because of the unique power and character of Churchill, his remarkable egomania, his imperviousness to argument. He would not, as we have seen, brook any curtailment of his powers, and at times he would deny that his power was as great as he often claimed. When he made the decision to remove Wavell and to replace him with Auchinleck, he wrote: 'I found that these views of mine encountered no resistance in our ministerial and military circles in London.'

What he must have meant was that the resistance was not strong enough to make him change his mind: it seldom was. Yet Dill had expressed his grave misgivings about the change, and so had the Viceroy of India, and Amery, the Secretary of State. Auchinleck himself was uneasy about the change, and 'in two minds'.

Generals Wavell and Auchinleck, unique in their great roles, faced their tasks with fortitude and resolution; their tasks to hold

[1]*Grand Strategy*, vol. III, part I, p. 163.

at all costs through the lean years, to make do with the poor tools to hand, confident that the British Armies would grow steadily in strength, and that the finest equipment and weapons would be put into the hands of their successors.

Churchill consistently refused to face the facts of modern warfare. He refused to recognise the inevitable growth of the tails of armies brought about by advances in technology, the rapid development of new and complex weapons, the growth of workshops, of virtual factories behind the lines, and the growth of organisations like R.E.M.E., the Royal Electrical and Mechanical Engineers, striving to keep armour and armoured vehicles in action, servicing and repairing the great fleets of transport always breaking down under the fierce heat and sand, the natural conditions of war in the Western Desert. Also the immense administrative problems absorbed many men in non-combatant roles.

Churchill incessantly questioned, and in effect denied, the sober and accurate reports provided from time to time by Wavell and Auchinleck in turn. Infuriated by an 'Appreciation' of Auchinleck's, he sent General Nye, the V.C.I.G.S., and Sir Stafford Cripps to look into the situation on the spot. Nye was 'armed with a formidable list of twenty questions'. Their reports fully supported and confirmed the facts supplied by the Commander-in-Chief in the field.

General Auchinleck was not as competent as Wavell in coping with the Prime Minister's incessant questioning, particularly his attempts to interfere in tactical matters, his demands for premature offensives from positions of weakness, and his 'private' war dispositions of Auchinleck's troops. In late July 1941 Churchill challenged Auchinleck's placing of fifty division in Cyprus. Having written to the C.I.G.S. on this and other matters Auchinleck replied briefly to Churchill: 'If you wish I can send you detailed reasons which actuated me and which appeared to me incontestable. I hope you will leave me complete discretion concerning dispositions of this kind.'[1]

This was the beginning of the kind of attitude General Dill feared. He knew Auchinleck very well indeed, and the future looked ominous from the outset. General Brooke, who replaced Dill as C.I.G.S., went so far as to suggest to Churchill that Auchinleck and Wavell should again change places. Churchill minuted in reply: 'I could not do this.'

[1] John Connell, *Auchinleck,* p. 262.

Such a change, had it been made, might have gravely disturbed parliament, and aroused misgivings in the people throughout the country, and could not have helped the struggle in the Western Desert.

Where were the generals to be found of the calibre of Wavell and Auchinleck, capable of the vast administrative and command burdens these men bore; where were good army commanders to be found? Slim and Alexander were fast discovering their virtues and abilities in the Far East, but neither of these could have undertaken the roles played by Wavell and Auchinleck.

Perhaps only General Paget, unpopular with Churchill, and deeply involved in building the Home Army, not simply to defend the Island—for that threat had passed—but to provide reinforcements for overseas, and above all to train an army to assault across the channel when the time came, might have taken on such a vast and complex command with some hope of success.

Wavell and Auchinleck were cast in their tragic and heroic roles, Churchill's scapegoats for his own failures, for his almost certain postponement of victory in North Africa. Could either man be blamed for the set-backs in the Western Desert through the lean years, while they achieved their unsung victories, avoided disastrous defeats, and put total victory into the hands of their heirs?

Could Sir John Dill, or his successor General Brooke, be blamed? If so, it is only because they might have resisted Churchill's pressures and bludgeonings more powerfully, and devised some means whereby his constant flow of messages could have been stopped before reaching the commanders in the field. It is only necessary to suggest such a course to realise its hopelessness.

In May 1941, within a month of Wavell's replacement, Sir John Dill told Churchill: 'You must not forget, Prime Minister, that we started the war without an army... and it is not easy to build it up and to fight at the same time.'

Churchill's answer, if he had given one, might have been: 'Maybe not, but that is what we are doing and going to do.'

Wavell had stressed the inferiority of British tanks and armoured cars in comparison with German armour and equipment. Churchill was furious. He had no patience with facts like these, no patience with delays. Nevertheless Britain could not send reinforcements. All that she could hope to do was to replace losses in men and equipment.

II

The changeover in command in the Middle East induced Dill and his Director of Military Operations, General Kennedy, to consider the old situation and the new with infinite care. While Sir John Dill composed a thoughtful letter to Auchinleck, welcoming him to his command and warning him of the pressures he must expect, Kennedy summed up the situation. He tended to blame Wavell for not resisting the Prime Minister more forcefully.

> From Whitehall great pressure was applied to Wavell to induce him to act rapidly, and, under this pressure, he advanced into Syria with much less strength than desirable, and in the Western Desert he attacked before in fact he was fully prepared. The fault was not Wavell's except in so far as he did not resist the pressure from Whitehall with sufficient vigour.[1]

But surely, if Wavell had made the position clear, as he had done, the fault was also with the Chiefs of Staff for not opposing Churchill 'with more vigour' at the source.

Why, oh why had Wavell not taken Tripoli, Greece or no Greece, Churchill or no Churchill! Kennedy wrote:

> It is inconceivable to imagine men like the Duke of Wellington or Douglas Haig acquiescing in a strategy such as that which has been, to all intents and purposes, dictated to the Middle East over the last six months. There have been at least four or five situations when a great commander would have preferred to resign rather than follow the course which has been suggested. Nothing can take the place of proper direction by the commander on the spot.[2]

The last brief sentence is the crux. It is, of course, incontrovertible, yet Churchill must have believed that his remote command in the field was preferable. The Chief of the Imperial General Staff could not and did not believe it, and did everything possible short of refusing flatly to permit Churchill to

[1]Sir John Dill to Auchinleck 'personal secret'. *Grand Strategy*, vol. II, pp. 530–2.
[2]Kennedy, *The Business of War*, pp. 137–141.

interfere in the way that he did. Both Dill and Wavell were ready to resign, and both offered to, yet they had a duty to go on serving while it was possible to do so with any advantage to Britain's cause. They were great men in their own right, and patriots. Dill urged Churchill either to 'back or to sack' Wavell, but this only served to infuriate the Prime Minister.

Kennedy's comparisons with Wellington and Douglas Haig seem to me to reveal the weakness of his case against Wavell. It may be inconceivable to imagine Wellington or Haig taking the kind of treatment Churchill meted out to Wavell, and afterwards to Auchinleck, but it is equally inconceivable to imagine the kind of incessant pressures Churchill exerted in 1940–1942 by means of high speed communications being exerted in 1815 or 1915.

I feel that both Dill and Wavell should have offered to resign in favour of Churchill taking command in the field, but denying him the right to 'command in the field' from Whitehall or Washington or wherever he happened to be. Surely Churchill might have been confronted with the meaning of his interference, however great an explosion it may have provoked. The fact is that Churchill was never forced to face the results of his actions, and he learned nothing from his mistakes.

John Connell in his brilliant studies of Wavell and Auchinleck, has stated the tragedy with compassion and profound understanding:[1]

> He [Churchill] would give Auchinleck everything but his confidence; he would do anything for him except let him alone to carry on with the heavy tasks which had been allotted to him. Churchill misunderstood Auchinleck just as he had misunderstood Wavell before him; but the origins of this misunderstanding lay in defects, not of their character or temperament, but of his own . . . the Prime Minister's will to victory was indomitable and tireless; he spared himself less than he spared anyone else, but had he not been so self-willed and so stubborn in his refusal to concede to his commanders the patient but vigilant understanding which they merited, many reverses and tribulations, much sorrow and many deaths might have been averted. He not only wore them down spiritually, he compelled them to act in haste or fatigue, and against their own judgment. The hurt which he did to them

[1]Connell, *Auchinleck,* p. 250.

counted nothing beside the damage which he wrought to the cause to which they, no less than he, devoted their skill, experience, courage and patriotism. The grief, therefore, must not be on Auchinleck's behalf, but on Churchill's and the country's.

At the time of the change in command Dill told Kennedy, 'I suppose you realise that we shall lose the Middle East?' But Kennedy did not take such a gloomy view, and neither did Auchinleck. It was true that if all the possible threats developed, not only from Libya, but from the north through Turkey and the north-east through the Caucasus and Persia, the British position would be desperate if not hopeless, but that these threats would all develop at once or in the immediate future was highly improbable.

It is worth repeating that the most important commitment in the Middle East was not to hold Egypt, but Abadan oil. Churchill might banish this to the back of his mind, but the Commander-in-Chief, Middle East could not do so. That was the 'citadel', and if a British Army had to fight to 'the death' it would be in defence of Abadan and not of Egypt. That is why, whatever Churchill might choose to believe, the Commander-in-Chief had to have a plan for 'the worst possible case'.

In spite of the reinforcements Britain had been able to provide, the British became slightly weaker when Auchinleck took command. Losses had been severe: 30,000 men with all their equipment, and 8,000 vehicles had been lost in Greece and Crete. Not all of these had been made good, and the fighting strength available to Auchinleck had not increased. Moreover so complex had been the operations in which Wavell had been involved that a complete re-grouping of forces was necessary, while new arrivals needed training and acclimatisation.

Perhaps the greatest difficulties in Middle-East Command arose from the great distances involved. It was 3,000 miles to India and 12,000 miles to Britain by the Cape route. Internally communications were bad. Egypt, as the Official Historian points out, had to supply 'three operational areas, Cyrenaica in the West, Palestine and Syria in the North East, the Soudan and Abyssinia in the South'. The numbers of men needed for the staging and for transport were great, and these were not the kind of facts and figures Churchill cared to contemplate, but which were essential to the understanding of the command and its ability to fight.

Infuriated by the situation, Churchill appointed General Haining, V.C.I.G.S., under Dill, to the role of 'Intendant General of the Army in the Middle East'. It was a good idea but it would not work. It led to the appointment of a 'Minister of State' to represent the War Cabinet on the spot. General Haining stayed on as a member of the Minister's War Council.

Thus the stage was set in the first days of Auchinleck's command. Both sides had suffered severely in the last ill-omened Wavell offensive, and neither side would be ready to strike again for at least three to four months. Churchill would for once have to abide in patience.

III

The battle, which Auchinleck and the newly formed Eighth Army fought in the Western Desert from the end of November until its final resolution in the first week of July, is, I believe, unique in the history of warfare. It may be difficult for those born in the first days of the Second World War, and growing through youth to manhood to be confronted by the unspeakable outrage 'war' has become, to believe that there was a time when it was otherwise, when human beings were not regarded as insects to be exterminated by subhuman devices of ever increasing obscenity, but it is true. I am not one to attempt to glamorise human conflict, yet at its best it did reveal the best as well as the worst of which human beings are capable.

The battle that ebbed and flowed over the vast 'natural' battlefield of the Western Desert, from one end to the other and back again, army against army, one kind of people against another kind of people without civilians intervening, was won and lost by men and not by machines. If this were the tragic game men had to play, or believed they had to play, this was one of the few natural arenas on which to play it. Those who played it were isolated, alone with each other in a wilderness of sand and heat and cold and insects, in which it was possible to pass within a few yards of the enemy without knowing it. It was a battle impossible to describe, made of a multitude of pieces, parts of an insoluble puzzle, and solved in the end by sheer nerve and courage and by a greater exhaustion on one side than the other. It was fought out to a standstill. It was obscured constantly by 'the fog of war', a succession of encounters, of advances and retreats demanding iron nerve, intuition, will and often great individual gallantry from commanders. From the soldiers it demanded faith in their commanders, their weapons, and in themselves. It also demanded endurance of a very high order.

It was almost certainly the last fight of a race of amateurs and romantics against professionals. In the end the amateurs prevailed, but by that time they had become 'professional' amateurs. They had set out to defend their interests in the Middle and Near East and they succeeded. The enemy had set out to conquer, and they failed. It was in a way the last great fight of the British, with all their vices and virtues, including the inability of most of their leaders in the field to know when they were beaten. It was a triumph on both sides for human values in the midst of killing. The British had, in the main, put down their plough-shares to take up the sword. Admittedly their plough-shares had become rusty; but so had their swords. It was a battle demanding the highest qualities of generalship, and in the main the enemy had the advantage in that respect, except that the British had a Commander-in-Chief—not the Army Commander—who was, in the view of his enemy, the greatest British general of the Second World War. It was this man who won, inasmuch as one man may win a battle involving many thousands of men.

It was, and is still, a sign of the times that the great struggle of the Eighth Army and its triumph over terrible difficulties, a battle that changed the course of war and the course of history, a battle compared with Gettysburg, is without an official name. Only belatedly was it acknowledged except by the enemy. The army that fought the battle has not been recognised. It does not wear the 'Africa Star', bestowed upon its successor army for capitalising upon its victory. It has nothing to show, but its honour in the last hours before honour vanished from the human scene. Henceforth people began to outnumber human beings at an ever increasing rate.[1] Soon it would be machines against machines; soon what once had been war would reach its ultimate obscenity; slaughter by remote control, extermination. Victory would seldom be to the brave.

The final outcome of the battle, known in its first phases as 'Crusader', is 'writ in sand'.

When Auchinleck arrived to take over his command it was all new to him. His chosen battlefield was 500 miles long from

[1]The old Indian in the film, *Little Big Man*.

the Egyptian frontier to the Gulf of Sirte: it was infinitely broad.
It was easier to get lost than to find the way; like the sea it
demanded good navigation. The general on the British side who
knew most about it was a prisoner of war.[1] A new man had to be
chosen to command the army which had yet to be formed,
trained and equipped. Meanwhile Auchinleck had come under
immediate fire from the Prime Minister. General Dill's 'secret
and personal' letter dated 26th June had not arrived, and did
not reach Auchinleck for a month. The pressures against which
Dill had warned him had not waited upon anything, and before
the end of July the Commander-in-Chief, Middle East, was in
London to meet the super-general and his Staff, and to resist
Churchill's pressures for an early offensive with all his skill and
knowledge. The facts Auchinleck presented impressed and convinced Churchill's Staff, but not Churchill, yet his Commander-
in-Chief impressed him deeply. Auchinleck was a magnificent-
looking man, a warrior, and there was no doubt almost from
the beginning that Churchill wanted this man, not to step down
from his high position, but none the less to command the new
Eighth Army in battle, and to defeat the German general,
Rommel. Only in dire emergency could Auchinleck take command of the army in the field, and such an emergency was not
to be thought of in these early months.

Auchinleck's first problem was to appoint an Army Commander for the new army. Whitehall favoured the appointment
of General Maitland Wilson, whose experience in the Western
Desert might have proved invaluable. In Auchinleck's view
Maitland Wilson would be more useful in commanding in the
north, preparing to meet any threat that might develop through
the Caucasus, to wind up the Syrian campaign and to deal with
the myriad administrative and defence problems with an army in
process of building, and low in the priorities. In the event
Auchinleck appointed General Sir Alan Cunningham to command the Eighth Army, to train and rebuild it with the utmost
speed, and to launch an offensive against the enemy at the earliest
possible moment. The pressures from Whitehall to attack prematurely would fall upon Auchinleck, but the pressures upon
Cunningham would be very great and far greater than any in
his previous experience. It is easy to see now—and some saw at
the time—that Cunningham was not a good choice. He had
done wonderfully well in the East-African campaign, but was

[1] Major-General Richard O'Connor.

without desert experience. Moreover the force he had commanded bore no comparison with the great army he must now
mould into a great attacking force. The job awed him as it
would have awed any man confronted with such a command for
the first time, but Cunningham was aware too of his lack of
seniority and experience in the company of his corps commanders. His Brigadier General, Staff, Galloway, was far more
experienced and his knowledge should have been invaluable,
but it is clearly not ideal for an army commander to feel in
certain vital ways inferior to his principal adviser. Galloway was
a forceful and outspoken character.

Meanwhile for the first time arms and equipment, trucks,
armour and aircraft, were reaching the Middle East in quantities
reflecting the seeming miracles of production being achieved at
home. Not only on paper, but to the casual eye it looked a
magnificent army in the making. The grave flaws were not
casually discernible. It was not apparent to the spectator that the
Crusader tanks had been rushed too swiftly into action, and much
else besides, including troops short of experience and training.
It proved impossible to make Churchill understand this even
when his own teams of advisers led finally by Attlee, the Deputy
Prime Minister, confirmed the worst: 'The upshot of his long
report of 2nd June was that the Crusader tank was pressed into
production before the pilot model had been adequately tested
and before defects had been detected and rectified. It was a
sad story.'[1]

Indeed it was. It confirmed the reports of Auchinleck, Stafford
Cripps, General Nye and others, but it was too late to be of
service. The Australian Minister, R. G. Casey, who replaced
Oliver Lyttelton as Minister of State, Middle East, wrote in his
diary, 24th June, 1942:

> After two and three-quarter years of war we are not making
> a tank that is any good. Our radio sets can't stand up to the
> jolting of a car or truck. We do not have amongst our anti-
> aircraft guns the equivalent of the German 88mm used in
> an anti-tank role . . . There is an understandable reason for lack
> of quantity, but lack of quality was another matter.[2]

The list of faulty equipment from leaky petrol-containers to
armour is formidable. It is, however, not quite true to say that

[1]*Grand Strategy,* vol. III, part II, p. 441.
[2]Ibid.

England had not an anti-aircraft gun the equivalent of the 88mm. German weapon, for as General Pile, C-in-C, AA Command, pointed out, the 3.7 could have been used in an anti-tank role. Mistakes which we could ill afford were made constantly until the end of the battle. Our armour, outgunned by the enemy, should not have engaged in direct confrontations with the enemy armour. Nor should it have been split up into small groups against which the enemy was always able to concentrate superior force. The infantry was an essential ingredient on both sides, and on the enemy side it was properly integrated with the armour. The British infantry was too often naked against enemy onslaught, deserted, it believed, by the armour that should have been its shield. Infantry, armour and artillery were not integrated as a fighting force.

The great battle was fought in four main phases, the first a prelude, followed by three sombre movements. By the time the prelude was at an end the new army commander was overwrought to the point of nervous exhaustion. The strain had been very great.

Immediately before the battle opened in the first week of November, Auchinleck wrote to his old friend, General Ismay, at the very core of Whitehall power, and gave a clear insight into the nature of the battle about to be fought. He wrote:

> I am not nervous about CRUSADER, but I wonder if you and others who sit at the council table with you realise what a peculiar battle it is to be, and how everything hangs on the tactical issue of one day's fighting, and on one man's tactical ability on that day. It is something quite different to battles as we knew them. All these months of labour and thought can be set at nought in one afternoon; rather a terrifying thought?[1]

Almost certainly General Cunningham, the Army Commander, was aware of the magnitude of the task confronting him, if not of the nature of the battle, and that he faced a master of desert warfare and tactics, a commander of exceptional dash and boldness, supported by generals of great experience. The British did not lack good generals at a divisional level, but as an army they did not feel 'commanded' as did their enemy; they lacked the spiritual, mental and physical cohesion of an army

[1] Ismay, *Memoirs,* p. 271.

under a commander of absolute professional competence and confidence. Moreover the British tended to be individualists, capable of great deeds serving under the right man, but the right man was not to be found, save in those moments of grave crisis, confusion and defeat when the Commander-in-Chief left his post at the heart of his command to save the army.

General Cunningham launched his army into the attack on 18th November, taking the enemy by surprise, but not off balance. Early reports created the impression of success, but it was soon clear that communications between units, formations and Army command were often inaccurate. Reports of enemy losses were greatly exaggerated, and British losses underestimated. News released prematurely from Cairo gave a misleading and over-optimistic impression, and on Sunday, 23rd November, Churchill, who had been studying the battle-ground with General Kennedy at very long range, and impatient for hard news, sent a telegram to Auchinleck 'pointing out the possibilities of bold and far-reaching action in the enemy's rear'.[1] This was almost at the precise moment when the enemy planned a daring action to drive through to disrupt the British rear, Rommel, with some reason, believing that he had the mastery of the British armour and that the Eighth Army was as good as beaten. It was a bold gamble designed to create confusion and undermine morale. It was typical of Rommel. The German armour had proved itself superior to the British in all departments, save only gallantry, and gallantry was not enough. No one on either side knew precisely the shape of the battle, or how grave were the losses on either side.

On the night of the 23rd Rommel ordered General Ravenstein to muster all available armour, motorised infantry and anti-tank guns, and make a dash for the Egyptian frontier straight through the centre of the Eighth Army. He was convinced that he had the chance to snatch victory out of confusion. At the same time Rommel directed his main armour to strike against Eighth Army Headquarters while he followed up Ravenstein's drive in person.

On the 24th, Cunningham, preparing his own drive against a 'beaten enemy', suddenly realised the extent of his armoured losses and sent urgent messages to Auchinleck. The C-in-C reacted instantly. That night he reached Cunningham's H.Q. to find the General resolved on retreat 'to save Egypt'. Galloway,

[1]Kennedy, *The Business of War*, p. 180.

Eighth Army Chief of Staff, left a clear account of Auchinleck's immediate effect. It is not your business to save Egypt, Auchinleck told Cunningham. The Army would not retreat, nor would it go on the defensive. It would attack. The key passages of Auchinleck's bold appreciation and orders were:

'You will continue to attack the enemy relentlessly using all your resources even to the last tank. Your main immediate object will be as always to destroy the enemy tank forces. Your ultimate object remains the conquest of Cyrenaica and then advance on Tripoli.'[1]

The Directive then set out how the immediate tasks should be tackled. Auchinleck's presence had changed everything. Galloway, who had been deeply worried and had sent his own urgent messages to Cairo, was deeply impressed. Unhappily Cunningham was no longer able to respond with the drive and enthusiasm essential.

The events of the three days and nights of 23rd, 24th, and 25th November, 1941, are a microcosm of the desert war waged by Auchinleck and his generals from November to July 1942. There had been nothing like it before, nor was there afterwards. It was a campaign of bluff, faith, intuition and high courage. Morale was as important as all the armaments in the sense that without it all would be lost. The 'dense fog of war' was the central danger.

Auchinleck was one of the rare commanders with the character, and the unrelenting resolution and offensive spirit to fight and win such a battle. The misfortune, and a source of constant frustration to Churchill—and to others—was that the generals chosen by Auchinleck to command Eighth Army were not only too junior, but lacking in the high qualities to wage a campaign of this nature against a brilliant and bold commander like Rommel. Auchinleck was more than a match for Rommel, but he was too senior to step down from his great command. It is difficult to imagine a more exasperating dilemma. It happens, to a degree, up and down the chain of command.

The battle within a battle fought in those early days, the near defeat turned into victory by Auchinleck, could only be fought by men on the spot. There was no clear pattern. Neither Churchill, nor anyone else in Whitehall could know what was going on, or give useful advice, but Churchill was fully aware of Auchinleck's achievement: 'By his personal action Auchinleck

[1]Connell, *Auchinleck*, p. 365.

thus saved the battle and proved his outstanding qualities as a commander in the field.'

Rommel was discovering the same truth, recording it in his diary. The situation added to Churchill's exasperation. Immediately upon his return to Cairo Auchinleck had felt it essential to remove Cunningham. He did it with sorrow, writing a personal note to Cunningham, and to his brother, the Admiral commanding the Mediterranean fleet. No one disputed Auchinleck's decision, but Churchill and his advisers longed for Auchinleck to take command in person. It was not enough that Auchinleck should keep a close watch on his new appointment to command the Eighth Army, Major-General Ritchie, lately his deputy Chief of Staff. No one liked the appointment, and there were others better qualified, but Auchinleck considered that it would be dangerous in the extreme to risk removing generals, like Godwin Austen and Willoughby Norrie, or Gott, while they were involved in the battle. The German drive, careering right through the centre of 30 Corps and several lesser headquarters, created appalling confusion, but confusion is seldom one-sided. British transport was roaring headlong back to the frontier, but the troops forward in contact with the enemy, bravely led by men like Gatehouse, not only stood firm, but attacked with great flair and gallantry.

Meanwhile on the night of 24th Rommel himself was within a hair's-breadth of capture. Having spent the night at the 4th Indian divisional headquarters, unknown to anyone including himself, he managed to get a lift back to safety with his general, Cruewell. The one enormous piece of luck the British had was that the enemy passed within easy striking distance of the two field maintenance centres, on which the Eighth Army depended.

Throughout this crisis of many and obscure parts Auchinleck was a rock of absolute confidence and strength. He thought that: 'Rommel was probably in as bad shape as we were. I certainly gambled,' he wrote. Rommel's senior staff officer recorded that Auchinleck's 'decision to order the offensive was certainly one of the great decisions of the war'.[1]

In the midst of battle Auchinleck was impervious even to the demands of Churchill. Back in Air Vice-Marshal Coningham's caravan, enjoying a brief hour of relaxation he exuded

[1]Connell, *Auchinleck,* p. 369 (and see: Eve Curie, *Journey among Warriors,* p. 52).

an impression of remarkable tranquillity, noted by Eve Curie, the war correspondent, who had the good fortune to be sitting quietly in a corner. She recorded Auchinleck as saying, almost to himself: 'He [Rommel] is making a desperate effort, but he will not get very far. That column of tanks simply cannot get supplies. I am sure of this.'

The second movement of the battle had begun, and at first it seemed that success would crown Ritchie's offensive. By the first week in January hopes were beginning to be disappointed, and it was clear that Ritchie, not lacking in confidence, was a very difficult man to control, self-opinionated, and difficult to advise. While appearing to take the advice, even of his Commander-in-Chief, he went his own way. Moreover he had begun to interfere directly with the tactical handling of troops in various small actions, by-passing his corps and divisional commanders, so that Godwin Austen felt compelled to resign. Auchinleck, unhappily, felt bound to support his Army Commander, but his grave doubts of Ritchie were hardening.

Before the end of February the British offensive had petered out very far short of victory, and both sides began to regroup, to heal their wounds, and to prepare for what must be the final movement, the decisive battle. Early in March, Brigadier Dorman Smith, Auchinleck's Deputy Chief of Staff, who had contributed to O'Connor's great victory and probably knew as much as or more than anyone else about the handling of armour in the desert, went forward to examine and report on the command situation. Dorman Smith formed the opinion that Ritchie was lacking in imagination and stubborn. A new commander of the army should be found.

Auchinleck and Dorman Smith, knowing and understanding each other very well, met gloomily and alone to consider the situation. Auchinleck felt that it would be dangerous to morale to sack a second army commander within three months. He resolved to keep as tight a rein as possible on Ritchie while preparing for the final decisive clash. It was a tragic mistake. In retrospect it is clear that Auchinleck should have taken command himself. It would have pleased Churchill, fuming in growing impatience, unable to reconcile himself to the long pause while both sides prepared, and nagging Auchinleck constantly. Immediately after Cunningham's failure Churchill had tried to cajole Auchinleck into taking direct control of the Army:

'C.I.G.S. and I both wonder whether, as you saved the battle once you should not go up again and win it now. Your presence on the spot will be an inspiration to all. However, this of course is entirely for you to judge.'

Auchinleck replied: 'I considered very carefully whether I should not myself take Cunningham's place in command of Eighth Army, I realise well what hangs on this battle, but concluded that I was more useful at G.H.Q. where I could see the whole battle and retain a proper sense of proportion. I shall go forward to visit [Ritchie] of course as required.'

This might have been wise had Ritchie been amenable and co-operative, providing his Chief with accurate reports of his actions. He could not think that Ritchie would deliberately flout his authority and ignore his advice, and even his orders.

Auchinleck was justified in his first refusal to take command, but in early March I am sure that he was wrong. The appointment of Ritchie had been regarded as temporary, and it was a pity that Churchill, fully aware of this, should have announced the appointment in a way that led parliament and people to believe that Ritchie was permanent. No doubt Churchill could have found a way out of this embarrassment, and had Auchinleck taken command in March he would have been relieved of the intensive pressures Churchill brought to bear. Churchill remained incapable, despite the irrefutable facts, of grasping the simple necessities and the dangers of going off at half-cock.

The 'Crusader' battle had petered out in early January, Rommel withdrawing to regroup and Ritchie failing to appreciate the skills of his opponent, or to learn from his experience. He had held a victorious position and failed dismally to grasp his opportunity. In spite of clear warnings from Auchinleck, Ritchie went his own way, failing to understand that it was fatal to dissipate his armour and offer it up to the enemy in 'bits and pieces'.

'They have been trained to fight as divisions, I hope, and fight as divisions they should,' Auchinleck wrote, 'Norrie must handle them as a corps commander, and thus be able to take advantage of the flexibility which the fact of having two formations gives him.'[1]

For Ritchie, while appearing to agree and to carry out his commander's wishes, ignored his advice and instructions.

The British weakness in handling their armour had long been apparent to the enemy, as well as to Auchinleck. Ritchie's

[1]Connell, *Auchinleck*, pp. 506–7.

failings had given the enemy strength beyond his true resources, and at a crucial phase in the decisive battle Rommel wrote in his diary: 'I was full of hope about the further course of the battle. For Ritchie had thrown his armour into the battle piecemeal and at different times and had thus given us the chance of engaging them on each occasion with just enough of our own tanks. This splitting up of the British armoured brigades was incomprehensible. [1]

In January a counter-stroke by Rommel at a moment when Ritchie had his forward troops off balance enabled the enemy to regain Cyrenaica. The consequent loss of British forward airfields added to the grave threats against Malta. At the same time the disasters in the Far East demanded reinforcements from wherever they could be found, and the Middle East was weakened.

The price of Ritchie's failure was heavy, and the three months March to May presented Churchill with opportunities to harass Auchinleck unmercifully. In March he had urged the Commander-in-Chief to come to London, but Auchinleck had felt unable to comply. There was nothing he could say to Churchill that the Prime Minister did not know already, and it might have been a dangerous moment for Auchinleck to leave his post at the heart of the Middle-East Command. The course of the immense struggle in Soviet Russia remained unpredictable and ominous, posing a threat to the British northern flank should the Germans decide to break through the Caucasus. Churchill believed, of course, that Auchinleck was merely avoiding further direct confrontation with him.

It was a period of extreme crisis, yet lacking the inspiration of a Dunkirk, and giving rise to misgivings at home, and growing discontent with Churchill's leadership. Indeed Churchill was exposed to greater pressures than any he imposed upon others, but they were pressures of his own making, of the immense task he had undertaken, no particle of which would he relinquish. The struggle was the breath of life to him and too often the breath of life seemed to be getting short. Age was beginning to tell, and poor health beset him increasingly and added to his impatience, without seeming to diminish his mental energy. He was answerable to no man, save only to himself and to 'parliament'.

While the Middle East was the only battlefield where the British might hope for success, Churchill naturally focussed upon

[1] *The Rommel Papers* (edited by Liddell Hart).

it, but it seems doubtful that he fully realised its importance, that in the Middle East the war could be lost. Churchill needed success as a means of impressing his powerful allies. In the spring of 1942 success seemed very far off.

In March General Alexander had taken over command in Burma in the hour when the Japanese threat to Rangoon was overwhelming. Joined by General Slim from Persia to assume command of an army corps, Alexander conducted the evacuation of Rangoon with great skill. The British were beginning to find their generals, but there was not much light as yet in the Far-Eastern sky, nor anywhere else.

Thus the delays in the Western Desert irked Churchill gravely, and he would not let Auchinleck, whose offensive mindedness and resolution were beyond all doubt, fight his own campaign in his own way. At the same time his messages, suggestions, exhortations to General Wavell in the Far East had shown very little sign of abating, while growing marginally less offensive in tone from those to which he had subjected his general in the desert. Moreover the Far East was far away, and would not be decisive for Britain. Auchinleck now bore the brunt of Churchill's long-range super-generalship patiently, courteously and resolutely. His appreciation of the situation in late February had angered Churchill, partly because he could find little support in it for his own views. On 2nd March, the C.I.G.S. noted:

> Another bad Monday . . . found P.M. had drafted a bad wire for Auchinleck in which he poured abuse on him for not attacking sooner. Without it being possible for him to be familiar with all aspects of the situation . . . he is trying to force him to attack at an earlier date than is thought advisable and, what is more, tried to obtain his ends by an offensive wire. Thank heaven we were able to stop the wire and re-word it.

Perhaps they should have let the wire go in its original form, perhaps provoking Auchinleck to a blunt, but courteous reply. A series of telegrams now passed between the Middle East and Whitehall, as though the commanders-in-chief of the three services and the Minister of State were a bunch of incompetents. On 15th March Churchill telegraphed:

'Your appreciation of February 27 continues causing deepest anxiety here, both to the Chiefs of Staff and Defence Committee. I therefore regret extremely your inability to come home for consultation. The delay you have in mind will endanger safety of Malta.'

The telegram continued full of pained suggestions, revealing Churchill's absolute disbelief in Auchinleck's assessment of the Army's strength and readiness. 'I have done everything in my power to give you continuous support at heavy cost to the whole war. It would give me the greatest pain to feel that mutual understanding had ceased.'

Churchill, of course, was incapable of mutual understanding, nor was he receptive to facts which conflicted with his fixed view. This was the time when Churchill decided to send Sir Stafford Cripps and the V.C.I.G.S., Sir Archibald Nye, to examine the situation for themselves. His distrust of Auchinleck seemed absolute, and it was wrong that Auchinleck should continue in command, alone, without support on the eve of decisive action. General Dill would have been adamant about that. The truth was, I believe, that Churchill dared not sack his great commander. Had he done so and the decisive battle been lost in consequence, as it surely would have been, irreparable disaster would have befallen not only the Prime Minister but Britain. His dreams of North-African and Mediterranean conquest would have been over, and all that might have confronted Britain would have been a miserable compromise peace. There would be time enough to vent his spleen when the battle was won, and he was safe.

Meanwhile Cripps and Nye confirmed every paragraph of Auchinleck's appreciation, and Cripps telegraphed: 'If you accept situation as detailed in my long telegram, as I much hope you will, it would I am sure help if you could send Auchinleck a short friendly telegram expressing your satisfaction and that he will have all possible help from you to hit the target at the appointed time.'

It was a forlorn hope. Churchill was furious. He sent an urgent telegram to Nye ordering him to go into the situation more deeply, but the result was the same. There was now no possibility that decent relations could be restored between the super-general at home and his commander in the field, nevertheless Churchill would not hesitate to use Auchinleck for his salvation when the time came.

In more normal circumstances Auchinleck must have resigned, but the struggle in the desert transcended personalities, and Auchinleck in his setting was even more indispensable than the Prime Minister was in his. The battle must be won in spite of Churchill. If the battle should be lost it would not be simply Malta that would be lost, but the war. There were few then, and there may be some even now, who doubt the calamity that would have faced Britain. Auchinleck and the German high command certainly understood, and saw clearly the strategic realities. The British Prime Minister and the German General, Rommel, in the desert 'concentrated their attention on the Mediterranean and North Africa'.[1]

It is doubtful if Churchill was capable of seeing the situation in its true light. An aura of the romantic did not simply cling to him; he was a romantic, and also a lone adventurer, a seeker of power who had been training himself to fight a war since the nursery, and now he had a war it was his war. The present, immensely real to him, was at the same time a projection of his life. War was for him basically a game, *the* game, the most exciting and dramatic game there was, but it was too personal, he was too involved in the destruction of Rommel, to understand the strategic context. It was an obsession. The struggle was not an up-to-date version of Kitchener and Omdurman, when the Empire was still in flower, or of Allenby and Lawrence. It was in 1942 a struggle for survival.

Nevertheless, seen in isolation, the struggle in the Middle East was as 'romantic' in its fashion—and braver—than all that had gone before. Wavell and Auchinleck, together with O'Connor and with Stirling, leading his long-range desert group, could take their rightful places in any gallery of heroes out of the past. But these men of 1940/41/42 were not adventurers, even though they were adventurous. Adventurers are often wonderful men, but in the context of modern war their day is done. Wars of this magnitude could not be won by them or even influenced by them, and Churchill was an adventurer, an adventurer in war, politics and on the world stage. It was his terrible weakness. And now, angered and frustrated, his mind ranged over the military hierarchy seeking a replacement for Auchinleck, while knowing and resenting bitterly his feeling that Auchinleck alone might save the day. Brooke and Ismay constantly attempted to dissuade Churchill, and succeeded, but Churchill could never forgive Auchinleck for not being a vassal, his general, his champion. Worse still, Churchill did not fully understand the make-up of Auchinleck's command, the urgent demands upon it, the difficulties within it.

[1] See: Connell, *Auchinleck,* p. 481.

Brooke, a 'Flanders' man and without real sympathy with the 'Indians', nevertheless wrote to the Commander-in-Chief:

> I am sorry that you should have had the difficult times that you have been through lately, and I can assure you that it was not owing to lack of efforts to save you from it ... We have now got the P.M. to accept your dates and arguments, but not in a very pleasant manner. He is accepting the delays only under protest, and with little grace! It was a pity you could not come home ... I do not think you realise how difficult he is to handle at times.

Ismay wrote in similar vein, but Ismay was under the spell of Churchill, and absurdly sentimental. He had himself been called every name under the sun, he wrote, except coward. He took the rough with the smooth, day after day, and did not understand that that was exactly what he was for: he was not commanding an army in a distant field, but was his master's voice and whipping boy. 'The outstanding point is that although the P.M. is at present at cross-purposes—and even loggerheads—with you,' he wrote to Auchinleck, 'this is a purely temporary phase of a relationship which is marked by mutual esteem, and I might also say affection.'

Dear old faithful Ismay, protected by his innocence, hero-worshipping the 'head boy', the 'captain of school'! 'One more point,' he wrote, 'you are both indispensable, the P.M. as the only possible national leader; and you as a universally admired commander of perhaps the most important force we have. And so you have *got* to make it up.'[1]

Shades of Mrs. Everest!

But there was no way of making it up, not even by launching a heterogeneous army prematurely into battle, unevenly trained and difficult to weld into a tight command. The dominion governments retained an absolute right to control the manner in which their troops should be used, and Auchinleck and his Army Commander always had to take account of their feelings and the special powers of some of his most important divisional commanders. He could not simply order and command Australians, New Zealanders, South Africans to do this or that. Their agreement must be sought, often causing grievous delays. And they were among the finest troops he had. He had also lost some of his best Australian divisions to the Far East, and

[1] Ismay, *Memoirs*.

thus to the more immediate defence of their homelands. The disasters in the Far East drained his strength, not dangerously, but sufficiently to compel him to adjust his timings. He pressed ahead as fast as he could, consistent with reasonable hopes of victory over his German and Italian opponents. He was very much alive to the grave dangers threatening Malta, and the need to regain Cyrenaica. Moreover, he had always to be alert to the dangers threatening his northern front, to the possibility that the Germans might decide to thrust through the Caucasus in strength, especially if Rommel were successful in Egypt. The progress of the great battles looming on the German southern flank in Soviet Russia was, therefore, of overwhelming importance, and in the early summer of 1942 the outcome was unpredictable. Unlike Churchill and Rommel he could not focus his entire attention on the Western Desert to the exclusion of all else. Tobruk, for example, had become an obsession with Churchill, whereas it was a serious running sore to the Mediterranean fleet, as well as an irritant to Rommel, and in certain favourable circumstances a useful sally point. Many thought that Wavell had made an error in holding Tobruk after the failure of 'Battle Axe'. It had proved very costly, and Auchinleck had warned Whitehall, in complete agreement, that it might be wise to evacuate Tobruk in certain circumstances. Churchill, of course, knew this very well.[1]

One thing was certain, Churchill would never forgive Auchinleck for being Auchinleck any more than he could forgive Wavell for being Wavell. They were servants of Britain, Britain's generals, and not Churchill's.

Churchill would never understand the strategic realities in the Middle East, and as that year of disasters everywhere moved towards the final crisis, he was under very heavy political pressures from which only military success could save him. And he was resolved to survive at all costs. Meanwhile Auchinleck was his champion.

Late in May the issue of when the Eighth Army would attack was resolved as Auchinleck had believed it would be by Rommel launching his final assault on 26th May. The Eighth Army was well placed to defend itself, and General Ritchie faced his final test.

[1]Operation Instruction no. 110, 19th January, 1942.

CHAPTER ELEVEN

Climacteric of a Super-General

I

IN JUNE 1942, CHURCHILL FOUND HIMSELF FACING A CENSURE motion upon his return from the Washington Conference, while Mussolini was preparing for a triumphal entry into Egypt, and disaster seemed imminent in the Middle East. The battle of Gazala began in favourable circumstances, for Eighth Army had never developed a clear theme. Ritchie had never understood confusion, and was incapable of the kind of leadership demanded in the circumstances. Before the end of June it was clear that, as the Official Historians commented, 'the battle was slipping away from him'. It is an understatement; Ritchie had never got hold of it. He had been devious with his Commander-in-Chief and failed to carry out his precise orders. His corps and divisional commanders, without clear orders, were equally confused.

In that desperate hour when it at last became clear that the Eighth Army was rapidly retreating in virtual defeat, General Auchinleck, Commander-in-Chief, Middle East, despite the threats from the northern front, took personal command of the Eighth Army in the field, resolved to keep the army in being at all costs, resolved to win. He took with him his Deputy Chief of Staff, Major-General Eric Dorman Smith, to fight the battle with him, to live rough with the troops, to lead them as they had not been led before.

On 28th June Churchill telegraphed Auchinleck: 'I am very glad you have taken command. Do not vex yourself with anything except the battle. Fight it wherever it flows. Nothing matters but destroying the enemy's armed and armoured forces. A strong team of reinforcements is approaching. We are sure you are going to win in the end.'

Churchill's faith in Auchinleck as an army commander in battle was immense, and he had never understood why the Commander-in-Chief of a vast area, seriously threatened on all sides, could not take command of an army at any given moment, whatever else might demand his urgent attention.

The next day, 29th June, Churchill telegraphed Auchinleck a second time: 'When I speak in the vote of censure debate on Thursday, about 4 p.m., I deem it necessary to announce that you have taken the command in supersession to Ritchie as from June 25.'

This was not only the time of decision in the Middle East, and perhaps for Churchill himself, but also the climax of the war for Britain. In the true meaning of words all that followed would be anticlimax, the events flowing naturally from that hour. It would be, whatever happened, Churchill's climacteric as a super-general, the end of his interference on the battlefields and his attempts to command and control Britain's generals, but not without a struggle. When it was over, and he knew that he was 'saved' he reacted in a manner that will forever reveal the flaws in his character, without detracting from his immense service to Britain at the time of Dunkirk. He wanted, when he saw his opportunity to recreate that image, for here was another Dunkirk, at least as terrible in the event of failure as the first. Churchill wanted to make it his own, and for at least eleven years until the first official histories, and a mass of information slowly became available, he was successful. The best that may be said of it may be that it was not done by malice aforethought, but by day-to-day perception of his opportunities. It is not a pleasant story.

As soon as Auchinleck reached the battlefield to discover that troops which he had believed to be forward were in fact retreating to the Egyptian frontier, it became clear that Ritchie's intention to stand at Mersa Matruh was no longer tenable.

Dorman Smith wrote: 'The primary decision was whether the defensive battle now projected in the Matruh area should be fought to a finish or whether Eighth Army should be given time to regroup by a further withdrawal.' Dorman Smith believed the dispositions of the Army at Matruh were unsound, and could not be readjusted in time.

Had Auchinleck taken over on June 22nd it would have been possible to deploy Eighth Army at Matruh on much the same lines as were adopted at El Alamein from July 1st onwards and the results would have been similar, but Ritchie was still in command and his two corps were divided by a gap of some twenty miles with an almost undefended gap between and the bulk of the armour even further south. Rommel had only to keep motoring to place himself between the separated portions of the Eighth Army and everything indicated that the Army command and the corps commanders lacked the nous to be able to close the gap. Correctly both of Eighth Army's Corps should have been deployed for battle, 'shoulder to shoulder' . . . Had this been done and the armour moved from the southern flank into central located Army reserve, Rommel's impetuous advance would have met a powerful force in place of a vacuum . . .[1]

Auchinleck and his C.G.S. had done some vital homework in the aircraft on the way to the battlefield. By the time the aircraft landed they had decided to withdraw Eighth Army from Matruh to El Alamein and there to stand and fight. Moreover they had decided on entirely new methods of fighting Rommel. The Army would fight as one, all formations and units working together, all with an integrated role. Above all the front would be kept fluid.

The 25th June was almost too late. The dispositions were so bad that 'no matter who was actually in command, the Eighth Army, so handled, was doomed to failure'. Chaos and confusion were escalating by the time Auchinleck was able to impose himself upon the Army, to strip it of all excess baggage. Lorry after lorry carried bulging loads of non-essential gear away from from the battlefield. Personal caravans were dispensed with. Mobility and comfort did not go together, and Auchinleck himself pitched his tent beside his map wagon on the sand, sleeping in his bedroll with his C.G.S. close at hand.

He had cracked down heavily on the Rommel myth. He instructed all his commanders that the adversary was no superman and no more talk on these lines would be tolerated.

Early on 1st July Auchinleck's tactical headquarters lay just east of 30 Corps some eighteen miles east-south-east of Alamein, and from that place one of the great decisive battles of the Second World War was fought over the next four days. At daybreak of 1st July the guns of 30 Corps were going full blast and Dorman Smith wrote in his pocket diary: 'Battle of El Alamein.'

[1] Private papers of Dorman Smith.

By evening on 3rd July Auchinleck believed that Rommel had shot his bolt, and he began to take the German-Italian Army apart, concentrating upon the Italians, compelling the German armour to rush about to their rescue. The danger was over for Britain, and 4th July was finally recognised as the end of Rommel's threat. The resolution then was to destroy him. On 13th July Rommel's counter-strokes met devastating artillery fire, and at last 'Rommel was dancing to our tune,' and was forced onto the defensive. It proved impossible to destroy him, mainly because the corps commanders were unable to respond to their orders with sufficient speed. The British Army had, like Rommel's, fought itself to a standstill. There were other factors. The command of dominion troops was never easy. Pienaar, the South African, had been consistently difficult, and had to be handled with care. For a precious forty-eight hours Auchinleck tried in vain to persuade the Australian, General Morshead, to attack. The discussion, in spite of its dreadful urgency, was conducted with calm and courtesy, but Morshead, as he had a right to do, insisted on consulting his Government. Freyberg, the very brave New Zealand commander, a friend of Churchill's, was invariably difficult.

Meanwhile 'on the other side of the hill' Field-Marshal Rommel was keeping a diary and writing regularly to his wife:

> It was essential to do everything possible to bring about a British collapse in the Near East before any considerable shipments of arms could arrive from Britain or the United States. The British were sparing no effort to master the situation. They organised the move of fresh troops into the Alamein line with admirable speed. Their leading men had clearly realised that the next battle in Africa would determine the situation for a long time to come, and were looking at things very cool-headedly.

For five weeks of incessant fighting Rommel tried everything he knew, in vain. 'General Auchinleck had taken personal command of the operations at El Alamein,' he wrote, 'handling his forces with remarkable skill...His appreciation of the situation seemed admirably cool: he did not allow himself to be led by any of our moves into adopting a second-class solution. This became very clear as the battle went on.'[1]

[1] *The Rommel Papers.*

Auchinleck has paid glowing tribute to the genius of his C.G.S. Major-General Dorman Smith. It was Dorman Smith's plan to destroy the Italian formations, forcing the Afrika Corps to rush about in constant attempts to save their allies, but in the end that was impossible.

'We were forced to conclude that the Italians were no longer capable of holding their line,' Rommel wrote, and 'On July 17th every last German reserve had to be thrown in to beat off the British attacks . . . we were going to have to count ourselves lucky if we managed to go on holding our line at all.'[1]

It was, as it transpired, a tragedy for Auchinleck and Dorman Smith that they were unable to complete the destruction of the enemy, even though they had saved Egypt and Britain. Liddell Hart states very clearly Auchinleck's insoluble difficulties:

In analysis it becomes evident that the Commonwealth composition of the forces did not work out well for the commonweal . . . During the course of the battle the commanders of the various Commonwealth contingents were subject to a bombardment of anxious questions and cautionary admonitions from their respective Governments . . . This bombardment 'from the far rear' was a serious distraction for commanders in the midst of a decisive battle. It was a command problem which would have defied a Marlborough.[2]

'One last push and P.A.A., stretched so tight, might burst and collapse like a pricked balloon, and Eighth Army had nothing left with which to deliver a coup de grace,' wrote Dorman Smith.[3]

Meanwhile Dorman Smith and Brigadier Kitsch, Chief Engineer of the Eighth Army, designed the impregnable defence plan from which a new attack could be mounted by mid-September, at the same time Dorman Smith had devised the Alam Halfa trap, praying that the day would come when, the enemy, in desperation, would invite his own total destruction.

On 26th July Dorman Smith worked all day and night in the map caravan to produce his appreciation and plan, dated 27th July. This appreciation 'was to acquire a unique historical importance as the major piece of documentary evidence which

[1] Ibid.
[2] Liddell Hart, *The Tanks,* vol. II.
[3] Private papers of Dorman Smith.

was strong enough over a period of eleven years, to supply grounds for challenging the elaborate apparatus of myth, misunderstanding and mischief by which Auchinleck's handling of his command and his removal from it were surrounded'.[1]

It was eighteen years before the official histories recorded this forgotten and suppressed battle. A Panzer army report of 21st July revealed that 'the Germans and Italians had lost much of their field artillery and about half their anti-tank guns: their men were reduced to a third of their strength and it was stated that since the 10th July the Italians had lost the equivalent of four divisions.'

Auchinleck continued to strive for the destruction of the enemy until the end of the month, and then concluded that he would have to wait for mid-September before he would be able to gain the necessary strength. 'Plans were to be made for a new British offensive, but the programme of reinforcements would not allow this to start before mid-September.'[2]

In paying tribute to the Eighth Army the Official Historian wrote:

A special word of recognition is due to those who fought through this period in the most trying conditions, parched by heat and sandstorms and pestered by loathsome swarms of flies. That horrible affliction, the desert sore, was common. These and other forms of the ten plagues had to be endured day after day in cramped or exposed positions or in roasting hot tanks. Small wonder that tempers were short or that strain and malaise set hasty tongues wagging. But it is to the lasting credit of the troops that, although they suffered heavily, they nevertheless responded to every demand made upon them. This could not have happened with a dispirited army . . . But underlying all this was the plain fact that the fabulous Rommel had been stopped.[3]

None of this was recognised, neither their great fight, nor their morale. Their Army 'wore no star'. The 'hasty tongues' had achieved more than all the fighting, and the Eighth Army and its commanders were discredited.

'It was left to the enemy,' as Liddell Hart wrote, to put

[1] Connell, *Auchinleck*, p. 684.
[2] I.S.O. Playfair, *The Mediterranean and the Middle East*, pp. 359–60.
[3] Ibid.

Auchinleck's achievement in true proportion and be first in paying him due tribute.' Steadily there were others. Some had been dedicated to the task from that time onwards.[1]

John Connell has written:

> By what strange and ugly combination of factors 'were Auchinleck, and the officers and men of the Eighth Army who served under him, not merely deprived of the full credit of this victory, but told to their faces by lesser men that they had not even achieved it, that they had gone down in defeat and retreat, from which miraculously they were retrieved more than a month later.'[2]

II

July was a month of suspense and strain, in Churchill's own words. It was a great deal more than that. It was the month in which the direction of the war was moving out of his hands, but that was not immediately apparent. It had been evident to the very well informed at the time of *Arcadia* that this day would come, that the United States would be the dominant partner, the callers of the tune. Perhaps even Churchill had known it, accepted it, and sought to delay the take-over, and even to retain a kind of joint command with the President until the end. When he had called himself the President's 1st Lieutenant he had perhaps realised very well how things must be. But he had hoped, and worked, and played the super-general, striving to bring the conflict to a point where he could not be superseded.

I think it is doubtful that Churchill allowed such thoughts

[1]Compton Mackenzie, *Eastern Epic,* was among the first in 1951; John Connell, *Auchinleck,* came in 1959, Corelli Barnett, *Desert Generals,* in 1960; I.S.O. Playfair, *The Mediterranean and the Middle East,* vol. III (H.M.S.O.) in 1960; *The Rommel Papers,* edited by B. H. Liddell Hart, in 1953; R. W. Thompson, *The Montgomery Legend,* in 1967; and some others. But for a generation the 1st Battle of Alamein, the decisive battle marking the turn of the tide in the Second World War, was unknown to the British people and 'had not taken place'. In 1958 Sir J. Wheeler Bennett, in *King George VI,* p. 542, wrote: 'The actual turning of the tide in the Second World War may be accurately determined as the first week of July 1942. After Rommel was repulsed at El Alamein on July 2 and turned away in deference to British resistance, the Germans never again mounted a major offensive in North Africa.'

[2]Connell, *Auchinleck,* p. 637.

to have more than a momentary occupation of his full consciousness. It was an inner knowledge, never to be openly
admitted, but giving him, in the end, a profound sense of personal
failure, of being robbed of victory. His entire *raison d'être* was to
make this war his triumph, to fight this war, his war, his way,
and to win. It was his tragedy that he failed.

It is essential to try to understand some of the innermost
feelings of the Prime Minister in July in order to understand his
actions in August. Perhaps it is impossible; there are no facts
about a man's innermost feelings.

The month opened in the hour of the supreme crisis in the
Western Desert, the crisis for Egypt. In Cairo the 'chairborne
army', convinced of defeat, was burning papers, its morale non-
existent. Cairo 'seethed and bubbled like some hell-brew, the
ingredients of which have got out of control of the presiding
warlock; Connell wrote:[1] To Churchill it was a stewpot of wild
rumour, malice, and the lies of disappointed defeatist men. Yet he
listened to the rumours and lies, unaware of the true evil.

Rommel had produced a stampede behind the front even
though he was unable to produce one on the battlefield.
Auchinleck had purified the army of its defeatist elements, and
it found itself when the crisis was upon it.

Liddell Hart described the scene in Cairo with a detachment,
difficult for others closely involved:

> Clouds of smoke rose over the city, and charred paper rained
> down upon it, from the frantic burning of files in that hive
> of rear staff bureaucracy—the day came to be popularly
> called 'Ash Wednesday'. But on July 2 the great 'flap' began
> to subside. The situation had never been so bad as it looked
> from a distance—from Cairo or Whitehall. Forward there
> had been no such 'flap'.[2]

Clearly the situation may have seemed more grave than it was
to Churchill, and in a way he wanted it to be grave, to give
him a chance to act as hero and saviour. He was in the midst
of his personal crisis, and his crisis and the crisis in the desert
coincided, as his cables to Auchinleck clearly show. He emerged
from his personal crisis at home at exactly the time that the Eighth
Army emerged from its last crisis in the desert.

[1]Connell, *Auchinleck,* p. 639.
[2]Liddell Hart, *The Tanks,* vol. II, p. 197.

'I sent my encouragement,' he wrote, 'on the morrow of the Vote of Censure debate, which had been an accompaniment to the cannonade.'

On 4th July he cabled Auchinleck: 'I cannot help liking very much the way things seem to be going.'

There is a reserve about this message in contrast to his cable on the same day to Air Chief Marshal Tedder:

Here at home we are all watching with enthusiasm the brilliant, supreme exertions of the Royal Air Force in the battle now proceeding in Egypt. From every quarter the reports come in of the effect of the vital part which your officers and men are playing in this Homeric struggle for the Nile Valley. The days of the Battle of Britain are being repeated far from home. We are sure you will be to your glorious army the friend that endureth to the end.

It is true that he calls the army 'glorious', but there is a marked lack of praise and enthusiasm in his cable to Auchinleck, and its glory did not endure for many days in his mind. The Air Force had played a great and vital part, but would any airman consider his role more utterly wearing, more demanding on sustained physical courage, on all the resources of endurance men somehow found in the depths of their beings in the midst of an Homeric, and long sustained struggle on the ground? There is no relaxation for the man on the ground, no mess to return to, no decent bed to lie on, nothing but resolution to fortify the weary and battered body and spirit. I doubt that Churchill had any real concept of these things.

I doubt whether Churchill's mind was ever properly open to realise or to consider the nature of the victory won in those grim days by the Eighth Army commanded by Auchinleck. Churchill is not to be blamed for craving more. He was fighting for his own position, not only at the top of Britain, but at the top of the strategy of the Western Allies in Europe, to play the super-general. Because of these pressures he urged upon Auchinleck the destruction of Rommel and his army at a time when it was impossible, as the C.I.G.S. and Kennedy, the D.M.O., knew very well. Brooke remarked that 'a false move would be fatal, and that Auchinleck might lose Egypt in five minutes if he made a mistake'. Auchinleck was unlikely to make a mistake, but Churchill was well able to make one, fortunately not fatal. This was because the defeat of Rommel was far more decisive than anyone other than those on the spot realised even in mid-July.

Churchill's order to Auchinleck was a bad order, but Auchinleck had no alternative but to accept it and do his best. Defeat is one thing, destruction is another. 'Destruction' is a very tall order. Even Montgomery with an astronomical advantage in men, armour, artillery and all the equipment of war was unable to achieve Rommel's destruction after the terrible attrition of second Alamein, when the enemy lay at his mercy. Even Hitler's senseless order to Rommel to stand and fight when he was already withdrawing his last remaining strength with skill and success failed to deliver the enemy into Montgomery's hands. Montgomery's caution was remarkable, and astonishing to Rommel and to everyone else.

But in July 1942 there was no overwhelming strength or superiority, and the destruction of Rommel's army was impossible.

Immediately after the censure motion Churchill's urge was to leave at once for Cairo to see as near to first hand as he could get, what was going on. He had been irked by Lord Winterton's criticism of his behaviour as a Generalissimo rather than as a Prime Minister: 'His appearance, on occasion, in uniform with ribbons, to both of which he was most honourably entitled, gave the impression that he was a Generalissimo and not a Prime Minister: further it is suggested that he was more responsible for strategy and tactics than either was the case or ought to have been.'[1]

Undoubtedly Churchill did act as a Generalissimo and was more responsible for strategy and tactics than he should have been. His attempts at tactical interference constantly undermined the authority of his generals and inhibited them at crucial times. But he was neither dismayed nor repentant. His emotional state alarmed Brendan Bracken, and the C.I.G.S. feared the havoc Churchill's presence could create at a crucial time in the Middle East. Both men strove to deter the Prime Minister from rushing off to the battlefield, yet his visit when he set off a month later was far more dangerous and destructive. John Connell wrote that had Churchill gone as he wished in the first week of July many melancholy consequences might have been averted:

[1]Connell, *Auchinleck*, pp. 644–5. Orders of the Day, Earl Winterton, p. 285.

Churchill and Brooke would both have seen for themselves at the time what was happening both in Cairo and in the Desert. Brooke would have grasped at once the military implications of Rommel's defeat... The Prime Minister's anger and suspicion following the wound the loss of Tobruk had inflicted upon him would have been swallowed up in the recognition of hard-earned victory. Nor would there have been time for those who had been beaten by Rommel to recoup their self-esteem by unloading the blame on to better broader shoulders than their own.

That is true, but there is more to it than that. Churchill needed a personal victory urgently. Had he been in the Middle East he could have claimed, and believed, that he and Auchinleck together 'had saved Britain'. The Old Man would have had little difficulty in identifying himself with victory. He could have claimed credit for persuading the Americans to give up their proposed cross-channel assault in 1942, however hopeless (and impossible) such an enterprise would have been; credit for the acceptance of *'Gymnast'*, the landings in North Africa, would have been his. In fact Auchinleck had made these things possible. The frustrated Generalissimo-Prime Minister nursed his rancour, and since he had failed to be in at the kill, he denied the kill. He denied Auchinleck's victory, denied the first battle of Alamein, disgraced the old Eighth Army, and created a new victory nearly four months later, one for which he could claim the 'credit'. As it was, in those first days of July, Auchinleck had usurped Churchill's prerogative as champion. He would not be permitted to enjoy his triumph.

Throughout July Churchill was in a dangerous mood. He was under greater strain, perhaps, than at any time since he assumed Supreme Command. The course of the war, even possibly defeat or victory, might hang upon decisions off the battlefield, and upon success or failure on the battlefield in the Middle East. Perhaps no one apart from Auchinleck and Dorman Smith in the midst of their decisive battle realised fully what was at stake.

The Middle-East Command was also very much aware of the very grave threat developing on their northern front. The German offensive in Russia was making startling progress on the right flank. Sevastopol was in German hands and was followed by the fall of Voronezh. A new Army Group was 'about to start an attack aimed eventually at the Caucasus'.[1]

[1] *Grand Strategy,* vol. II, part III, p. 613.

In the event of the Eighth Army failing to halt Rommel decisively at Alamein, Dorman Smith visualised the possibility of an immediate invasion from the north, considering that Hitler would seize his great chance, hold on the Russian front, and order Von Kleist to swing south. No one could have predicted Hitler's insane obsession with Stalingrad, which, perhaps more than anything else, cost him not merely an Army, but the war.

After the war Dorman Smith wrote:

Had it [1st Alamein] not been won there'd have been no invasion of Europe... Starting from the premise that by mid-July 1942, Rommel had taken Cairo and Alexandria, and Hitler, instead of becoming obsessed with his Stalingrad objective, had directed von Kleist across the Caucasus into northern Persia and towards the Persian Gulf. Turkey joins the Axis, so does Spain. No American–British expedition to French North Africa and the U.S.S.R. now properly isolated. I think also, no cross-channel invasion in 1944. The V1's and V2's dominating British skies indefinitely. India possibly lost and no come-back in Burma. Hitler and Mussolini remain in the saddle, Musso supreme in a true *mare nostrum*. It is a bit of a nightmare but few except Auchinleck and myself know how close we were to it.[1]

That was the 'abyss' from which Auchinleck dragged us all back in July 1942.

The Middle-East Command (Defence Committee) recognised the threat which might develop even after Auchinleck had held and halted Rommel for good. On 9th July the Defence Committee asked London for guidance, drawing attention to the fact that the demands of the Far East had caused serious inroads into British strength in the Middle East, and that if things went badly for the Russians (and it was touch and go) a choice between two serious decisions would have to be made:[2]

whether to transfer forces from Egypt to the northern front, thus securing the Persian oil fields but losing Egypt, or to continue to put the defence of Egypt first, thus risking the loss of the Persian oil fields. 'We have not got the forces

[1] Personal correspondence, from Major-General E. Dorman Smith to the author.

[2] Playfair, *The Mediterranean and the Middle East*, pp. 363–4.

to do both, and if we try to do both we may fail to achieve either. We request your guidance and instructions on this issue.'[1]

This infuriated Churchill. He was determined that Auchinleck should attack and destroy Rommel, and the Chief of Staff, even with Ismay's help, was unable 'to restrain the Prime Minister's impulse to attack too soon'. It was, or might be, 'Battle Axe' all over again.

Churchill at once assumed the mantle of Generalissimo: the Eighth Army, battered as it was, had to be launched at once into a fresh series of offensive operations.

General Auchinleck replied that he took [this] to mean that the Prime Minister accepted the risk to the northern front, and hence to Iraq and the oil. Whether it was a justifiable risk he himself could not say. He would continue to apply all his available resources to destroying the Germans in the desert as soon as possible.[2]

Auchinleck had no option but to accept a direct order and to act upon it, however unfortunate it might be. It was unlikely that he would be able to destroy Rommel, and the attempt to do so must delay the eventual destruction of Rommel's Army by several weeks.

Churchill's memoirs exaggerated his position on the eve of the censure motion in July, and certain important statements are omitted from his account. The battle in the Western Desert was no longer 'in the balance'. He omits the strong objections of Brooke, the C.I.G.S., and Kennedy, the D.M.O. to his blaming Auchinleck for the loss of Tobruk. They pointed out that although they had expressed a strong hope that Tobruk might be held, 'no order to this effect was ever sent from London'.

In his speech Churchill had stated:

The decision to hold Tobruk and the dispositions made for the purpose were taken by General Auchinleck, but I should like to say that we, the War Cabinet, and our professional advisers thoroughly agreed with General Auchinleck beforehand, and although in tactical matters the Commander-in-

---

[1] Sir Arthur Bryant, *Alanbrooke Diaries, The Turn of the Tide*, p. 420.
[2] *The Mediterranean and the Middle East*, vol. III, p. 364.

Chief in any war theatre is supreme and his decision is final, we consider that if he was wrong we were wrong too.[1]

Nevertheless the fall of Tobruk, and the manner of it, was a shock, especially to Churchill, who heard the news in Washington. Ever since Wavell had decided to hold the fortress, the heroic defence by the Australian garrison had made of it a symbol out of all proportion to its strategic and tactical value. It was a source of constant aggravation to Rommel, and finally an obsession. It was also 'a running sore' for the Mediterranean fleet, whose task it was to sustain the garrison. The cost was severe.

When Auchinleck inherited the command and the Australians were withdrawn, the Commanders-in-Chief agreed that Tobruk should not be held if the pressures became too great. Whitehall accepted the decision.

In December, 1941, Anthony Heckstall-Smith wrote, 'Tobruk was no longer a fortress—a bastion against which Rommel's panzers had battered themselves senseless for months. It was a supply dump. All the guts have dropped out of the place.'[2]

Its end was miserable and confused and unworthy of its beginning.

The loss of Tobruk rankled with Churchill, but there were many other factors governing his growing determination to get rid of his general, not least his dislike of the Indian Army. Connell, and others, seeking for some excuse, rather than for an explanation of Churchill's conduct, regard Tobruk as one of the main causes, however unjustified.

I believe the causes more subtle and quite unprovable. Simply Churchill felt at a disadvantage with men of the stature and integrity of Auchinleck, and was always uncomfortable with such men. The memoirs, written in retrospect about this crucial period are loaded, for he knew even in early July that the tide had turned, yet he wrote: 'During this month of July, when I was politically at my weakest, and without a gleam of military success, I had to procure from the United States the decisions which, for good or ill, dominated the next two years of the war.'

Later he wrote of the month of July:

I had now been twenty-eight months at the head of affairs, during which we had sustained an almost unbroken series

[1] This passage is omitted from Churchill's *The Second World War*, vol. IV.
[2] Anthony Heckstall-Smith, *Tobruk, the Story of a Siege*.

of military defeats. We had survived the collapse of France and the air attack on Britain. We had not been invaded. We still held Egypt. We were alive and at bay; but that was all. On the other hand what a cataract of disasters had fallen upon us!

Having listed faithfully the principal disasters, Churchill continued: 'Was it strange that the whole system of the war direction, for which I was responsible, should have been brought into question and challenge?

It is indeed remarkable that I was not in this bleak lull dismissed from power, or confronted with demands for change in my methods, which it was known I should never accept. I should have vanished from the scene with a load of calamity on my shoulders, and the harvest, at last to be reaped, would have been ascribed to my belated disappearance.[1]

Thus he set the stage for the 'scapegoats', and for the climax of the story he told so well. July was a bad month. In the first twenty-five days decisions were made that would decide on the future of the Atlantic theatre of war, the future shape of Europe, the Middle East and doubtless much more besides. Decisions of great importance must have repercussions far beyond the immediate areas upon which statesmen, and their advisers are focussing their minds.

III

When July opened and the great battle for Egypt was still in furious progress, the President and his advisers in Washington watched developments as keenly as did Churchill and his Chiefs of Staff in Whitehall. There was the crucial area. This was the climax.

Churchill in his map room in 'The Hole' was shadow-boxing the enemy from Africa to the North Cape, longing to plunge his right into the 'soft under belly' on the Northern shores of the Mediterranean, and to left hook at North Norway. The convoys to the U.S.S.R. were being gravely harassed, and it was a high price to pay to help an ally from whom there was at best a churlish acceptance, and usually harsh criticism.

[1]Ibid. Readers' Union ed., pp. 444–5.

There was nothing intrinsically wrong, or unsound, about Churchill's desire to attack north Norway, 'Operation Jupiter', except that there were not the resources available to achieve it. There might not be the resources, even with the fullest determination of the United States, to carry out the North-African landings Churchill had planned for and hoped for under the code-name of 'Gymnast'. For certain, in the British view, which was indisputable even though bitterly disputed by the Americans, it would be impossible to carry out a cross-channel assault in 1942 under the code name 'Sledgehammer' or any other name. Moreover in the decisive battle of the Atlantic, always 'in the background' and which Churchill followed on his charts as keenly, and more anxiously, than the struggle on land, losses were sacrificial, 400,000 tons of shipping, all the cargoes and many men, lost in two weeks in that fateful month of July. On the control of the Atlantic must depend the troops, arms and equipment the United States could hope to build-up in the United Kingdom against the day of assault on Western Europe— upon which the Americans were resolved, unless they turned their backs on the Atlantic theatre of war and switched their main effort to the Pacific. Until 18th July this was a very clear possibility. The issue was in doubt. General Marshall, the President's trusted Chief of Staff, was inclined to throw in his lot with the naval Chief of Staff, Admiral King, for whom America's war was clearly in the Pacific. Europe and the Atlantic came a very poor second. The Admiral also agreed with General Marshall that the Mediterranean was a 'grave-yard' where it would be profitless and wrong-headed for the United States to become involved.

The future did not sound promising, but it was more promising than it seemed because President Roosevelt was sympathetic to the proposed North-African landings, and very much aware of the importance of the Middle East. The President's concern was to get U.S. troops into action in 1942 at all costs, and if not in a cross-channel assault, where?

This was, of course, domestic politics dictating the military tune. Churchill was well briefed on developments in Washington by Field-Marshal Dill, who enjoyed the confidence of General Marshall in particular. On 12th July Churchill wrote to Dill underlining the impossibility of 'Sledgehammer' which, if attempted, would make cross-channel attack in 1943 impossible. He pressed for 'Gymnast': 'Gymnast affords the sole means by

which United States forces can strike at Hitler in 1942 . . .
'Gymnast' does not interrupt the vast preparations and training
for 'Round-up' [the President's name for a 1943 cross-channel
assault] now proceeding on this side.'

This was true as far as it went, but it was almost certain
that an assault on North Africa would render a cross-channel
assault impossible in 1943. Landing craft, of which there was an
acute shortage, were perhaps the vital key. There would not be
enough: there were never enough, not even a bottom more than
enough in 1944. Every assault project in the Far East, the
Mediterranean, Europe, depended upon an adequate supply of
landing and support craft. At any rate, Churchill wrote, without
'Gymnast' both countries 'will remain motionless in 1942'.

The Prime Minister could not bring himself to believe that
a switch to the Pacific would be adopted. Two days later he
wrote very briefly to the President. 'I have found no one who
regards "Sledgehammer" as possible. I should like to see you
do "Gymnast" as soon as possible, and that we in concert with
the Russians should try for "Jupiter" . . . All this seems as clear
to me as noonday.'

It did not seem as clear as noonday to the men in Washington,
although the President was perhaps three-quarters of the way
towards believing that 'Sledgehammer' would have to be
abandoned.

In mid-July Roosevelt had debated the outstanding questions
with Hopkins and Marshall, and drawn up a masterly appreciation
and directive. On 15th July Field-Marshal Dill warned Churchill
bluntly and precisely of the American mood:

'Marshall leaves for England with Harry Hopkins and King
tomorrow evening.'

Dill listed four main objections to 'Gymnast' of which the
last is of the greatest importance: 'Gymnast would build up
into such a large commitment as to destroy any possibility of
"Round-up" in 1943.'

Vague plans for action in Pacific have been put to President . . .
There is no doubt that Marshall is true to his first love, but
he is convinced that there has been no real drive behind the
European project . . . King's war is against the Japanese. I have
a feeling . . . that there are highly placed Americans who do
not believe that anything better than a stalemate with
Germany is possible . . . Marshall believes that your first love

is 'Gymnast', just as his is 'Bolero' [new code-name for 'Round-up'] and that with the smallest provocation you always revert to your old love. Unless you can convince him of your unswerving devotion to 'Bolero' everything points to a complete reversal of our present agreed strategy and the withdrawal of America to a war of her own in the Pacific, leaving us with limited American assistance to make out as best we can against Germany.[1]

In June the U.S. naval victory of 'Midway' in the Pacific, which marked the turn of the tide against the Japanese, may have been an important factor in the American desire to switch to the Pacific. It was too early to understand just how dramatically the war was swiftly moving against the enemy.

At least until 10th July Marshall, supported by U.S. intelligence sources, believed that Egypt would be lost with dire consequences. Against this the President's Directive was cool and balanced. Key passages were:

1. You will proceed immediately to London as my personal representatives for the purpose of consultation with appropriate British authorities on the conduct of the war.

Paragraph (e): It is of the highest importance that American ground troops be brought into action against the enemy in 1942.

The vital importance of 'Sledgehammer' is then emphasised, but that it might be impossible is understood.

6. Only if you are completely convinced that 'Sledgehammer' is impossible of execution with reasonable chances of serving its intended purpose, inform me.

7. If 'Sledgehammer' is finally and definitely out of the picture, I want you to consider the world situation as it exists at that time, and determine upon another place for U.S. troops to fight in 1942.

The President then underlined the decisive nature of Auchinleck's great battle for Egypt; and what failure might mean:

Such loss means in series:
(1) Loss of Egypt and Suez Canal.
(2) Loss of Syria.

[1]Churchill, *The Second World War*, vol. IV, Readers' Union ed., p. 361.

(3) Loss of Mosul oil wells.

(4) Loss of the Persian Gulf through attacks from the north and west, together with access to all Persian Gulf oil.

(5) Joining hands between Germany and Japan and the probable loss of the Indian Ocean.

(6) The very important probability of German occupation of Tunis, Algiers, Morocco, Dakar and the cutting off of the ferry route through Freetown and Liberia.

(7) Serious danger to all shipping in the South Atlantic and serious danger to Brazil and the whole of the east coast of South America. I include in the above possibilities the use by the Germans of Spain, Portugal and their territories.

By that time as we know, and Churchill and the Chiefs of Staff knew, Auchinleck and the old Eighth Army had won the decisive battle, and the 'nightmare' would not happen.

The final paragraph of the President's Directive makes it clear that Germany was the main target for the Allies: '. . . it is obvious that defeat of Germany, or the holding of Germany in 1942 or. in 1943 means probable eventual defeat of Germany in the European and African theatres and in the Near East. Defeat of Germany means the defeat of Japan, probably without firing a shot or losing a life.'[1]

In the early morning of 18th July the C.I.G.S. met the American delegation at Euston Station. They had ignored Churchill's attempt to have the train stopped for them to meet him at Chequers, determined, as Brooke wrote 'to avoid the temptation from the great "diversionist"'. At Chequers Churchill, aware of the implications, was furious, knowing in his heart that the Americans were taking over the direction of the war and that henceforth he would be very much a 1st Lieutenant, often ignored, often shabbily treated. When Roosevelt wrote to Churchill at the end of the month that they were now 'shoulder to shoulder' it was clear whose shoulder was doing the pushing. There was nothing Churchill could do about it, but there might have been a great deal he could have done about it had he not been Churchill and half American, had he not been dazzled by U.S. power—and later by Soviet power—to the point where he was unable to realise British power. It was Churchill, far more than America, who craved for an alliance of 'the English-speaking

[1] Sherwood, The White House Papers, vol. II, p. 606. Also Churchill's memoirs, et al.

peoples'. Bluntly, although the Americans were fond of Churchill they did not like the British, and Hopkins, as neither Churchill nor the Chiefs of Staff realised, was wholly Roosevelt's man. He became in a sense a 'spy' in our midst, trusted implicitly as though he were a shared man, the binding ingredient.[1]

Churchill at once telephoned Hopkins in London, and Hopkins reported to Roosevelt: 'The Prime Minister threw the British Constitution at me with some vehemence. As you know, it is an unwritten document, so no serious damage was done.' He had done his best over the telephone, he wrote, to persuade the Prime Minister that no rudeness had been intended. 'Rudeness!' Hopkins visited Churchill the next day, and smoothed matters over, but the situation was beyond 'rudeness' and smoothing over. Meanwhile in the staff talks there was stalemate, but the U.S. Admiral Stark understood much better than his fellow countrymen the hopelessness of 'Sledgehammer'. By the 25th the matter was settled, and 'Gymnast' now in its final cloak of 'Torch' was agreed.

For the Americans 'Sledgehammer' died hard, as 'Round-up', renamed 'Bolero' was to die hard. They did not trust the British, even though the British effort to make cross-channel assault possible was monumental and decisive. When it happened it would belong to Britain first, even though we were doomed to become a poor second. That writing was on the wall in July, 1942.[2]

It is perhaps not surprising that throughout Auchinleck's great fight Churchill's harassment of the General had been continuous and often churlish. The prime role of war direction was slipping away from the Prime Minister on two levels at once. Auchinleck's victory was not Churchill's personal victory, and it would remain for the Official Historian summing up the July achievement to write:

By his determination and his imperturbability, Auchinleck had once again saved the situation. He was now confidently holding a position from which a further assault from Rommel could be repelled and an Allied offensive resumed when decisive superiority in men and materials had been created.[3]

[1] *T.L.S.* 'front' essay, 'Chemistry of the Cold War', (22nd September, 1972), assessing *The Semblance of Peace* by Sir John Wheeler Bennett and Anthony Nicholls (Macmillan).
[2] Sherwood, *The White House Papers,* vol.   , pp. 608–9.
[3] *Grand Strategy,* vol. III, part ii, p. 615.

The defensive strength of the Alamein position created by Brigadier Kitsch, Chief Engineer, Eighth Army, and by Dorman Smith, was virtually impregnable and ideal for launching an offensive. By mid-September Auchinleck planned to be ready to attack and encompass the final defeat of the enemy. He knew nothing of the decision for the Allied landings in North Africa, which would render the enemy position untenable.

In view of the distortion of the facts that was about to be perpetrated, it is important to establish the mood of Auchinleck, and his relations with the C.I.G.S. as July drew to a close. On 17th July the C.I.G.S. wrote:

> You have been constantly in my thoughts since Rommel started his attacks, and I have so well realised the difficult and anxious times that you have been through. I only wish that it was possible to do more to help you from this distance.
>
> It is such a joy to see you gradually regaining the mastery over the enemy. I do hope this heavier equipment in the shape of six pdr tanks, and the latest American tanks will arrive soon enough to provide the additional striking power you require.
>
> I did not answer your very kind wire (in regard to the removal of General Ritchie from command of Eighth Army) more fully, as I had seen the Prime Minister's wire to you expressing full confidence. It is his confidence that is the important factor. You know how temperamental he is apt to be at times, so I hope you do not attach too much importance if occasionally his telegrams are not quite as friendly as they might be . . . I feel for you in the difficult times you have been through . . . you can rely on me to do all I can to help you from this end.

The letter ends after discussing some plans for the northern front:

> I have every hope of being able to escape to pay you a visit before long, and am preparing plans. Shall let you know results as soon as I can fix something definite. Am looking forward to it tremendously.
>
> With *very* best luck to you in your trying and difficult task.

In his reply of 25th July, thanking Brooke not only for what he had said, but for the way in which he had said it, Auchinleck reported on the position. He drew attention to the need to appoint a commander for the Eighth Army, and thought that General Gott might do the job. He praised Corbett, his Chief of Staff, in Cairo, and had praise for General Ramsden, commanding 30th Corps. Dorman Smith had been 'most invaluable'.

This correspondence is of the utmost importance in view of the totally undeserved fate awaiting most of those mentioned. Gott, for whom alone a better fate may have been destined, was tragically killed before becoming involved one way or the other.

The last paragraphs of Auchinleck's letter are of particular importance: '... we have now got a strong defensive position, organised in depth for thirty miles or more, based on strong points, within supporting field artillery range of each other, and sited to command all the intervening ground and to deny this essential observation to the enemy...' The letter further outlines the strength of the defensive position, and ends:

> *A propos* of this demand for a 'second front', we feel that you have already a 'second front' of no mean importance here! As to it being necessary to establish a 'second front' in Europe, Northern Africa and the whole of the Mediterranean basin is, I suggest, really Europe for strategical purposes, and inseparable from it. Would it not be a good thing to try to make the public understand this?[1]

Churchill, despite all possible attempts to dissuade him, was about to take matters into his own hands. His journey was totally unnecessary, as the historians would underline. Nothing called him to the Middle East, save his resolution to establish his 'hero image'. He would become the maker and sender of news, the old 'war-correspondent' role. 'Instead of sitting at home waiting for news from the front I could send it myself. This was exhilarating.' He would also 'make' it himself.

On 25th July Auchinleck addressed a special Order of the Day to all ranks Eighth Army from C-in-C:

[1] The exchange of letters is quoted fully in *Auchinleck* by Connell, pp. 676–680.

You have done well. You have turned a retreat into a firm stand and stopped the enemy on the threshold of Egypt. You have done more. You have wrenched the initiative from him by sheer guts and hard fighting and put HIM on the defensive in these last weeks.

He has lost heavily and is short of men, ammunition, petrol and other things. He is trying desperately to bring these over to Africa but the Navy and Air Force are after his ships.

You have borne much but I ask you for more. We must not slacken. If we can stick it we will break him. STICK TO IT.

Unhappily where Rommel failed Churchill succeeded. The struggle of the Eighth Army, and its great fight, was to be denied for more than a generation, and its last great commander and his principal aides banished.

CHAPTER TWELVE

The End of the Super-General

I

DURING AUGUST, 1942, THE PRIME MINISTER DISMISSED WITHOUT warning or opportunity for defence, and then traduced, the two men who had saved him from almost certain dismissal from power, for the loss of Egypt would have carried that in its train. Aneurin Bevan, speaking in the House of Commons on 2nd July, 1942, the second day of the 1st Battle of Alamein, stated the position bluntly:

> You have got to change it, and you will have to change it. If the House of Commons has not got the guts to make the Government change it, events will. Although the House may not take any notice of me today, you will be doing it next week. Remember my words next Monday and Tuesday (6th, 7th July). It is events which are criticising the Government. All that we are doing is giving them a voice, inadequately perhaps, but we are trying to do it.

The answer came from Auchinleck's guns at Alamein. Egypt was saved, and Churchill—at least for the time being. Nothing else saved him. The men who had saved him would be his scapegoats.

There is no doubt that Churchill felt challenged very seriously in July and August. He was no longer personally identified with salvation, as he had been, and he had, somehow, to identify himself with victory, to make it his own. It was his last chance, for leadership was passing into the hands of the Americans. It is sad to remember his words in his Vote of Confidence speech on 27th January, 1942:

If we have handled our resources wrongly, no one is so much to blame . . . Why then should I be called upon to pick out scapegoats, to throw the blame on generals or airmen or sailors . . . Therefore I feel entitled to come to the House of Commons, whose servant I am, and ask them not to press me to act against my conscience and better judgment and make scapegoats in order to improve my own position, not to press me to do the things which may be clamoured for at the moment but which will not help our war effort . . .

The march of events had now driven the Prime Minister to make scapegoats 'to improve his own position'. The Churchill dedicated to and identified with Britain gave way to Churchill the adventurer, the opportunist, the Man on the Spot, the war correspondent and super-general who, when things didn't happen, 'made things happen'. He did not go to Cairo merely to observe, but to act, to refurbish the Churchill of Dunkirk and the dark days he had made bright by his words and indomitable spirit, so indelible in the minds of all those who lived through those days in England. He was a power politician at bay, his mind inflamed by the evil rumours emerging from Cairo, and resolved to seize whatever opportunities might occur to put his own indelible mark upon events.

In the light of what Churchill did on his journey the conclusion of the Official Historian hides far more than it reveals:

'His [Churchill's] presence, though stimulating, and ensuring prompt action, was not essential. The C.I.G.S. was quite competent to perceive and recommend the necessary changes in command.'[1]

The last sentence is perfectly true. The C.I.G.S. had to choose a commander for the Eighth Army in agreement with Auchinleck. They agreed that Montgomery was the man, rather to Brooke's surprise. The C.I.G.S. had also to consider most urgently the threat to the northern front and to decide with the Commander-in-Chief and the Middle-East Defence Committee what must be done. It was a problem demanding quiet and careful thought.

'The Prime Minister and his principal adviser were going to the Middle East with radically differing conceptions of what should be done when they got there,' wrote Sir Arthur Bryant. 'Brooke had hoped to form "calm, unhurried judgments" before making his recommendations. Now he would have to take

[1] *Grand Strategy,* vol. III, part II, p. 657.

decisions affecting the whole future of the war with his "impetuous master at his elbow".'[1]

Moreover his impetuous master would not be alone. He had summoned his old crony, Field-Marshal Smuts, to be present, knowing that he could count on the old man's support for whatever he chose to do. He had also summoned Wavell from India. Churchill's personal choice for command of the Eighth Army was General Gott. In spite of the obvious weariness of Gott and the General's own insistence that he needed rest badly, Churchill persisted in his choice until Gott's unfortunate death on 7th August left Montgomery as the clear answer.

But Churchill's preference for Gott is important, and acquits the Prime Minister of any Machiavellian scheme to achieve his ends. Gott would never have been a party to the denigration of the Eighth Army, or to the denial of Auchinleck's victory. It is unlikely that such an idea was in Churchill's mind when he reached Cairo. The Prime Minister simply seized, and made, his opportunities.

His first resolve was to get rid of Auchinleck. It was not simple to do so. A replacement would have to be found, and this would prove impossible. Moreover, Auchinleck could not simply be banished to 'outer darkness'. Something would have to be thought of, for the obvious task for Auchinleck as C-in-C India was already in the hands of Churchill's first scapegoat, General Wavell. With Smuts at his side the two old men would think of something.

The unsavoury story of Churchill's behaviour is told clearly, lucidly and with restraint, by John Connell. It has also been dealt with from a rather different angle by the author.[2]

I shall not go over it again, save to emphasise certain points. Churchill's own account is grossly distorted and heavily edited to eliminate his praise of Auchinleck and the Eighth Army.

On 4th August he discussed the business alone with Smuts, and in the late afternoon attended a meeting of 'all the talents', as he called it, in which Auchinleck reported the situation clearly, and his views on the situation in the north. He was in complete agreement with all present except Churchill and Smuts. Churchill began at once to argue with Auchinleck's plans for an offensive, and the target date for it in mid-September. Brooke commented: 'I could see that he did not approve of his replies. He is again

[1] Bryant, *Alanbrooke Diaries,* pp. 443–4.
[2] In the background to *The Montgomery Legend.*

pressing for an attack before Auchinleck can possibly get ready. I find him almost impossible to argue with on this point.'[1]

Churchill had begun to work himself up into a fury. 'There was a lot of tension at the meeting,' R. G. Casey wrote. Those present 'could almost see his mind working,' and Brooke suffered some of it until late into the night. It was clear that Auchinleck's date for his renewed offensive would be Churchill's immediate pretext for Auchinleck's dismissal.

Very early in the morning of the 5th the Prime Minister and the C.I.G.S. set off for Eighth Army Headquarters in the desert. It was an uncomfortable journey, and when Churchill arrived, he breakfasted in what he described as 'a wire-netted cube, full of flies and important military personages'. It didn't improve his temper. It was not the manner in his experiences of long ago in which a Commander-in-Chief should live. He did not seem to understand that he had pleaded with Auchinleck to fight the battle himself.

It was clear that he had very little idea of the great struggle that had taken place, or that his hero, Rommel, fought and lived forward with his troops without thought of comfort. Churchill was in a vile temper. He was disgusted to learn that Auchinleck and his Staff slept in their bedrolls on the sand. To Churchill, accustomed to luxury, wherever he might be, cushioned by a more than adequate staff of every kind from secretaries to cooks, the whole thing was distasteful and unnecessary.

Alone with Auchinleck and Dorman Smith in the map caravan the Prime Minister revealed his feelings, stabbing his fingers against the talc covering the battle map, demanding attack. Auchinleck was quiet, courteous and firm.

'No sir, we cannot attack again yet.'

Churchill at once turned to Dorman Smith, demanding 'Do you say that too! Why don't you use the 44th Division?'

'The 44th Division isn't ready yet, sir.'

The Prime Minister did not attempt to hide his anger. He wanted the 44th Division committed immediately to the offensive. Auchinleck quietly explained his reasons for not committing a green division, untrained in the desert, and not yet acclimatised. The Prime Minister argued angrily. Auchinleck remained courteous, but adamant, when perhaps only anger—which would have been justified—might have achieved some reaction from the

[1]Bryant, *Alanbrooke Diaries: The Turn of the Tide.*

Prime Minister, for even he must have known that the division could not be committed by any commander fit for his job.

'Because these two officers acted as they did that morning, a division was not squandered and many men's lives were saved, but they set the seal on their own professional doom,' wrote Connell.[1]

General Sir Brian Horrocks later commented upon Auchinleck's moral courage under extreme pressure from Churchill. The 44th Division 'might well erect a monument to Auchinleck who unquestionably saved them heavy casualites'.[2]

I do not believe that this event decided the fate of the two soldiers. Their fate was already decided upon. Churchill left the caravan without a word, and stood with his back to the two soldiers, seeming an alien, menacing figure, a visitor from another world. Dorman Smith wrote in his private notes: 'I wondered if Churchill was thinking himself into Lincoln's shoes when Lincoln dismissed McClellan at Harrison's Landing after the "seven days" ... The old man might be thinking of having us both shot ... He hadn't spoken a kind word since his arrival at Bourg el Arab.'[3]

Without even a word of common courtesy Churchill drove off to lunch in the comfort of the Royal Air Force Headquarters, enjoying all the luxuries provided by Shepheard's cuisine, a long way from the Commander-in-Chief's 'wire-netted cube full of flies'.

The Prime Minister returned to Cairo invigorated, his mind fully made up, not simply to get rid of Auchinleck, but to sweep away all those who had risen to Rommel's final challenge; Corbett, Chief of Staff in Cairo, who had held the fort, Dorman Smith who had been at Auchinleck's side throughout the battle, and played a vital part, Ramsden, who had commanded a corps with skill and resolution, and was second-in-command, Eighth Army. For Churchill to sack Auchinleck's staff was grossly improper, usurping the role of his C.I.G.S. and the War Office.

Meanwhile the C.I.G.S., having visited 5th Indian Division, returned to Auchinleck's Headquarters to study the war maps and plans, of which he warmly approved. The situation was clearly very good indeed, and the plans for the second battle of Alamein,

[1]Connell, *Auchinleck*, p. 697.
[2]Horrocks, *A Full Life*.
[3]The analogy with Lincoln-McClellan is remarkable. See (among others): Bruce Catton, *This Hallowed Ground*, for a clear brief account.

impeccable. They would be adopted by Montgomery, and claimed as his own with the connivance of Churchill and the C.I.G.S.

Auchinleck accompanied the C.I.G.S. to Cairo, leaving Dorman Smith alone to await the arrival of Wavell the next morning. Together Wavell and Dorman Smith went quietly through the July story, and the appreciation of 27th July. 'I stressed the desirability of Rommel attacking prematurely via the 13th Corps southern flank,' wrote Dorman Smith.

After listening in silence and studying the situation with care Wavell said: 'Eric, you are very strongly posted here; have you considered making a feint withdrawal to entice Rommel into the net?'

The idea had been considered, but Auchinleck hoped that Rommel would march into the net at Alam Halfa. That would have spelled disaster for the German Army, as Rommel himself recognised when in desperation he attempted the impossible. It was not even a gamble, as Kesselring warned, but it was intolerable for Rommel to be compelled to wait for a British offensive in which he would have no chance of victory.

Fortunately for the Panzer Army Auchinleck was no longer in command when Rommel committed himself into British hands at Alam Halfa, and was, for reasons never explained, permitted to escape when his situation was hopeless.[1] Even Montgomery's extreme caution may not be a sufficient explanation, and it may be that Churchill wanted a full-scale offensive against Rommel with the entire propaganda machine in full blast, and a simple destruction of the German Panzer Army at Alam Halfa would not do.

Auchinleck's position of strength and his plans (fully adopted by his inheritors) made no difference to the Prime Minister's attitude. His mind was fully made up, not only to get rid of Auchinleck but to sweep the whole command structure out of his way. He had come to hate it, whatever the facts might dictate. The northern front, and the enormous responsibilities of the Cairo Command, had denied him, as he saw it, total victory in the desert. The whole area must be cut in two, one looking west, even if the northern front must rely mainly on luck. On the night of the 5th Churchill sent a brief signal to the Deputy Prime Minister in London. Paragraph 2 is revealing: 'I am discussing the whole situation with Smuts, who is a fount of wisdom.

[1] Barnett, *The Desert Generals*, p. 249.

Wherever the fault may lie for the serious situation which exists, it is certainly not with the troops, and only to a minor extent with their equipment.'[1]

Ergo it must lie with the commanders. But there was no serious situation, and Churchill was very well aware of it. Moreover, his brief visit to Eighth Army Headquarters had not provided an opportunity for personal observation of the troops or of their equipment. When the troops did see him, two weeks later, they were less than enthusiastic, as Denis Johnston wrote:

> ... the Ridge was thinly lined with phlegmatic soldiers, who seemed to be in two minds about the warmth of the reception they were going to give the Old War Horse. The over-all direction of the war does not inspire much jollity in men who have consistently been chased by superior numbers with better equipment. Besides, they like Auchinleck, and do not see why he should be kicked out for General Alexander and some new Army Commander from England.[2]

Early on 6th August Churchill burst in upon the C.I.G.S. to find him 'practically naked', and at breakfast he gave Brooke an outline of the plans rapidly formulating in his mind, and told of his intention 'to remove Auchinleck to Persia-Iraq Command as he had lost confidence in him'.[3] He then offered Brooke the new Near-East Command, with Gott as his new Army Commander. The C.I.G.S., sorely tempted, wrote that he felt that his place was with Churchill: 'I had discovered the perils of his impetuous nature. I was now familiar with his method of suddenly arriving at some decision as it were by intuition without any kind of logical examination of the problem.'

Moreover, Brooke wrote, he could not bear the thought that 'Auchinleck might think that I had come out here on purpose to work myself into his shoes.' It is highly improbable that Auchinleck would have thought anything of the kind. No one would fill Auchinleck's shoes, for he was the last man to be asked to take control of what had been known as the Middle-East Command.

At once Churchill sent for General Alexander to take over the new Near-East Command, with General Montgomery as Army Commander, as soon as the death of Gott was known.

[1]Churchill, *The Second World War,* vol. IV, Readers' Union ed., p. 377.
[2]Denis Johnston, *Nine Rivers of Jordan,* p. 43.
[3]Bryant, *Alanbrooke Diaries,* pp. 444–5.

By this means, in spite of Brooke's efforts to explain the command situation to Churchill, the Prime Minister laboured under
the delusion that he would have two army commanders with
the sole task of destroying Rommel. Nor did Brooke succeed
in influencing his master against the new plan, in spite of understanding his master's methods of reaching his decisions.

All through the 6th and into the night Churchill worked on
his plan, the new Middle-East Command becoming little more
than an appendage, uncertain from what it appended, whether
it should look to Cairo or to India for maintenance, supply,
reinforcement. As it stood it would be hopelessly incapable of
meeting the real possibility of a German break-through in the
Caucasus, and the threat to Abadan oil. In effect Churchill
decided to take a chance on the northern front, and stake all on
a quick victory over Rommel to gain political capital at home,
and to impress the Americans.

Time was not on his side, politically. He wanted victory in
the desert in August or September, and Auchinleck was his only
hope for that, but he could not and would not recognise it.
Moreover he persuaded himself that his idea of splitting the
command would provide him with a plausible way of getting rid
of Auchinleck, by offering him the new Middle-East Command.

In a long message dated 6–7th August Churchill gave a brief
account of his resolution to the Deputy Prime Minister and War
Cabinet in London. The War Cabinet did not like the idea and said
so. 'In any case they thought that the appointment suggested for
General Auchinleck would convey the impression that a command
was being created in order to let him down lightly. He would be
unlikely to retain confidence in himself or inspire it in others if
he were transferred to a reduced, though important, position.'[1]

The Official Historian continues: 'Mr. Churchill then took
up the cudgels for General Auchinleck in whom, as the head
of an army with a single direct purpose, he said he had
complete confidence.'

His message to the Deputy Prime Minister and War Cabinet
contained two passages of such glowing tribute to Auchinleck
that it would have been an impossible embarrassment to include
them in his war memoirs.[2]

[1] Playfair, *The Mediterranean and the Middle East,* vol. III, p. 368.
[2] Note: it was not until the publication of the above volume, and of volume
III, part II of *Grand Strategy,* p. 654, that it became possible to reconstruct
Churchill's message of 6–7th August.

There was no time to be lost if Churchill's plans for the Middle East were to be set irrevocably in motion, for on 11th August he was due to fly to Moscow with his advisers for what promised to be a difficult meeting with Stalin. 'A decision has now become most urgent,' he telegraphed to the War Cabinet, 'since Alexander has already started and Auchinleck has of course no inkling of what is in prospect. I must apprise him tomorrow . . .'

In short Churchill's mind was made up, and all objections and criticisms, however valid, were swept aside. The presence of Field-Marshal Smuts ensured his domination. These two old men out of the past, in which they still lived, generated a ruthlessness, resolution and power none could oppose with effect. The C.I.G.S., in spite of imagining that he would have to make great decisions, would have done better to have stayed at home. He might even have emerged more honourably, perhaps daring at long range to protect Auchinleck's staff from 'his impetuous master'.

On 8th August, Colonel Sir Ian Jacob, 'feeling as if he were just going to murder an unsuspecting friend,' delivered the Prime Minister's letter of dismissal to General Auchinleck in his Desert Headquarters. Jacob was deeply impressed by Auchinleck's quiet dignity, 'a great man and a great fighter'.

On the following day Auchinleck had a brief interview with the Prime Minister, described by Churchill as 'bleak and impeccable'. There is no record of what was said.

Auchinleck's rejection of the proposal could not be in doubt. He had remarked to Jacob in Churchill's anteroom that it had 'crossed his mind that the offer was made to him in the certainty that he would refuse'. He had remarked to his close friends that rather than accept 'a sop' when his time came, he would prefer 'oblivion'. And this, as Connell wrote, was 'a grimy sop'. Many, including the War Cabinet, regarded it as a mean way of trying to fob off a great man and a great commander.

Meanwhile a committee was set up under the chairmanship of Major-General Dorman Smith to study and report on the Persia-Iraq Command. Churchill wanted to go ahead with his plans immediately upon his return from Moscow.

Dorman Smith reported to his Chief that the new command was unsound and unworkable, and advised very strongly against it, though Auchinleck's acceptance would have meant Dorman Smith's promotion to Lieutenant-General.

Auchinleck studied the report carefully, and wrote to the C.I.G.S.:

> I have studied the report of the Committee on the implication of setting up an independent command. I do not myself think that the scheme is workable in practice, and I feel there is a grave risk of it breaking down under the stress of active operations. I do not therefore feel able to accept the responsibility of this new command, and I have informed the Secretary of State accordingly.

It is barely conceivable that Churchill imagined Auchinleck's acceptance, but it is possible that the offer was serious. Both Churchill and Smuts were remarkably ignorant of all that the administration of armies and areas entailed, as Churchill constantly revealed in his attitudes to the Middle East and India. Both old men had a broad and often sound grasp of strategy, but were often completely naïve about tactics. Their own war experiences in the field were from a long distant age, the Soudan, the Boer War, and even the vastly different situation in the First World War. Particularly they did not understand the problems of the Middle and Near East, while Churchill's attitude to India was, as Amery noted to Wavell, rather like that of George III to the American Colonies.

If Churchill was serious in his offer it could not have been in his mind at that time to denigrate Auchinleck and his Staff, to deny the victory of 1st Alamein, to attempt to erase the battle from the records, to ignore the old Eighth Army after its immense service to Britain over two years of fortitude and grave hardship. With Auchinleck in employment it would have been impossible to perpetrate such a distortion of the truth.

II

Churchill's return to Cairo from Moscow to find that Auchinleck was now out of the way, and that the new command had taken over, not quite as planned, marked a change in Churchill, and a change in the nature of war. These changes all flowed naturally out of the events preceding them, and would have occurred whether Churchill had been in Cairo or not. Even the change in

Churchill was not sudden. There is a moment in time when actions produce visible results. Churchill's behaviour at this time sullied his reputation, and that is all. His creation of a fictional situation did not make it true, nor affect in the smallest degree the course of events. Inasmuch as the course of events was changed it was the natural outcome of changing commanders in mid-stream. The fictional situation was for home consumption, for the mass of anonymous people from whom, and from whom alone, his position at the top derived. For them (and for himself), he had to create the need for the huge pitched battle he was resolved to stage, supported by the entire publicity machine of the nation.

Meanwhile the Prime Minister had had a difficult time in Moscow, and it is not easy to understand why he found it necessary to confront and placate an oriental potentate when he was in a weak position, and when neither he, nor even the oriental potentate himself, could have any effect whatsoever on the immense struggle in which the German and Russian armies were locked. Nor would he learn of Russian intentions in the Caucasus. The only human being whose intentions could or would affect the course of the conflict was the man who had become the tyrant of the German nation.

The Russians demanded a great deal from Britain, most of it impossible to provide, save at crippling cost to the British war effort. They also demanded a second front in Europe at a time when even a small cross-channel assault against Dieppe, comprising little more than a division and a concourse of 252 ships, taxed available resources to the limit, and was a disaster.[1] The second front about to be established in North Africa by the Anglo-American landings in late autumn was real enough to Stalin, and probably a potential threat to Russian aims.

Churchill emerged from his difficult meeting with the Russians at the cost of at least half a lie, otherwise unscathed. 'By every statement short of an absolute promise, Stalin had been given to understand that his Western Allies would launch "a very great operation in 1943"'—the cross-channel assault.[2]

On 24th July the British Cabinet had been informed by their own Chiefs of Staff, as well as the Chiefs of Staff of the United States, that a cross-channel assault was unlikely in 1943. 'Torch',

[1]Operation Jubilee, Dieppe Raid (Thompson, *Dieppe at Dawn*), 19th August, 1942.

[2]*Grand Strategy*, vol. III, part II, p. 663.

the North-African landings, would make it impossible if nothing else would.

The Prime Minister and his party arrived back in Cairo on 17th August. A week later Churchill and the C.I.G.S. were home in England.

As Liddell Hart pointed out: 'An ironical sequel to his [Auchinleck's] removal was that the renewal of the British offensive was postponed to a much later date than he had contemplated, and the impatient Prime Minister had to bow to the new high command's determination to wait . . .'[1] Mid-September had been too late, now it would be 23rd October, less than two weeks ahead of the North-African landings which would leave Rommel with no alternative but to retreat, even without fighting 'the Battle without Hope', as he described 2nd Alamein.

The Official Historian wrote:

> In all the stir of the Prime Minister's visit it was perhaps natural that thoughts should dwell more upon the future than upon the past . . . the vital importance of the July fighting stands out clearly, and to General Auchinleck belongs the credit for turning retreat into counter-attack. His forecast of mid-September as the earliest date by which the Army could be ready for an 'all-out' offensive may not have been popular in London, but it was realistic and reasonable. In the event, this offensive began on 23rd October, and its success should not be allowed to overshadow the earlier achievements of those who made it possible.[2]

We must be grateful even for this mild attempt to keep the record straight, but such truths could not prevail against the determination of Churchill to erase the record and substitute a victory arising out of his genius and leadership. It is necessary to look at 'all the stir' of the Prime Minister's visit to Cairo from Moscow, which created a succession of what have been called in recent years 'non-events', to prepare the way for the real event of the 2nd Battle of Alamein. Churchill heard at once that Montgomery had 'seized' command of Eighth Army on 13th August, two days ahead of the date agreed for the new command to operate. Immediately after this insensitive act, Montgomery signalled to Alexander in Cairo and left Eighth Army head-

[1]Liddell Hart, *The Tanks*, vol. II, p. 214.
[2]Playfair, *The Mediterranean and the Middle East*, vol. III, p. 377.

quarters for a tour of the battlefields to put himself out of reach of a reprimand. His action was an insult to General Ramsden, who was the acting Commander of the Eighth Army until 15th August.

Montgomery's behaviour, unimportant in itself, may have given Churchill the idea of creating a sense of crisis and extreme danger in Cairo. He could be seen at the centre of 'action', playing the lead. He at once re-created the myth of the 'fabulous Rommel', a myth Auchinleck had been at pains to destroy. He was observed by Sir Ian Jacob and others pacing his room and growling, 'Rommel, Rommel, Rommel'. Rommel was, in fact, a sick and weary man trying to regain some strength to face a hopeless situation.

Churchill's account of his deeds in Cairo is remarkable:

> During the last days of my visit all my thought rested upon the impending battle. At any moment Rommel might attack with a devastating surge of armour. He could come in by the pyramids with hardly a check except a single canal till he reached the Nile, which flowed serenely at the bottom of the Residency lawn. Lady Lampson's baby son smiled from his pram amid the palm trees. I looked out across the river at the flat expanses beyond. All was calm and peaceful, but I suggested to the mother that it was very hot and sultry in Cairo and could not be good for children. 'Why not send the baby away to be braced by the cool breezes of the Lebanon?' But she did not take my advice, and none can say she did not judge the military situation rightly.[1]

Nevertheless, at once Churchill created a sense of extreme urgency and danger. Every man must spring to arms immediately, and so on. All was bustle. None of it was necessary. The defence of Cairo had been wonderfully organised in the days of possible danger from 25th June to 2nd July.

And there he was, the old warrior, at the very heart of the non-event he had created, yet he must have known that he would not be able to 'fool all of the people all of the time' not even himself. It was simply creating a background to make it easier to deny Auchinleck's victory and prepare the fanfare for the new heroic offensive in overwhelming strength against the weak and desperately weary enemy. It is reminiscent of his

[1]Churchill, *The Second World War,* vol. IV, Readers' Union ed., p. 423.

remarkable early novel, *Savrola*. Again he is creating the heroic setting for himself. Reinforcements in all departments of war were pouring in; armour, artillery, ammunition, men. The activity was tremendous.

On 19th August Churchill visited Montgomery's comfortable Headquarters, inspected the powerful gun positions established by the previous command, and saw troops, both new arrivals and veterans, all glad to see the immense strength safeguarding their future.

With the C.I.G.S., the Prime Minister listened in admiration to Montgomery expounding plans almost identical to those prepared by Auchinleck, as though they were his own. This was essential to Montgomery, and not deliberate. Like Churchill he was incapable of accepting any idea whatever unless he could be persuaded that it was, in some mysterious way, his own. A myth was in the making and Churchill seized upon every part of it. The stage was set. It would be impossible to lose the forthcoming battle.

Immediately upon his return to Cairo Churchill telegraphed the Deputy Prime Minister, for the War Cabinet, and General Ismay and others concerned:

> 21st August, 1942. Have just spent two days in the Western Desert visiting H.Q. Eighth Army. Brooke, Alexander, Montgomery and I went round together ... I am sure we were heading for disaster under the former regime. The Army was reduced to bits and pieces and oppressed by a sense of bafflement and uncertainty. Apparently it was intended in face of heavy attack to retire eastwards to the Delta. Many were looking over their shoulders to make sure of their seats in the lorry, and no plan of battle or dominating will-power had reached the units.
>
> So serious did this appear that General Montgomery insisted upon taking command of the Eighth Army as soon as he had visited the front, and by Alexander's decision the whole command in the Middle East was transferred on the 13th.[1]

The message is painful to quote in full. As Connell wrote: 'The ritual smearing of the scapegoat had begun with gusto.' He described the message as 'this disagreeable, inaccurate and

[1] Ibid., p. 421. See also: Connell, *Auchinleck*, pp. 718–9.

offensive document.' No doubt there is virtue in understatement. The document is a deliberate and gross misrepresentation of the facts, and fortunately there were men who knew the truth and were not afraid to say so, but their voices were not heard above the uproar of the Prime Minister's drums and bugles. It was a triumph for the defeated and failed men who had stirred the brew in Cairo. Now their poison had achieved what Rommel had failed to do, and ironically Rommel was among the first to set the record straight.

It was Churchill's last battlefield, and it is a tragedy that it was to be an inglorious ending. As for his battle, or Montgomery's battle, when it took place it was a battle of attrition in which the British could afford to exchange two for one and finish with such immense strength against the enemy that it would have been impossible for Rommel's tiny remnant to withdraw, or survive. It is a strange story. Montgomery's Army followed Rommel's remnant from Alamein to Tunis.

In Liddell Hart's summing up of Montgomery's generalship, he formulated four basic questions:

Whether the commander's plan and conduct of the battle (a) gained victory as economically as possible; (b) attained victory without losses so heavy as to jeopardise the certainty of success inherent in the initial odds; (c) attained victory without exposing his army to defeat by counterstroke; (d) succeeded in achieving the complete victory that was promised by the overwhelming odds in his favour.[1]

Montgomery fulfilled only the third of these points, but this is a generous judgment. For Rommel, as he wrote in his diary: 'It was a matter of getting the best out of a hopeless situation. Armed with a pitchfork, the finest fighting man can do little against an opponent with a tommy gun in his hand . . . there was never any chance of the army achieving success at Alamein.'[2]

On his long and skilful withdrawal Rommel found it difficult to believe in his astounding luck. He was at the mercy of Montgomery at Alamein, after Alamein, and for weeks thereafter. 'He [Montgomery] risked nothing in any way doubtful and bold solutions were completely foreign to him . . .' So Rommel simulated activity to make Montgomery even slower,

[1] Liddell Hart, private papers, November, 1958.
[2] *The Rommel Papers*, p. 333.

until he was 'quite satisfied that Montgomery would never take the risk of following up boldly and over-running us, as he could have done without any danger to himself...'[1]

III

Churchill's exhilaration was short-lived. He had recognised Montgomery at once as a 'man on the make', and also a man with a mind of his own. A suggestion to the new general that one of his corps commanders was not satisfactory brought the immediate rejoinder, 'You stick to your job; I'll stick to mine.' The Prime Minister soon realised that the new general would go his own way, and that General Alexander, the Commander-in-Chief, with whom he was never at ease, could not be harassed, nor could he be induced to drive Montgomery on a tight rein, or on any rein at all.

The appointment of the new command was Churchill's swan-song in his unfortunate attempt to play the super-general. His urgent messages, exhortations and suggestions to the commanders in the Middle East and the Far East still went out in some profusion, but they had lost their bite. He had begun to lose his zest for playing that part, and other more important parts demanded his attention. Nevertheless he relinquished the role unwillingly. It had always been an impossible part to play, and could only bring about disaster, as it would do for Hitler and Germany. As it was, Churchill had come very close to bringing disaster in the Middle East, and only the dedication, fortitude, and skill of Wavell and Auchinleck had saved him (and Britain) from reaping the bitter harvest.

It is of course, impossible to command an army at long range, and very difficult to command an army on the spot. Auchinleck's message to Ismay before 'Crusader' is perhaps explanation enough. A battle is an exercise in confusion, and it requires a particular kind of genius, a remarkable instinct, perhaps a sixth sense, all allied to a profound knowledge of the military craft, not to fear that confusion, and to use it.

The original six weeks Churchill had lost by appointing Alexander and Montgomery to command in the new Middle East, which was now the Near East, drew out to six months or more, as Montgomery went doggedly but noisily, on his slow

[1]Ibid.

and cautious march from the field of Alamein to the Baltic. His re-groupings of his army or armies, his massive build-ups, his huge demands on shipping space and transport to feed his voracious appetite for 'ironmongery', served by astronomical quantities of fuel and ammunition, caused grave delays. For Britain to have any chance to impose her ideas on the pattern of the new Europe the war had to be won by the autumn of 1944. By that time, Britain's manpower and industrial output had reached and passed their peaks, while the power of the United States, on and off the field, grew with every hour of every day, and with that her domination.

Industrial production, providing armies with far more than they could possibly need, or use effectively, became the governing factor, so that the momentum and the drive of armies slowed as their tails grew longer and heavier. Montgomery was the high priest of the new abundance, but also the victim of logistics. He might have done better with half the war materials and half the transport he demanded. He forged his own ball and chain.

From the turn of the tide of war in the late summer and autumn of 1942, the course of the war in the West lost its heroic content and became in a sense tedious and inevitable. The great days of Dunkirk, the Battle of Britain, of Wavell's fortitude and vision, of O'Connor's great victory over the Italian armies in Africa, of Auchinleck's brave stand in that terrible ebb and flow of battle in the Western Desert, could stand with the finest deeds in Britain's past.

On the new battlefields, as General Fuller observed, the old order had given way to the new 'Cadocracy', and the 'Iron-mongers'. Churchill did not truly belong in this new warfare. He was a natural romantic. His tactical ideas were those of the kind suited to the adventurous spirits he had always admired, from d'Artagan; by way of Lawrence of Arabia, to young General Wingate towards the end. When he eagerly embraced Wingate, perceiving rightly a valiant spirit, but making himself look ridiculous by calling him 'the Clive of Burma', and suggesting that Wingate should replace General Slim in command of the 14th Army, he revealed not only his romanticism, but his total lack of understanding of the qualities needed for the command of an army.

When Hitler's obsession with the fight for Stalingrad cost him an army it was clear that he hastened his own defeat. Germany was over-stretched on all fronts, not only in Soviet Russia, in the Balkans and in the Middle East, but over the immense coast-line of Europe and Scandinavia she must ceaselessly guard and prepare to defend. Except from that coastline, which she dared not abandon, her Armies began to move back, never again to move forward. In the Pacific in that year of 1942 the United States had gained the upper hand, and after Midway and the Battle of the Coral Sea, the tide of Japanese victory was on the ebb. In India and Burma, under Wavell, Auchinleck and Slim, and soon with the valuable addition of Lord Mountbatten as Supreme Commander, South-East Asia, Britain's armies, fortunately denied the excessive 'fat' available in the Western theatre of war, remained 'lean' to hold and defeat the Japanese on land.

Only in the Atlantic did the deadly battle rage on, un-diminished and always threatening disaster until the early summer of 1943.

The heroic mood of Britain inevitably began to wane, and the longing for security and peace was greater than the stimulus of danger. In the field, General Montgomery was the ideal hero and symbol, promising safety.

CHAPTER THIRTEEN

The Bitter End

I

CHURCHILL'S TRUE BATTLEFIELDS WERE THE CONFERENCE TABLES, and from Casablanca to Teheran by way of Washington and Quebec, at last to Yalta and Potsdam, Churchill the statesman fought bravely but in vain for Britain's strategy, and for her role in the aftermath of war. On these battlefields Churchill and Britain were doomed to defeat. I believe that it was a blunder of the first magnitude, and not a blunder dictated by destiny or the tides of history, to rush into the arms of Soviet Russia and the United States with indecent haste. The illusions of Soviet Russia and the United States about each other and the rest of the world, were profound. Russia's ignorance of the United States, and of China, was matched by the ignorance of the United States about Europe, China, and the nature of Soviet Communism, and the grand strategy she must pursue.

Because Churchill was aware of the immense strength of the two giants, he tended to under-estimate the strength of Britain. In spite of the professionalism of the British Chiefs of Staff, and the brilliant arguments of Churchill, British influence waned steadily. In the end his task, as James Gould Cozzens wrote,[1] was to palter. American distrust of British intentions was paramount.

Nevertheless Churchill fought doggedly for his concepts of strategy to the bitter end. He understood the ancient and modern trends of power. He understood the strategic objects of the Soviet Union. He was a political animal, and for him, naturally and rightly, war and politics were inseparable.

When Roosevelt suddenly (as it seemed) brought out his

[1] J. G. Cozzens, *Guard of Honour*, Longmans Green.

proposal for unconditional surrender at Casablanca, pretending that the formula had simply 'popped out' on the spur of the moment, whereas it was in his notes for the conference and carefully calculated, Churchill was taken by surprise, and agreed. It seems unlike Churchill, but his close associates at the time assure me that it was so. He did not immediately realise the implications. Perhaps, at first, he did not take it seriously, believing that it must be modified, that it could not be final. It became the bar to peace and delayed the end of the war, but it delighted Stalin, the Soviet dictator, who knew exactly what his object was.

Hitler, too, had known his object, fortunately too grandiose and ambitious ultimately to prevail.

It was at Casablanca that Churchill finally realised that Britain's destiny, and the destiny of Europe, was in other hands. To his dismay he had to observe the United States and the Soviet Union growing closer together, and endure the insult at Teheran of being virtually excluded from some vital discussions. In addition, the United States embraced the old bandit, Chiang Kai-Shek and his Madame, and seemed unaware of the importance of Mao Tse Tung.

It was understood in Moscow as early as 1941 that Britain would not act in Europe or commit herself to a statement of aims without American agreement. Conversely in Germany, Britain was recognised as the main enemy until much later: 'The fact that Britain had lost its freedom of political and military action, and the extent to which it was already dependent on the United States were entirely unknown in war-time Germany. Even until late in 1942 Britain was still regarded as the principal of Germany's enemies.'[1]

Bravely at Yalta and Potsdam Churchill battled on, standing by that enigmatic man, Charles de Gaulle, who believed himself to be, and was, France. The Americans had grossly under-rated him, revealing themselves unable to read the position in Europe.

Churchill was growing old, and feeling old. His indomitable spirit kept him going, with the aid of Sir Charles Wilson, his physician (Lord Moran), the devoted and often exasperated General Brooke, the C.I.G.S., and Churchill's devoted wife and daughter, Mary. He survived severe illnesses and crises, and from his sick beds his messages, his almost anguished pleas to Roosevelt, went out unheeded. He clung to his strategic aims

[1] Albert Seaton, *The Russo-German War, 1941–5*, p. 519.

to the bitter end, the aims that Hitler feared, and Stalin frustrated. Thus Roosevelt and Stalin welcomed the American plans to launch an attack on the South of France (code-named 'Anvil') in conjunction with the cross-channel assault. The Western Allies would be safely clear of the Balkans.

Churchill never gave in, but the seeds of failure were in himself. He was at least as much an American and a tycoon, as he was an Englishman (with the blood of the Spencers and Churchills) and a European. He tried to unite the two sides in himself in his dream of a union of the English-speaking peoples. It was impossible, and undesirable.

Britain, even in 1940, when Churchill took command of the nation, was a very great power. Moreover she was not alone. The dominions had stood by her side, Australian, New Zealand, Canadian and South-African divisions fought with the British on many battlefields with the many divisions of the Indian Army, with the Free French, the Poles, the Dutch. These peoples had not come to Britain empty-handed, but with treasure, with ships, with great territories still under their control. On the seas, and, thanks to the dedication of Air Marshal Dowding, in the air also, Britain was a match, and often more than a match for her enemies.

Of course it was great good fortune for Britain when Germany attacked Soviet Russia, and a few months later when Japan attacked the United States base at Pearl Harbour. We were allies whether Britain liked it or not, and, of course Britain liked it. But if Soviet Russia and the United States did not need Britain, there could not be a truly fruitful alliance. Soviet Russia and the United States of America and Britain together with her Commonwealth and European allies all over the world were compelled to fight a common enemy, and the common enemy of all was Germany. Anything that could be done to help each ally was, of course, of the highest importance, and plain common sense. But could Britain persuade Soviet Russia to defend herself more steadfastly than she did? Could Britain hope to influence Russia's war aims one way or the other, or with all her support in kind—which was considerable and given at a truly frightful cost to Britain—make the slightest difference in her defeat or victory?

I believe not. Certainly it seems to have been a grave mistake in Britain to have subjected herself to Soviet insults and calumny—for absolutely nothing.

As for the United States, despite her admirals, she either regarded the Atlantic theatre of war and the defeat of Hitler as of vital importance to her interests, or she didn't. Britain could not exert real influence on the choice—Britain was either of immense value to the United States, or she was not. I believe that she was.

There was no need for Britain to cast herself in the role of poor relation with her begging bowl. She was not. Without Britain, her fleet and her island, the United States could not have hoped to defeat Nazi Germany, or even to get there. Churchill's strange attitude gave him an inferiority feeling, and led him to under-estimate British power. It led him to forfeit his strategy. His search for allies had been wise, especially in a European context, while Turkey, Spain, and important areas of French North Africa, might be won. His desire to attack in the Balkans was frustrated by the United States, and 'Churchill's urging of a reluctant Roosevelt was not enough', as Seaton wrote.[1] The same writer also states that von Weichs, the German Commander in the Balkans, warned Hitler that he held 5,000 kilometres of frontage with ten divisions, some of them of poor quality. He wanted to evacuate the Balkans. Britain was not short of friends over the area.

It is naïve to believe in altruism between great powers. Power knows no altruism. The United States could not ignore the Atlantic theatre as Roosevelt clearly recognised. Britain could give her ally every facility to mount a cross-channel assault against Normandy, or wherever she might select. Britain and the United States were fighting a war together, not only in the Atlantic, but in the Indian Ocean and the Pacific. Our Commonwealth allies were of the greatest importance to the United States.

It is, of course, possible, and even probable, that America might have decided to put the Pacific first, as she frequently threatened to do. Such a course would have left Britain in Supreme Command of all Allied forces in the Atlantic theatre.

Provided such forces were concentrated upon the right places; provided Churchill could have been restrained from attempting too much, the 'Great Amphibian' might have come into its own.

1943 was the last possible year of decision for Britain. By then, as others have pointed out, Britain had to make a choice about herself; she could not remain an empire power and a European power. That is not to say that she could have, or should

[1] Albert Seaton, *The Russo-German War, 1941–5.*

have, abandoned the empire to which she owed a vast obligation, but it does mean that the recognition that the winding-up process of the British Empire was inevitable would have released the minds of powerful elements in the complex structure of British political power to devote themselves to a new future as the cornerstone of a new Europe, a Europe moreover, resolved to rebuild in her own fashion. If the United States helped it would be because she had to, because her huge industrial machine would not run down, and her immense surpluses would choke her.

If these were two of the options which might have helped to curb Soviet power in Europe, and limit American power in Europe, it must seem to a European that a more balanced, perhaps a less deadly world pattern might have emerged. For there was one other factor of overwhelming importance, the atom bomb. In Quebec in 1943 Churchill and Roosevelt signed an agreement about the atom bomb that would have far-reaching consequences. It had been a joint project, but it was basically a British project, and work could have gone ahead on it in Canada, had there been the faintest suspicion that the United States would seize a monopoly of this dreadful weapon. Many scientists were extremely uneasy. Niels Bohr had written to Roosevelt to express his fears, foreseeing that it might divide the world into two nuclear camps—'since the Russians, he realised as a physicist, would ultimately produce a bomb.'

Early in 1944 Professor Lindemann (later Lord Cherwell) persuaded Churchill to meet Bohr. It was in vain.

> So far as post-war problems were concerned he [Bohr] was told there were none that could not be solved between Churchill and his friend President Roosevelt. 'He appears to have felt,' says one who was close to Churchill at the time, 'that by making the grand gesture embodied in the Quebec agreement, he would remove all obstacles to co-operation on the part of the United States to take unfair advantage of it'.[1]

II

Even when and while Britain's freedom to pursue her strategy, and to act independently, were seeping away at the conference tables, there were many chances on the battlefields, to the

[1] Ronald W. Clark, *The Birth of the Bomb.*

eleventh hour, to shape the course of the war, before and after the United States assumed Supreme Command. The most far-reaching and tragic choice for which Churchill was largely responsible was the decision to build up a great bomber force. The strain on war production was out of all proportion to the value, even though by means of the bomber the enemy attempts to produce an atom bomb, as we suspected, and secret weapons which we knew about, Germany's efforts in that terrifying field of destruction were hampered. But this was an objective which could have been pursued with a far smaller specialised bomber force.

Churchill, almost certainly, could have refused the choice of the bomber as the principal means of winning the war. It would not have been easy. The Army had been a poor relation for many years, and the Air Force seemed to offer a chance of victory, and make the possibility of another Passchendaele—always a British fear—highly improbable.

Professor Lindemann worked out to his satisfaction, and to Churchill's, the virtual certainty that by strategic bombing the war could be won. The heads of Bomber Command and of the Royal Air Force were enthusiastic. Air Chief Marshal Sir Arthur Harris (Bomber Harris) was a fanatic. Air Chief Marshal Portal, one of the Chiefs of Staff, was both brilliant and determined. The moral issues do not seem to have weighed with these men, yet Churchill was soon unhappy about the choice. There were also practical considerations. Tizard and Blackett were among those who believed that strategic bombing would fail. In the military field, Liddell Hart observed, 'You cannot surrender to a bomber in the sky'.

Strategic bombing swiftly escalated from military to civilian targets, the appalling destruction of Hamburg and Dresden, the fire raids on Tokyo, to the horror of Hiroshima and Nagasaki. That was not the end, but a new beginning, as men, striving to avoid personal combat, and driven by a fearful frustration—and despair—resorted to weapons of almost unimaginable horror from the sky, while all the time the nuclear threat hung over the world in ever-increasing power.

Meanwhile Britain's choice of strategic bombing in the early days of the Second World War condemned the Army to third place in the priorities, starving it not only of adequate support aircraft, but of armour and artillery to match the quality of armour and artillery deployed by the enemy in the first three years of war. It also meant that Britain could not use her strength in the role of the 'Great Amphibian' until very late in the day, using her Army, Navy and Air Force as a most potent striking force, a single instrument of warfare.

There were many other choices, as the reader of this book will know, but none, I think, as momentous as the choice of the bomber.

For the rest, even in Britain's weakened position, resigning the concept of political-military strategy to the American concept of military strategy divorced from political considerations, there were still opportunities on the battlefield to shape the final issue more in line with British needs even without persuading the Americans. This might have been achieved by speed. Immediately after Montgomery's successful battle for Normandy, the Field-Marshal's task was done. Britain could no longer afford his extreme caution, and there were two possible generals who might have gone farther faster. The C.I.G.S., General Brooke, could have been spared from his nursing of Churchill, or General Sir Bernard Paget, whose job it should have been to lead 21st Army Group in the first place. An Army Commander should have been given the freedom to act without Montgomery's, or anyone else's, tight rein yoking him.

Could such an Army Commander have been found—a British Patton? Could Dempsey, commanding the 2nd Army, given his head, have achieved the victory there for the taking in early September, 1944? Or had he been too conditioned, good soldier though he was, to submerge his own skills and characteristics in subservience to the inflexible hand of the Commander-in-Chief under whom he had served so long. And would the Commander of the Canadian Army on the left flank, acting on his own, and of necessity in close conjunction with the British 2nd Army, have had the necessary vision to take the tide at the flood? Often opportunity has found the man.

It would have been bold, but not rash, to thrust with all speed beyond the Scheldt to the north, deep into Holland on both flanks.

Given such an object, and given the leadership and drive, the impetus of the spearhead armoured divisions, which petered out at Antwerp and Brussels could have been maintained. The enemy had left a vacuum. It was filled before the British girded themselves for the next move, too late.

In those first days of September, Germany was wide open.

There was nothing to save her from collapse in the face of a determined Allied advance. Time was running out fast for Britain, and it was vital to win in 1944. Britain had reached and passed her peak, but there was still time to redeem something for Britain before the American Armies took over and called the final tune.

Even on the Rhine bank in early March, 1945, the British Armies waited for three vital weeks in overwhelming strength, and finally relinquished the command of U.S. 9th Army and the last opportunity for Britain to have a say in the pattern of the European Continent.

Churchill, the old warrior, hammered away to the last, urging the occupation of Prague, an easy advance to the Vltava by Patton and the U.S. 3rd Army, an occupation of Berlin before the Russians, but General Eisenhower, Supreme Commander of the Allied Forces in Europe, was adamant, and, supported by General Marshall, the U.S. Chief of Staff in Washington, no arguments would move him from his purely military purpose.

III

In common with all other heads of states, Churchill inherited a society, unique in itself, its strengths and weaknesses peculiar to itself alone. All history, all life, is a continuous story.

Churchill inherited a nation, together with a commonwealth of nations and an empire, a network of foreign alliances, a pattern of world trade, a pattern of industry, a pattern of hopes and fears. Much that was, as it were, in the pipe-line of history, was unalterable. The emergence of the British Empire—especially the emergence of the great Indian sub-continent—to self-rule, to independence, would have occurred irrespective of Churchill or anyone else. Men like Amery, Linlithgow, and many others whose families had served India and Britain for generations might recognise and aid the process; others might strive to hinder. No man could arrest the tide.

In terms of war and leadership Churchill inherited a pattern of the art of waging war, manifest in the Committee of Imperial Defence, an edifice of committees whose ramifications he understood very well. He inherited also an Army, Navy and Air Force whose patterns and present strengths were the result of attitudes and growths over many years. He inherited also a crisis in the military predicament of his country of extraordinary immediacy and danger.

And there was the personal inheritance in blood and breeding, in prejudices and ambitions, in dreams, in the upbringing and personal experience of Churchill, the man.

The problem always to be borne in mind is what could Churchill do to use the means to his and his country's ends? However powerful, however strong willed, his means and methods of using his power were governed by an immense and complex machine, and a society, in being. He had the overwhelming confidence of the nation.

All this is evident—even a platitude. I wish simply to indicate the limitations of power. Churchill's great power was not so much in his voice, but in the words he chose to match his voice and his whole powerful personality. His words, his inspiration, his energy, his drive gave the nation its awareness of its strength, its inheritance, and of its hopes. Thus, if Churchill changed the course of history, it was by his inspiration.

But the present is not simply the outcome of the past, it is also influenced by the future, the future we hope for, or fear, the objects we seek to achieve. In the Second World War the nations involved had widely different ambitions, desired different kinds of societies, different groupings of nations and peoples.

Each of the nations harboured powerful fears, and these fears governed many of their actions. In Britain and the United States we feared, in the context of war, the secret weapon upon which we were working with the utmost urgency in a race, as we believed against the enemy.

The fear that there was a deadly and horrifying race upon which we were embarked, cast a dreadful shadow over the minds of the men at the top. It was the horror that this secret weapon could invalidate all the victories and defeats, all the heroism, all the cowardice, all the errors, all the choices, the fear that this 'thing' could change the face of the world. And it did.

IV

The two devastating wars of this century in Europe were domestic upheavals, upheavals of a group of nations developing over centuries within a common context, the inheritors of what was known as Western Civilisation, an inheritance tragically squandered.

I believe that it must be disastrous for any outsider, however well intentioned, to intervene in any domestic quarrel, between husband and wife, or nations of the same basically 'domestic' family. Thus, in a sense, the wars in Europe were civil wars. If the United States had not become involved in the First World War, especially at a time when the antagonists were nearing stalemate, it seems to me almost certain that neither side would have been victorious, and that some sort of decent and sane pattern could have been worked out.

It is useless to pursue might-have-beens, but perhaps not useless to indicate that there were, and are, crossroads. Must destiny be absolute? Must it all be fore-ordained, and can men and peoples by their deeds and visions influence the patterns ceaselessly evolving, the one out of the other? I must believe that we are not merely puppets. 'The fault, dear Brutus, lies not in our stars, but in ourselves, that we are underlings.' Even Churchill.

One thing I believe is true: Churchill in 1940 was for a time as surely Britain as Charles de Gaulle was France. The British people roused to defend themselves, and at Dunkirk showed themselves at their very best. I believe it would have been difficult to find a man, woman or child who would not have 'rowed a boat' in those days, given the strength and opportunity. I believe that there were many who would have striven with all their courage and ingenuity to oppose an invasion of these shores, and to defend their homes.

The impetus of that mood was maintained almost to the end, and Churchill gave it drive and inspiration almost from the beginning, almost to the end. It was not his fault that in the end the Yankee should gain the upper hand over the Marlborough in him.

It was not the fault of the people that, as the danger receded, the surge of enthusiasm receded also. Men no longer thought of survival, or even of victory; they thought of peace—whatever that might be. The First World War had taken a tremendous toll of Britain's youth and genius; the degradation of the mean and bitter years between the wars had bitten deep into the consciousness of the people, and was imprinted upon the memories of their children.

It was magnificent that that old man could give tongue to greatness, and that those people could rouse themselves to match him, so that the dying candle flared, before it was quenched.

But it is not to be wondered at that in the end Britain went out with a whimper.

'Victory is a mirage in the desert created by a long war.'[1]

[1]B. H. Liddell Hart, *Why Don't We Learn From History?* Allen and Unwin.

Select Bibliography

This bibliography is intended as a brief guide to useful reading in this context.

Alexander of Tunis, Field-Marshal Lord, Despatches, H.M.S.O.
Auchinleck, Field-Marshal Sir Claude, Despatches, H.M.S.O.
History of the Second World War, United Kingdom Military History, H.M.S.O.:
> *Grand Strategy,* vol. II, J. R. M. Butler; vol. III, part 1, M. A. Gwyer; vol. IV, Michael Howard; vol. V, John Ehrman.
> *The Mediterranean and the Middle East,* vol. III, I. S. O. Playfair; vol. IV, I. S. O. Playfair and C. J. C. Molony.
> *The Strategic Air Offensive against Germany,* 1939–1945, Four Volumes, Sir C. Webster and Noble Frankland.
U.S. Army in World War II, Office of Chief of Military History, Department of the Army, Washington, D.C.
> *The Supreme Command,* Pogue, F. C.
> *Global Logistics and Strategy,* 1940–1943, Richard M. Leighton and Robert W. Coakley.
> *Command Decision.*

Amery, Rt. Hon. L. S., *My Political Life,* Three Volumes, Hutchinson.
Barnett, Corelli, *The Desert Generals,* Kimber.
Bryant, Sir Arthur, *The Turn of the Tide,* Collins;
> *Triumph in the West,* Collins.
Cadogan, Sir Alexander, *Diaries,* Cassell.
Casey, R. G., *Personal Experience, 1939–1946,* Constable.
Churchill, Winston, *The World Crisis,* Four Volumes, Thornton Butterworth;

The Second World War, Six Volumes, Cassell.

Clifford, Alexander, *Three Against Rommel,* Harrap.

Connell, John, *Auchinleck,* Cassell;
Wavell, Scholar and Soldier, Collins;
Wavell, Supreme Commander, Collins.

Cooper, Duff, *Old Men Forget,* Hart Davis.

Clark, Ronald W., *The Birth of the Bomb,* Phoenix House.

Cunningham, of Hyndhope, Viscount, *A Sailor's Odyssey,* Hutchinson.

Eade, Charles (Editor), *The War Speeches of Winston Churchill,* Cassell;
Churchill by his Contemporaries, Hutchinson.

Feis, Herbert, *Churchill, Roosevelt, Stalin,* Oxford Univ. Press.

Fuller, Major-General J. F. C., *The Conduct of War, 1789–1961,* Eyre and Spottiswoode;
The Second World War, 1939–1945, Eyre and Spottiswoode.

de Gaulle, General, *War Memoirs,* Four Volumes, Weidenfeld and Nicolson.

George, David Lloyd, *War Memoirs,* Six Volumes, Ivor Nicholson and Watson.

Grigg, Sir James, *Prejudice and Judgement,* Cape.

Gilbert, Martin, *Winston S. Churchill, 1914–1916,* Heinemann.

Hart, Capt. B. H. Liddell, *The Tanks, The History of the Royal Tank Regiment,* Two Volumes, Cassell;
Memoirs, Two Volumes, Cassell;
The Rommel Papers, Collins;
History of the Second World War, Two Volumes, Cassell.

Heckstall-Smith, Anthony, *Tobruk,* Anthony Blond.

Higgins, Trumbull, *Winston and the Second Front,* Oxford Univ. Press.

Hull, Cordell, *Memoirs,* Two Volumes, Hodder and Stoughton.

Ismay, Lord, *Memoirs,* Heinemann.

Johnson, Arthur Franklyn, *Defence by Committee,* Oxford Univ. Press.

Johnston, Denis, *Nine Rivers of Jordan,* Deutsch.

Kennedy, John, *The Business of War,* Hutchinson.

Mackenzie, Sir Compton, *Eastern Epic,* Vol. I, Chatto and Windus.

Mackesy, Kenneth, *Armoured Crusader,* Hutchinson.

Macleod, Col. R. and Denis Kelly, *The Ironside Diaries,* Constable.

Macmillan, Harold, *The Blast of War, 1939–1945,* Macmillan;

Tides of Fortune, 1945–1955, Macmillan.

Maund, L. E. H., *Assault from the Sea,* Methuen.

Neilson, Francis, *The Churchill Legend,* Nelson.

Seaton, Albert, *The Russo-German War,* Barker.

Sherwood, Robert (Editor), *The White House Papers of Harry Hopkins,* Two Volumes, Eyre and Spottiswoode.

Taylor, A. J. P., Plumb, J. H., Liddell Hart, B. H., Storr, Anthony, *Churchill, Four Faces and the Man,* Allen Lane.

Thompson, R. W., *The Eighty-Five Days,* Hutchinson;
The Battle for the Rhineland, Hutchinson;
The Price of Victory, Constable;
The Yankee Marlborough, Allen and Unwin;
The Montgomery Legend, Allen and Unwin;
Montgomery, The Field-Marshal, Allen and Unwin.

Winant, John, *A Letter from Grosvenor Square,* Hodder and Stoughton.

Wrinch, Pamela, *The Military Strategy of Winston Churchill,* Dept. of Government, Boston University.

Private Papers and Correspondence of Major Sir Desmond Morton, K.C.B., Major-General Eric Dorman Smith (O'Gowan), M.C. and Capt. Sir Basil Liddell Hart.

Index

Index

Winston Churchill is shown as W.S.C. throughout. Whenever possible, ranks shown are those ultimately held.

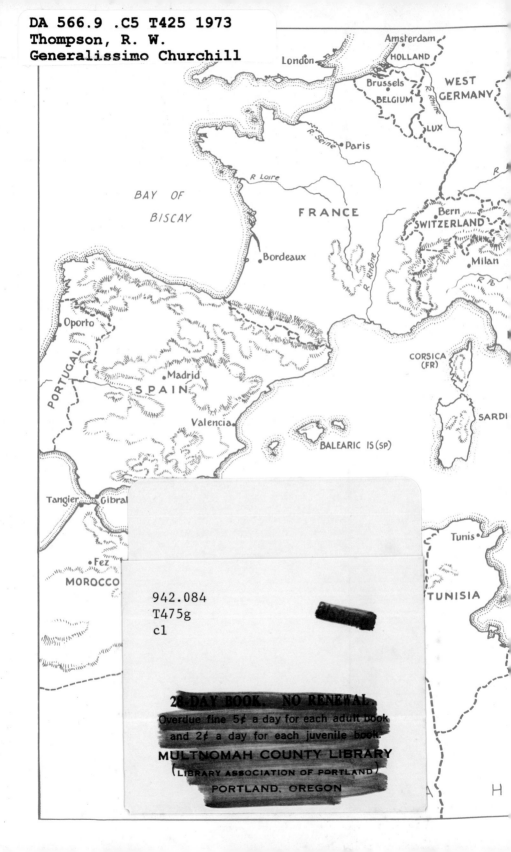